# *The Lives and Times of*
# The Presidents of Ireland

## About the Author

Kevin (Caoimhín) Kenna was born in Dún Laoghaire and educated at Presentation College, Glasthule, County Dublin. He qualified as a Chartered Accountant in 1967 and his professional career included five years in Oxford and seventeen years in Munich. He recently retired to devote his time to various writing projects.

*For Ciar,*

# The Lives and Times of
# The Presidents of Ireland

**Kevin Kenna**

*With special good wishes,*

*Caoin*

*Kevin Ke*

The Liffey Press

Published by
The Liffey Press
Ashbrook House
10 Main Street, Raheny,
Dublin 5, Ireland
www.theliffeypress.com

A catalogue record of this book is
available from the British Library.

ISBN 978-1-905785-84-1

'Immediate Man' by Brendan Kennelly is reproduced
with the permission of Bloodaxe Books

Printed in Ireland by Colour Books.

# Contents

This book is dedicated to the memory of my late parents, Kevin and Trassa Kenna. It is also for Margaret, Dervla, Cliona and Louisa.

# Acknowledgements

Firstly, I want to thank my wife, Margaret, for her unstinted support and encouragement in this project. A special word of thanks to Listowel man Jim McMahon, whose advice and help were invaluable. Thanks, too, to the staff of the National Library of Ireland, including those of the National Photographic Archive section.

I am especially grateful to President McAleese and to Gráinne Mooney, Communications Officer to the President at Áras an Uachtaráin, and to her staff for their help, and to Deirdre O'Gara of the Douglas Hyde Interpretive Centre. Thank you also to Nessa Childers MEP who kindly provided photographs, and to Maurice Mc Mahon who did likewise. I also thank my sister Stephanie Batt and her husband Kevin for photographic material.

David Coleman of the Bobby Studio, Dublin, was very generous with his time. I am indebted to Seán Dargan, General Secretary of Fianna Fáil, for permission to peruse the Fianna Fáil archive in University College Dublin, and to Seamus Helferty, Principal Archivist of the UCD Archive, School of History and Archives, and to his ever helpful staff for allowing me access to the Cearbhall Ó Dálaigh papers and other archival material. I also received very valuable assistance from Ed Penrose of the Irish Labour Historical Society. Aoife McGonigle of the National Print Museum also helped greatly by providing photographs and I'm very grateful to her, to the Museum and to photographer Fionn McCann.

A special word of gratitude to Sinéad McKenna who designed the excellent cover for the book.

I thank the various authors listed in the References section at the back of the book whose works were inspirational to me in the writing of the book.

Finally, I say a very sincere thanks to David Givens of The Liffey Press for his professional skills and unfailing courtesy to me, coupled with his patience and encouragement. I consider myself very fortunate to have forged such an easy working relationship with someone whose many talents have resulted in the production of such a high quality publication.

Kevin (Caoimhín) Kenna
Dublin
October 2010

# Foreword

It is now some seventy three years since the office of Uachtaráin na h-Éireann was established under our present Constitution. There have been eight office holders to date: an academic Gaelic scholar, four former prominent politicians, a judge, and two former law professors. Each of them in his or her own way has left a distinctive footprint on our history.

There have been great changes in this period: war years, post-war, stagnation, economic development, EU membership, tensions in the North, booms and busts. Despite the changing times and constitutional limitations on their role, the office holders have represented the country with honour and distinction. The functions of the office, while clearly defined, have allowed for a small evolution in the role played by each holder. Nowadays the office is more open and accessible and this, in turn, reflects a growing confidence of the country in 'its own skin'.

Kevin Kenna has done a great service to many, not least students and visitors from abroad who wish to get a view of our country from a vantage point somewhat removed from the political fray. His work is not that of a formal historian but from the perspective of an average citizen. The book brings between its covers something that will be of interest to a great many, especially now that retrospection will be more in vogue with the coming of the centenary of 1916.

The work for Kevin was painstaking, yet a labour of love, and will be savoured my many in the decades to come.

Jim McMahon
Killarney, June 2010

# Introduction

## Times Past

In 1170, the King of Leinster, Dermot Macmurrough, invited the Earl of Pembroke, known as Strongbow, to come to Ireland to help him in his battles against Rory O'Connor, then High King (Árd Rí) of Ireland. This was a new beginning of Ireland's struggle against unwelcome visitors which was to last for more than 700 years. Previously, the Vikings had been defeated by Brian Boru in the 'Battle of Clontarf' in 1014. From the thirteenth century onwards, however, rebellions against foreign occupation were numerous but failed in the face of superior forces or through poor organisation.

In 1845, Ireland was struck by a disastrous famine. Ireland's population in that year was 8 million. Based on the 1841 census the normal expected population by 1851 would have been 9 million. However, the 1851 census showed that the population was reduced to 6.5 million, an effective reduction of 2.5 million. Of these, 1.5 million emigrated and 1 million died of starvation. The legacy of failed rebellions and the famine left Ireland tired and weak.

*Brian Boru, High King of Ireland – figure over door in Dublin Castle*

The granting of limited legislative power to an Irish parliament in 1782 was beneficial mainly to the ruling classes. In 1800, these powers were taken back to the British parliament at Westminster by the Act of Union. Power remained as far away as ever for ordinary native Irish citizens.

## Modern Ireland

In 1916, there was a rising against British occupation in Ireland, led primarily by P. H. Pearse and James Connolly. Militarily it was a failure. However, in the wake of the execution by the British authorities of Pearse, Connolly and the other signatories of the 1916 Proclamation, the old flame of Irish nationalism was re-kindled and the War of Independence (1919–1921) against the British was commenced. It was fought under the military expertise of Michael Collins and the political guile of Éamon de Valera. It ended in a treaty which was ultimately accepted by a small majority vote of the Provisional Government in January of 1922, and it culminated in the establishment of the Irish Free State.

The concept of the Free State, a state remaining within the British Commonwealth of Nations and excluding six of the thirty-two counties

*Part of Dublin Castle, seat of British administration in Ireland up to January 1922*

of Ireland (these six now being designated 'Northern Ireland') was not acceptable to Éamon de Valera. A tragic civil war followed (1922/1923) in the course of which Michael Collins, who supported the Treaty, was shot dead. In the end, the Free State forces held sway. Despite the upheaval, the Cumann na Gael party (later to become Fine Gael), under the determined leadership of W.T. Cosgrave as President of the Executive Council, ran the country in very difficult economic and political circumstances. However, de Valera's newly formed Fianna Fáil party, having eventually accepted the de facto Free State status, swept to power in the general election of 1932. On assuming office, de Valera did away with the Oath of Allegiance to the British Monarch (which was a required undertaking for participation in the British Commonwealth of Nations), reduced the role of the Governor-General in Ireland (the Monarch's representative) to virtually nothing and halted payments to the British Exchequer under Land Purchase Acts (to buy back land confiscated by the British).

In 1937, de Valera introduced a new constitution for the country, now named Éire (Ireland). The new constitution foresaw the institution of the role of President, a non-political post.

## The Role of President of Ireland under the Constitution of Ireland

Article 12 of the Constitution of Ireland includes the following provisions:

> *There shall be a President of Ireland (Uachtarán na hÉireann) hereinafter called the President, who shall take precedence over all other persons in the State and who shall exercise and perform the powers and functions conferred on the President by this Constitution and by law.*

> *The President shall be elected by direct vote of the people.*

This Article also provides that the President shall hold office for seven years from the date upon which he or she enters the office, unless before the expiration of that period he or she dies, or resigns, or is removed from office, or becomes permanently incapacitated, such incapacity being established to the satisfaction of the Supreme Court consisting of not less than five judges.

The article further provides that a person who holds or has held the office of President shall be eligible for re-election to that office only once, and that where only one candidate is nominated it is not necessary to proceed to a ballot for his or her election.

Article 13 of the Constitution provides that the President shall, on the nomination of Dáil Éireann, appoint the Taoiseach (the head of the Government or Prime Minister) and shall also appoint the other members

*Presidential Harp Motif*

of the Government on the nomination of the Taoiseach with the previous approval of Dáil Éireann. Also, the President shall, on the advice of the Taoiseach, accept the resignation or terminate the appointment of any member of the Government.

Additionally, the Constitution provides that:

> *Dáil Éireann shall be summoned and dissolved by the President on the advice of the Taoiseach and that the President may at his/her absolute discretion refuse to dissolve Dáil Éireann on the advice of a Taoiseach who has ceased to retain the support of a majority in Dáil Éireann.*

It is also stated that every Bill passed or deemed to be passed by both Houses of the Oireachtas (Dáil and Seanad) shall require the signature of the President for its enactment into law, and also that the supreme command of the Defence Forces is vested in the President. Further, the President has the power to refer a Bill to the Supreme Court for a decision as to whether the measure is in any way repugnant to the Constitution.

4

## Author's Note

In this publication, the term 'President of Ireland' is that as described under the Constitution of Ireland, first introduced in 1937. This is different to the designation 'President' used in the period of the Irish Free State (1922–1937). For instance, during the period 1922–1932, the President of the Executive Council (Government Cabinet), Mr W.T. Cosgrave, was referred to as 'President Cosgrave'. In this capacity his role was similar to that of Taoiseach (Prime Minister), and therefore different to that laid down under the 1937 Constitution of Ireland.

*The Entrance Hall, Áras an Uachtaráin*

*Painting of the first meeting of the Council of State 8 January 1940
by Simon Coleman ARHA*

# Douglas Hyde
## First President of Ireland (1938–1945)

### Early Years

Douglas Hyde was born on 17 January 1860. He was the third son of the reverend Arthur Hyde Junior and Elizabeth Oldfield-Hyde. The family residence was at Kilmactranny, County Sligo and this is the place of birth shown on his birth certificate. However, it was thought that his mother, when nearing the end of her pregnancy, had travelled to her own family home at Castlerea in County Roscommon and that this was, therefore, the correct birth place of Douglas Hyde.

The Hyde family name is possibly derived from Norman or pre-Norman stock. In Britain in the middle-ages a 'hide' was a parcel of land sufficient to support one free family – about 100 acres. The name 'Hide' or 'Hyde' was often given to such land owners. The Hyde family held considerable property in Denchworth, in Berkshire, England. In St. James's Church in Denchworth there are sixteenth century brasses dedicated to Oliver Hyde, who died in 1567, and to his wife Alice, who died in 1584. The Hyde family was Catholic. It is not clear when at least some branch of the Hyde family adopted Anglicanism, but Arthur Hyde, who got a grant of land (of about 12,000 acres) in Munster from Queen Elizabeth I, was undoubtedly no longer a Catholic at that stage.

The family prospered and a junior line of the family built Castle Hyde on the banks of the river Blackwater in County Cork. Douglas Hyde's great grandfather married into the Frenches of Frenchpark in County Roscommon, and thus the family moved from the province of Munster to that of Connaught. Hyde's family was, therefore, of Anglo-Irish ascendancy stock. There followed a line of Church of Ireland clergymen, all called Arthur, the fourth and last of whom was Douglas Hyde's father.

The reverend Arthur Hyde Junior (Douglas's father), rector of Tibohine, moved his family from Kilmactranny to Frenchpark. Douglas was six years old at this time.

Prior to Douglas's birth, the reverend Hyde and his wife had produced two male offspring, namely, Arthur and John Oldfield (known simply as Oldfield). Hugh, a third son, died in infancy. Douglas's relationship with his older brothers was distant as there was a gap of six years between him and the younger of the two. However, despite a similar age gap between Douglas and his young sister, Annette, born on 19 May 1865, they became very close to each other.

Douglas inherited his father's love of the country life of hunting, shooting and fishing. Long hours were spent outdoors, irrespective of the weather. Douglas's roaming around the countryside brought him into contact with the local people with whom he developed an easy rapport. This was facilitated by his enquiring mind, an independent nature and despite a fairly formal upbringing. It was through one such contact in particular, namely, that with Seamus Hart, an employee of his father, that Doug-

*Glebe House – the Hyde family moved here when Douglas was seven years old*

las became fascinated with the Irish language and in the oral tradition of learning. From this he also developed an intense interest in Irish folklore and history. His voracious appetite for learning was satisfied by evenings spent at the hearth-side in Seamus Hart's cottage, or in the houses of other neighbours. With these people he started to speak Irish.

Apart from a spell of a few weeks at a school in Dublin (probably the former Kingstown Grammar School in Dún Laoghaire), ending when he contracted measles, Douglas received his formal education at home from his father. He was well schooled, especially in Latin, Greek, German and French. Certainly Douglas learned from his father about other aspects of Irish life too. His father would have had a very different historical perspective on the ownership and uses of the land from that of the local native people. There was certainly no evidence, therefore, of any sympathy by the family for the growing nationalist cause at that time. His father was firmly opposed to Home Rule for Ireland. The landlord class, including the few of the Catholic faith, considered that the Fenians were a dangerous group, supported by ill-informed Americans. It was from Hart, therefore, that Douglas learned about the suppression of the Irish language by the

British authorities over the centuries, the exploits of the Fenians, the Great Famine, Daniel O'Connell's struggle for Catholic emancipation, and the impact of the Land League.

From his diaries, which Douglas consistently filled, his interest and love of the Irish language are made clear. However, pronunciation and syntax did not come easily to him. In the early stages he concentrated on the spoken word. Grammatical knowledge and correctness were to come much later. He developed his own method of phonetic spelling to help him remember words and phrases. A typical example was: *"Vee Shamus in sho,"* later changed to *"Bhi Seamus an so"* (anso).

The influence of gamekeeper Seamus Hart on Douglas was enormous and Hart's death in December 1875 left him devastated. He became depressed but eventually continued his enthusiastic pursuit, study and collection of all things Irish. To him the songs and folklore of the Irish peasantry in the Gaelic tongue formed a kind of literature even though not written down. This, he contended, would last only as long as the language itself lasted. This thought spurred Hyde on during many summers spent in central Connaught collecting songs, ballads, proverbs and stories. His hope was that his collection would be of interest to an increasing class of people who took an interest in what he described as 'this oldest surviving branch of the Aryan languages which a hundred years ago was spoken throughout the length and breadth of our country, even up to the walls of Dublin'.

During this time, his father, the reverend Arthur Hyde, developed gout and was frequently unwell. Indeed, the regular consumption of strong drink by the male members of the Hyde family was common. It became a serious problem in his father's case and in that of his brother, Oldfield. When the Reverend Arthur was 'indisposed' it sometimes fell to Douglas to take religious services in his place, a chore which Douglas did not at all welcome. It was, nonetheless, made very clear to Douglas by his father that he was expected to follow him into the Church of Ireland as a minister. His father's wishes in this matter took on an even greater importance for him when Arthur junior and Oldfield both spurned similar suggestions.

## University Days

In 1880, at the age of twenty, Douglas Hyde entered Trinity College Dublin. His brother Oldfield was already there since 1875. Arthur, too, had attended Trinity, in his case commencing in 1871. But he had died on 14 May 1879 at the young age of 25, primarily from tuberculosis. Douglas graduated from Trinity in 1884 with a gold medal in modern literature. He then turned his attention, reluctantly, to the Divinity School and achieved a 'first' in his exam in 1885. However, to his father's annoyance, he decided to abandon holy orders in favour of law and graduated in 1888 in that discipline.

During his time in university Hyde immersed himself in debating and in other aspects of college life, especially those in the literary sphere. He contributed poems, mostly in Irish, to *The Shamrock* magazine and made many contributions to *The Dublin University Review*. An article entitled 'A Plea for the Irish Language' filled ten pages of one issue. This was an item of major significance on the formulation of ideas about the language and its contribution to the Irish ethos. Most of the ideas in the article were later to become the basic principles of the Gaelic League movement. Hyde also became active in the Gaelic Union, an offshoot of the Society for the Preservation of the Irish Language. By this time he wrote under the style of 'An Craoibhín Aoibhinn' (The sweet/delightful little branch). Not everything he wrote was in Irish. In 1880, his subject matter had turned to nationalism as shown in his writing, in English, of a work entitled 'Ballads of '98'. A sample of this was the following:

> *'But English gold, as were of old,*
> *Betrayed the rightful cause,*
> *And English lies and English spies*
> *And Bloody English laws.*
>
> *And the dungeon clay was Rossa's bed*
> *Cold and damp and bare,*
> *And the people were left without a head,*
> *And broken was their war.'*

Many of his contemporaries had different opinions to those of Hyde regarding the Irish language. Some were of the view that it was a dying language and therefore a lost cause. Another view, held by conservatives and unionists, was that in order to achieve peace with England, it was necessary for Ireland to lose its separate identity, especially its language. Unionists of a more liberal viewpoint, however, who had scholarly interests, joined with nationalists and revolutionaries and were fully supportive of the preservation of the language. During this period, too, Hyde was a member of various clubs such as the Pan Celtic Society, the France-German Society and the Theosophical Society. He was also a member of the College Historical Society, his input gaining for him a reputation as a gifted speaker. From the Society and clubs Hyde made a wide circle of friends. His membership of clubs was not confined only to college ones. For example, he attended meetings of the Young Ireland Society where papers on topics such as nationalism were discussed. Here it was that he pooled his views on these matters with those of W.B. Yeats. Whilst Yeats openly admired Hyde's work, he considered him at heart a country squire and distant from the ordinary people. For his part, Hyde thought that Yeats was condescending towards anyone he regarded to be of a different social standing. At the Young Ireland Society meeting, too, Hyde met the Fenian leader, John O'Leary, recently returned from exile, and Dr George Sigerson. At one such meeting he encountered Maud Gonne for the first time. Not only Yeats was smitten by this lady, as Hyde's diary records for December 1888 show:

> *'To Sigersons in the evening where I saw the most dazzling woman I have ever seen: Miss Gonne, who drew every male in the room around her. She was wonderfully tall and beautiful. We stayed talking until 1.30 am. My head was spinning with her beauty.'*

His head spun with less speed when, two days later, he met Maud Gonne again, but this time he recorded:

> *'I was not as dazzled as I was the first time.'*

Nevertheless, he gave Maud Irish lessons, calling to her house in Dublin's Nassau Street for this purpose. The lessons stopped after a short time, however, without much progress being made, her stimulating discourses on other topics taking up much of the time.

During this period at Trinity, his mother, who had been suffering from severe arthritis, fell seriously ill. She died on 25 August 1886 at the age of fifty-two.

Douglas Hyde's first book was published in 1889. It was entitled *Leabhar Sgeulaigheachta*. It comprised a collection of folk tales, riddles and rhymes and was the first such book to be published completely in the national language. A plethora of publications followed as befitted a consummate folklorist and talented poet. His opus magnum, *A Literary History of Ireland*, was first published in 1899 (a new edition appeared in 1967).

In 1890, having failed to secure a university post in Ireland, Hyde took up a post of 'interim professorship' for one year at the University of New Brunswick in Canada. This was a period of great enjoyment for him, both professionally and personally. He was greatly admired by his students and he struck up a close relationship with a local girl. This was some compensation to him as he had previously had to forego his relationship with a Frances Crofton whom he had met in 1882 in Dublin. He had, in fact, proposed marriage to her in 1886, but she declined informing him that she had no intention of marrying anyone. In Canada, Hyde enjoyed the social scene to the full including balls, card parties, dinners, concerts, tennis and sleigh rides. He was, nevertheless, happy to return to Ireland at the end of his sojourn. On 25 June 1891, he set sail for Ireland. He kept a close watch on the political happenings in Ireland, in particular the publicity given to Parnell's affair with Kitty O'Shea and his slump in political standing as a result, together with the consequential split in the nationalist party in Westminster. In that same year, Parnell died and the prospect of Home Rule being granted to Ireland receded once again.

## Vision for Ireland

At this stage of Hyde's young life it seemed that his views on the use of physical force to attain political freedom were ambivalent. In retrospect, however, it is clear that he decided that freedom of culture, through the Irish language, gained by peaceful means, was the better way forward.

The pursuit of freedom of culture became a driving force for Hyde. Nowhere is this epitomised more than in

*Douglas Hyde as a young man*

his lecture, delivered on 25 November 1892, before the National Literary Society in Dublin, under the heading of 'The Necessity for De-Anglicising Ireland'. His opening remarks included the following:

> 'I wish to show you that in Anglicising ourselves wholesale we have thrown away with a light heart the best claim which we have upon the world's recognition of us as a separate nationality ... what the battleaxe of the Dane, the sword of the Norman, the wile of the Saxon were unable to perform, we have accomplished ourselves. We have at last broken the continuity of Irish life, and just at the moment when the Celtic race is presumably about to largely recover possession of its own country, it finds itself deprived and stripped of its Celtic characteristics, cut off from the past, yet scarcely in touch with its present.'

Hyde also deplored the losing of traditional Irish surnames and Christian names. Part of his conclusion stated:

14

*"... I appeal to everyone whatever his position – for this is no political matter – to do his best to help the Irish race to develop in future upon Irish lines, even at the risk of encouraging national aspirations, because upon Irish lines alone can the Irish race once more become what it was of yore – one of the most original, artistic, literary and charming peoples of Europe."*

Hyde saw Ireland in an anomalous position – on the one hand imitating England, especially in the use of its language, and 'yet apparently hating it'. He posed the question: how could Ireland produce anything good in literature, art or institutions as long as it was motivated by motives so contradictory?

*'Besides, I believe it is our own Gaelic past which, though the Irish race does not recognise it at present, is really at the bottom of the Irish heart, and prevents us becoming citizens of the Empire, as, I think, can be easily proved.*

*... To say that Ireland has not prospered under English rule is simply a truism; all the world admits it, England does not deny it. But the English retort is ready. You have not prospered, they say, because you would not settle down contentedly, like the Scotch, and form part of the Empire.'*

Hyde considered that the decline of 'Irish training and knowledge' was adversely affected after 'the establishment of Maynooth and the rise of O'Connell. These two events made an end of the Gaelicism of the Gaelic race.' His criticism of the Catholic clergy was that they were apathetic in regard to the Irish language in that they preached in English. He was equally critical of the Anglo-Irish gentry because of their clear dislike of spoken Irish. He also bemoaned what he considered were the efforts of the National Board of Education to destroy the national language.

*'... But it may be said, roughly speaking, that the ancient Gaelic civilisation died with O'Connell. Largely, I'm afraid, owing to his example and his neglect of inculcating the necessity of keeping alive racial customs, language and traditions, in which with one notable*

*exception of our scholarly idealist, Smith O'Brien, he has been fol-
lowed until a year ago by almost every leader of the Irish race.'*

The soul of Ireland was to be re-discovered not in the descendants of
Cromwell and the Williamites who sat in Grattan's Parliament, but in the
descendants of the 'hewers of wood and drawers of water, the ordinary
people themselves'.

But Hyde also put the blame for the loss of the Irish language as a
vibrant every day language squarely on the Irish people themselves:

> *'In fact I may venture to say that, up to the beginning of the pres-
> ent century, neither man, woman nor child of the Gaelic race,
> either of high blood or low blood, existed in Ireland who did not
> either speak Irish or understand it. But within the last ninety
> years we have, with an unparalleled frivolity deliberately thrown
> away our birthright and Anglicised ourselves.'*

Hyde did, however, reserve praise for the Gaelic Athletic Association
(GAA) when he said:

> *'Our ancient national game Camán, or hurling, and Gaelic foot-
> ball, have done more for Ireland than all the speeches of politi-
> cians for the past five years.'*

Hyde's overriding fear was what the Irish people had become:

> *'What, I fear, we are largely at present, a nation of imitators, the
> Japanese of Western Europe, lost to the power of native initiative
> and alive only to second hand assimilation.'*

His conclusion was, therefore, that 'in order to de-Anglicise ourselves,
we must at once arrest the decay of the language'.

Later, while on a visit to Boston, Hyde clarified his position, saying
that whilst he wished to fully support the promotion of the native language he did not anticipate the replacement of English:

> *'What I wish to see is Irish established as a living language, for
> all time, among the million or half million who still speak it*

*along the west coast and to insure that the language will hold a favourable place in teaching institutions and government examinations.'*

## Literary Revival

In 1890, Hyde was making a weekly contribution to the *Nation* newspaper under the title 'Gaelic Folk Songs'. It was his prose, however, that won W.B. Yeats's admiration as indicated in this quotation:

> *'The prose narrative that flows about his "Love Songs of Connacht" ... the prose parts of the book were to me, as they were to many others, the coming of a new power into literature.'*

Hyde also had the distinction of writing the first ever play in Irish. *'Casadh an t-Sugáin'* ('The Twisting of the Rope') was first performed at the Gaiety Theatre, Dublin, on 21 October 1901 by members of the Gaelic League Amateur Dramatic Society. Hyde himself played the principal part.

In 1892, Hyde was made president of the National Literary Society in Dublin – an offshoot of the Irish Literary Society established some months earlier in London by Yeats and others.

## Marriage

The year 1893 was a momentous one for Hyde. In July, he recorded in his diary:

> *'... we decided firmly and finally that we were going to get married and we were publicly engaged.'*

He was referring to his relationship with Lucy Cometina Kurtz. This young lady he had met briefly some time previously but was re-introduced to her by his sister, Annette, when Lucy was visiting Frenchpark. Their relationship blossomed quickly, an outcome which was, indeed, envisaged by Annette. Lucy was tall, slim and attractive. She was the daughter of a German chemist, originally from Russia. When she returned to her home in England, she and Douglas corresponded in German. Later Hyde sailed for Liverpool and, on 10 October 1893, they were married in a Church of England ceremony. After a honeymoon spent in Paris and London, they returned to Ireland and settled in Ratra, a spacious Georgian house overlooking Lough Gara. Writing in his diary at the end of that year Hyde recorded:

> *'The greatest thing I did in the past year – indeed the greatest thing I ever did in my life – was that I got married.'*

## Gaelic League

In that same year, 1893, the Gaelic League was founded. This was done on the proposal of John MacNeill, who invited Hyde and a number of others to meet with a view to establishing an organisation to maintain and promote the use of Gaelic as a spoken language in Ireland. Hyde had been greatly inspired along these lines by Fr. Eugene O'Growney, Professor of Irish in Maynooth – a college at that time dedicated to the education of Catholics, especially those preparing for the priesthood (now a constituent member of the National University of Ireland). At the League's inaugural meeting Hyde was elected president. O'Neill emphasised that literature in Irish would be left to others; their own task was to spread Irish as a spoken language. Later, P.H. Pearse was to say that the Gaelic League was the most revolutionary influence that had ever come into Ireland, and that that meeting provided 'the germ of all future Irish history'.

By the third year of its existence the League had seventeen branches in Ireland, four in England and one in Scotland. Additionally, there were three Irish societies falling within the aegis of the League in the USA.

The growth of the Gaelic League coincided with the lessening of interest by Hyde's wife in her husband's work for the language. In truth, her interest had always been superficial, being more taken with the celebrity of the society he kept rather than in the language itself. Nevertheless, she was very supportive of him and was especially critical of those who did not give him due credit for his endeavours. Life was not easy for her because Hyde's schedule was hectic and he was frequently away on his travels. She also developed a dislike for Ratra which was too remote from Dublin for her taste. Hyde applied for the post of Professorship of Irish in Trinity College in Dublin but was rejected by the 'English fort in Ireland'. Meanwhile, Lucy was kept busy by the birth of their daughter, Nuala, in 1894. The arrival of a second daughter, Úna, was welcomed in June 1896. In that same year, however, Hyde's remaining brother, Oldfield, died.

*John Oldfield Hyde, elder brother of Douglas Hyde*

Hyde continued with his writing. In the summer of 1898 he met Lady Gregory, the close friend of W.B. Yeats, who became very supportive of him. Hyde wrote a number of plays which were staged at the Abbey Theatre. Playwright John Millington Synge and novelist George Moore were impressed by Hyde's work, the latter becoming also an enthusiast for the language movement. He actively advised Hyde regarding his play 'The Tinker and the Fairy'. The play was performed at the Gaiety Theatre in Irish in 1903 with Hyde in one of the principal parts. (One of the actresses was Sinéad Ni Fhlannagáin, later to become the wife of Éamon de Valera.) Moore's admiration did not last and he became critical of him as indicated in the first volume of his book, *Hail and Fairwell*, when he said that Hyde's acting was like that of the proverbial 'stage Irishman'.

By now, through his drive and enthusiasm, Hyde had brought 500 branches of the League into being. This he achieved in just over ten years of his leadership. The League's finances, however, were in poor shape. In 1905, following his father's death earlier in that year, Hyde made a fund raising trip to the USA on behalf of the Gaelic League. His tour in the USA was organised by John Quinn, an influential Irish-American millionaire. Quinn was instrumental in counteracting the reticence shown by some Irish societies in supporting the League because of Hyde's Protestantism. Hyde's lecture tour was extensive and he also had a meeting with President Theodore Roosevelt at the White House. The fundraising was a great success and Hyde was not slow to credit Quinn's endeavours in this regard. Hyde returned to Ireland in June of 1906.

In 1908, the National University of Ireland was established and in the following year Hyde was appointed to the chair of modern Irish, a post he held until his retirement in 1932.

## Sadness

Tragedy struck Hyde's family in 1916 with the death of his daughter, Nuala. She suffered a haemorrhage caused by tuberculosis and died on 30 September. She was a mere twenty-two years old. Attractive, outgoing and popular, she was most like Hyde himself. Her death was a big blow to the family. Nuala was buried in Portahard church graveyard near Frenchpark.

## Trouble Ahead

By 1913, the Liberal government in Westminster, after many years of pressing by Parnell, Redmond and others, became committed to granting Home Rule to Ireland. A Bill to this effect was passed by the Commons in January. This was welcomed by the majority of Irish people but rejected by a Protestant majority in the four north east counties of Ulster. The Protestants said that they would defy the British Government, by force, if necessary. A group called the Ulster Volunteer Force (UVF) was formed under the leadership of Sir Edward Carson with the support of many Conservatives. Their stated intention was to resist Home Rule. To counter this, in the paper *An Claidheamh Soluis*, an organ of the Gaelic League, Eoin MacNeill proposed the founding of the National Volunteers. Hyde was embarrassed by the use of the Gaelic League as a vehicle for a call to arms. He was concerned, too, by Pearse's oration at the grave of Wolfe Tone in June of that year, when Pearse drew a connection between Tone's aim of breaking the connection with England with the aims of the League. Hyde was firmly convinced that the League must preserve its independence of all political connections. In June he addressed the executive of the League in the following terms:

*Douglas Hyde and Eoin MacNeill, founders of the Gaelic League, c. 1923*

> *'I raise my voice strongly tonight against politics in the Gaelic League, and against the evils which all too often result from politics, as you yourselves know, ... I give you a warning tonight, a warning straight from my heart – if politics continue within the League that, one by one, the best people will be driven out of it ... and those who are left will be able to say (as perhaps they want to say) that they are the true patriots and that the rest of us are only useless good-for-nothings.'*

## Departure from the Gaelic League

With the outbreak of World War I, and the call of John Redmond (the leader of the Irish Party at Westminster) for Irish volunteers to enlist in the British Army, came a split in the Volunteers. Hyde referred to this as an example of the negative impact of politics on an organisation. At an Árd Feis (general meeting) held in Dundalk in 1915, the constitution of the Gaelic League was changed to include, in future, the realisation of 'a free,

Gaelic speaking Ireland'. On the announcement of the vote favouring this, Hyde vacated the chair and left the meeting and the League forever.

## The Rising and After

Hyde was not supportive of the rising which took place in 1916. During this period he continued in his university post. He had grave doubts about the use of physical force but he agreed in principle with the aim of achieving freedom from Britain.

In 1918, Sinn Féin won a general election but refused to take up their seats in Westminster. Instead, they set up their own parliament, Dáil Éireann. The volunteers, who supported this move, called themselves the Irish Republican Army (IRA). The War of Independence against the British commenced. A truce with the British was agreed on 11 July 1921. This was followed on 6 December by the signing of a treaty from which the Irish Free State came into existence. Hyde's view of the Treaty was that the country had achieved a measure of real freedom.

> *'So far as I can see, we have got almost everything we want under the new treaty … I think we got the very most we could have got without war, and war is too awful to contemplate again.'*

The Treaty was opposed by de Valera and his followers and a civil war followed. On more mundane matters, Hyde had hoped to be appointed to the new Free State senate and was disappointed when Yeats was appointed instead. Hyde assumed that his failure in this was due to the fact that Cosgrave, President of the Free State Executive Council, had not appreciated Hyde's support for the reprieve of Robert Erskine Childers, who was later executed by Cosgrave's government for being found in possession of a small revolver given to him by Michael Collins. In canvassing for Hyde's appointment, his old friend John Quinn of the USA said:

> *'… if it had not been for the Gaelic League there would have been no Sinn Féin. And with no Sinn Féin there would have been no Free State today.'*

Following the resignation from the Senate by Sir Hutcheson Poe on 4 February 1925, Hyde was unanimously co-opted. When, however, an election for the Senate took place in September of that year Hyde failed to be elected. From that time, until his retirement in 1932, his university work became his main preoccupation.

## President of Ireland

On his retirement from the university in 1932 he moved back to the family home, Ratra near Frenchpark. There, he once again immersed himself in county life which was so dear to his heart. Retirement for Hyde was to be relatively short-lived because, in 1938, he accepted the invitation to become President of Ireland. De Valera's Fianna Fáil party was in power as a minority government, relying on support from the Labour Party. The role of President was provided for in the newly introduced Constitution. Fianna Fáil and Fine Gael had vetoed nominations put up by each other for the Presidency, and Cosgrave, conscious of the Government's precarious position, proposed Hyde which was accepted by Fianna Fáil. The term was for seven years. His appointment being the unanimous choice of all parties, his election was unopposed. Hyde was then 78 years old.

*Douglas Hyde arriving at Dublin Castle for his inauguration*

*President Hyde leaving St Patrick's Cathedral on day of his inauguration*

Hyde's election formalities took place on 4 May 1938 in a simple ceremony in the boardroom of the Department of Agriculture in Government Buildings in Dublin's Kildare Street. The inauguration ceremony followed in Dublin Castle. His appointment was well received in Ireland, in the USA and in the other parts of the world with which Ireland had a close connection. De Valera was happy with the selection of Hyde too. He shared Hyde's love of the Irish language and, further, he felt that Hyde was independent in that he had no political favours to repay. However, some said that Hyde's selection was only a 'sop' to the Protestant minority.

Hyde moved to the Presidential official residence, Áras an Uachtaráin, in Dublin's Phoenix Park. Lucy, however, refused to leave home. This was ironic given that, prior to this, she had wanted Hyde to sell Ratra so that they could move to Dublin. However, a series of un-named illnesses may have been the reason for her change of mind. Certainly, the medical advice given to her was that she would not have been able to fulfil the duties of the wife of the President due to her nervous disposition. Among his wife's qualities which Hyde admired was the forthright way in which she

*Mr and Mrs de Valera greeting the newly installed*
*President of Ireland, Douglas Hyde*

expressed herself and the strength and sharpness of her mind. However, entertaining strangers and having to exercise diplomacy would have been difficult for her given her changed state of health. Hyde's sister, Annette, now widowed with no children, joined Hyde in Áras an Uachtaráin. In contrast to Lucy, she was well disposed to dealing with people, strangers or otherwise. She enjoyed good health and, like her brother, loved the outdoor life.

## Presidential Duties

Hyde carried out his duties with skill, diplomacy and with great dignity. His work schedule was honed by his Secretary, Michael McDunphy, and Hyde soon settled into a routine for dealing with his not inconsiderable paperwork and correspondence. The afternoons were generally reserved for receiving visitors from home and abroad – Hyde insisted that no reasonable request for an interview be refused. In particular, he insisted that certain old friends, including Maud Gonne, several Trinity College classmates and O'Siochfhradha, commonly known as '*An Seabhac*' ('The Hawk'), co-founder with Hyde of the Irish Folklore Society, be admitted whenever they came, irrespective of the planned schedule for the day. Outside this, Hyde got on with presidential visits, State banquets, public meetings and appearances as well as regular meetings with the Council of State. In 1938 he was visited by President Roosevelt's ambassador to Britain, Joseph P. Kennedy, and his son, Joseph P. Kennedy Junior. Hyde told them that he recalled meeting the young Kennedy's maternal grandfather, John F. Fitzgerald, in Boston in 1905.

One incident in that same year of 1938 caused him much distress. He accepted an invitation to attend an international soccer match on November 13 and duly did so. He was reminded, however, by the GAA, of which he had long been a patron, that membership precluded support for 'foreign' games. His attendance at the international match, he was informed, had violated this ban. Hyde was duly expelled from the GAA. He was deeply hurt by this action but chose to keep silent about the matter. It was not until 1984 that amends were made, after a fashion, when the Roscommon branch of the GAA had a plaque affixed to the entrance of the cemetery behind Portahard church to commemorate Hyde's early contributions to the Association. It now lies on his grave.

*First meeting of the Council of State – President Hyde is seated in centre and seated left are Sean T. O'Kelly and Éamon de Valera*

*Douglas Hyde relaxing with friends*

In 1938, too, it became clear that Lucy's health was deteriorating quickly. She died on 31 December of that year, at Ratra. Despite this great personal loss, Hyde continued to carry out the duties of his office. The advent of the Second World War had little effect on his role as President, the whole matter of Ireland's neutrality being the responsibility of the de Valera government.

In April 1940 Hyde suffered a stroke. He recovered gradually but was confined to a wheelchair. In the autumn of that year his doctors informed him that he would never regain the use of his legs. This was a bitter blow to someone as active as Hyde had always been. Nevertheless, he continued to attend to his duties as best he could.

A political crisis arose in May of 1944 when the de Valera government was defeated in the Dáil by a small majority over a controversial transport bill. There were two choices open to de Valera – to resign or to call a general election. Under the provisions of the Constitution, the responsibility for making the ultimate decision on this rested with the President. De Valera briefed President Hyde about the situation and then was asked to withdraw so that the President could discuss the matter with his Secretary, Mr McDunphy. Hyde decided that, given the state of play between the various parties, the interests of the country would be best served by calling a general election. De Valera was informed of this decision.

In 1945, Hyde was invited to stand for a second term but, now being eighty-five years old, he declined. He went to live in a house in the Phoenix Park near Áras an Uachtaráin which he called 'Little Ratra' and there he died on 12 July 1949.

At 8.30 am on 14 July 1949, the

*Statue of Douglas Hyde outside Portahard Church, Frenchpark*

remains of the first President of Ireland were taken from Little Ratra and with an escort of Army motorcycles brought in procession through the streets of Dublin. The procession halted for half a minute outside the General Post Office, the headquarters of the 1916 Rising, before continuing to St Patrick's Cathedral (Protestant) in the city centre. The service in the Cathedral was conducted by the Dean of St. Patrick's and benediction was pronounced by the Archbishop of Dublin, the Most Reverend Dr. Barton. After the service, the hearse again moved off through the local streets preceded by fifty civil guards and a battalion of infantry with arms reversed. The cortege then left the city and set off for Roscommon. Douglas Hyde was buried along side his wife in the cemetery at Portahard in Frenchpark.

> '*Reverence for our past history, regard for the memory of our ancestors, our national honour and the fear of becoming materialized and losing our best and highest characteristics call upon us to assist the Irish-speaking population.*' – Douglas Hyde

# Seán T. O'Kelly

## Second President of Ireland (1945–1959)

### Early Years

Seán T. O'Kelly was born on 26 June 1882 at 55 Wellington Street, near Mountjoy Street, Dublin. His father, Samuel O'Kelly, from Blackrock, County Dublin, was manager of a large shoe shop named Shorts, in O'Connell Street in Dublin. His mother, Caitríona Ní Dhea, was born in Dublin's Fishamble Street. Seán T. (as he was frequently called) had two brothers, Micheál and Maitiu. He also had a twin sister but she died when she was just under five years old. When Seán T. was about one year old his father moved the family to Berkeley Road where he later opened his own shoe shop. Both staff and customers from Shorts followed him there.

When Sean T. was five years old he was sent to school at Clochar Na Mban Rialta in Mountjoy Street. After three years he attended the Christian Brother's School in St. Mary's Place, and later O'Connell's School in North Richmond Street in Dublin. He didn't learn Irish until he started the preparatory grade of the Intermediate Certificate examination. Initially, he was not at all enthusiastic about Irish but this seems to have changed, and in fact, he was later singled out by his teachers for his proficiency in the language.

On leaving school O'Kelly was employed as a junior assistant in the National Library of Ireland, but after four years he tendered his resignation as he was unhappy receiving a salary from the British treasury. This was, he considered, like taking money from the enemy. When O'Kelly gave notice of his intention to quit, his boss in the library was furious. Where, he asked, could he ever expect to get such a good opportunity again? He was so annoyed by O'Kelly's decision that he tore up the resignation letter and threw it in the wastepaper bin. Nevertheless, O'Kelly left the library at the end of 1902. Ironically, it was through the good offices of one of the 'enemy', an English friend, that he got a job with the *Evening Mail* newspaper. He also worked as manager of the Irish language paper *Claiomh Solais,* of which P. H. Pearse was editor.

## Young Man

In 1889, O'Kelly joined the Gaelic League. He was also a member of the Celtic Literary Society where he first met Douglas Hyde and Arthur Griffith. O'Kelly was one of the founders of 'The Confederate Club' which sponsored lectures and discussions on politics and literature. The Club also promoted Irish music, held *céilí mór* and was engaged in the promotion of Gaelic games. O'Kelly remembered attending, in 1898, a commemoration of the 1798 Rising. A year later he attended a public meeting in Dublin's College Green in support of the Boers' struggle in southern Africa. Griffith and James Connolly were speakers and Maud Gonne McBride also attended. The meeting was broken up by the police. He witnessed many such 'subversive' meetings being similarly broken up. He also had a vivid memory of the huge funeral of Charles Stewart Parnell – the cortege passed his home in Berkeley Road. Mourners passed by continuously from midday to eight o'clock that evening. He joined the Irish Republican Brotherhood (IRB), the forerunner of the IRA, in 1900, around the time of the visit by Queen Victoria to the country. This visit most likely riled O'Kelly and his republican colleagues as it served as an unwanted reminder of the grip of the British administration on all matters Irish. His role in the

*Arthur Griffith, one of the founders of Sinn Féin*

IRB was that of organiser and his duties took him to all corners of Ireland. He also undertook extensive travel in Scotland and England.

In 1905, O'Kelly was, with Griffith, a founding member of Sinn Féin. With the growth of Sinn Féin the need for a way to reflect their views was recognised, and so a newspaper named, appropriately enough, *Sinn Féin,* was established. It was edited by Griffith and managed by O'Kelly. Shortly after the outbreak of World War I the newspaper was suppressed by the British authorities who feared its subversive overtones. It was immediately replaced by other publications such as *Éire* and *Nationality*. As soon as one was closed down another emerged under a new title.

World War I was to have a significant impact on Ireland. Irishmen in their thousands answered the British call to join their armed forces for the defence of 'small nations' and on the promise of the granting of Home Rule to Ireland – a promise later reneged upon. No doubt in some cases men enlisted for the sheer adventure of war and were influenced, too, by the lack of job opportunities in Ireland. Their participation in the fight for 'small nations' was seen by Republicans as contrary to the maxim that 'charity begins at home', believing as they did that those who joined up were joining the forces of Ireland's oppressors.

Sean T. O'Kelly stood as a Sinn Féin candidate in the municipal elections of 1906 and won a seat on Dublin Corporation. His work as an alderman saw him advocate the reform of public administration with special emphasis on providing decent housing for the poor of the city. He was chairman of various committees of the Corporation, including the Finance Committee, and obtained a wide experience of public matters.

## 1916 Rising

In response to the Loyalist formation of the Ulster Volunteer Force (to resist the granting of Home Rule for the country), a counter force, the Irish Volunteers, was set up in Dublin in 1913 and O'Kelly was to the forefront of its formation. This led, in turn, to his intimate involvement in the events that would later lead to the 1916 Rising. In preparation for this O'Kelly, at the request of Tom Clarke and Sean MacDermott, made visits to Britain to purchase arms.

In his autobiography, O'Kelly recalled a meeting held in the library of Conradh na Gaeilge on 9 September 1914 with Tom Clarke, Arthur Griffith, Patrick Pearse, Sean MacDermott and others in which the engagement of England in what was to be termed the Great War was discussed. It was acknowledged that England's preoccupation with matters of war would be to Ireland's advantage. It was agreed that the Fianna Éireann (a youth or scout movement) and Cuman na mBan (a quasi-military womens' organisation) were to be strengthened. It was further agreed that if German forces landed in Ireland they were to be helped, with the ultimate aim of assisting Ireland to achieve freedom.

In 1915, O'Kelly travelled to New York to advise Clann na Geadheal leaders (John Devoy, Judge Cohalon and Joseph McGarrity) of the plans for the Rising and to raise funds for it. By the end of that year, O'Kelly was appointed Staff Captain to Patrick Pearse, the Commander-in-Chief of the Republican forces. In April of 1916, O'Kelly was present at a meeting in Rathfarnham in Dublin with Patrick Pearse, Sean MacDermott and

Eoin MacNeill. A proposed rising was discussed. MacNeill was not happy about the proposal, but MacDermott subsequently said to O'Kelly that MacNeill would not be a problem 'as he changes his mind from one day to the next'.

On Easter Monday of 1916, O'Kelly went to his office (he was secretary of Conradh na Gaeilge) at 25 Parnell Square. Later in the morning he visited his mother. After 1.00 p.m. he went to Liberty Hall from where, on the orders of James Connolly, he marched with others to the General Post Office (GPO) in O'Connell Street (then Sackville Street). Later he was asked by Connolly to return to Liberty Hall to collect two special tricolour flags for raising on the GPO. Soon after his return they were informed that British soldiers were approaching O'Connell Street. Although formally assigned to Pearse, O'Kelly spent much of the day following orders from Connolly. At 3.00 p.m. he returned once again to Liberty Hall, this time to collect bombs and other armaments. These he arranged to be brought to the GPO by horse and cart! His work was still not done as he then had to get bread and milk. He used hand carts for this purpose and went 'shopping' in Capel Street, Bolton Street, Mary Street and Parnell Square. He was present when Pearse read the Proclamation at the main entrance to

*James Connolly's Irish Citizen Army outside Liberty Hall, Dublin, 1916*

the GPO. He recalled that between 300 and 400 members of the general public were present to witness this historic occasion.

The Proclamation read as follows:

**Poblacht na h-Éireann**

**The Provisional Government of the Irish Republic**

*To the People of Ireland*

*Irishmen and Irishwomen: In the name of God and of the dead generations from which she receives her old tradition of nationhood, Ireland, through us, summons her children to her flag and strikes for her freedom.*

*Having organised and trained her manhood through her secret revolutionary organisation, the Irish Republican Brotherhood, and through her open military organisations, the Irish Volunteers and the Irish Citizen Army, having patiently perfected her discipline, having resolutely waited for the right moment to reveal itself, she now seizes the moment, and, supported by her exiled children in America and by gallant allies in Europe, but relying in the first on her own strength, she strikes in full confidence of victory.*

*We declare the right of the people of Ireland to the ownership of Ireland, and to the unfettered control of Irish destinies, to be sovereign and indefeasible. The long usurpation of that right by a foreign people and government has not extinguished the right, nor can it ever be extinguished except by the destruction of the Irish people. In every generation the Irish people have asserted their right to national freedom and sovereignty; six times during the past three hundred years they have asserted it in arms. Standing on that fundamental right and again asserting it in arms in the face of the world, we hereby proclaim the Irish Republic as a Sovereign Independent State. And we pledge our lives and the lives of our comrades-in-arms to the cause of its freedom, of its welfare, and of its exaltation among the nations.*

*The Irish Republic is entitled to, and hereby claims, the allegiance of every Irishman and Irishwoman. The Republic guarantees religious and civil liberty, equal rights and equal opportunities of all its citizens, and declares its resolve to pursue the happiness and prosperity of the whole nation and of all its parts, cherishing all the children of the nation equally, and oblivious of the differences carefully fostered by an alien government, which have divided a minority in the past.*

*Until our arms have brought the opportune moment for the establishment of a permanent National Government, representative of the whole people of Ireland and elected by the suffrages of all her men and women, the Provisional Government, hereby constituted, will administer the civil and military affairs of the Republic in trust for the people.*

*We place the cause of the Irish Republic under the protection of the Most High God, Whose blessing we invoke upon our arms, and we pray that no one who serves that cause will dishonour it by cowardice, inhumanity, or rapine. In this supreme hour the Irish nation must, by its valour and discipline and by the readiness of its children to sacrifice themselves for the common good, prove itself worthy of the august destiny to which it is called.*

*Signed on behalf of the Provisional Government,*

*Thomas J Clarke*
*Seán Mac Diarmada*
*Thomas MacDonagh*
*P.H. Pearse*
*Eamonn Ceannt*
*James Connolly*
*Joseph Plunkett.*

It fell to O'Kelly to put up copies of the Proclamation in the streets near the GPO. O'Kelly reported to Pearse and was congratulated by him on the work he had done. On Wednesday he got word that one of his brothers had been injured. He got permission from Pearse to go to Temple Street to see him. Later, O'Kelly was detained overnight by British soldiers but was released the following morning because they thought he was one of a number of drunks picked up the previous night. He called again to see his mother

*Willie and Patrick Pearse – the brothers were executed for their part in the 1916 Rising*

and had breakfast there. Rifle and big gun firing made it dangerous for him to leave his mother's house. He tried to do so but was approached by soldiers and questioned. On Friday he ventured to Cumberland Street (linking Parnell Street to Seán MacDermott Street) but British soldiers were everywhere. He was shot in the foot by a sniper and was taken by

*Dublin in ruins following the 1916 Rising*

friends on a bicycle to the Mater Hospital where he was kept overnight. He was discharged reluctantly by a doctor who gave him a stick, and he went home. His brother scouted around for information and said that the GPO had surrendered and the leaders taken as prisoners.

After the suppression of the Rising by the British, O'Kelly was captured and jailed in England. He was freed on Christmas Eve only to be re-arrested a few weeks later and deported to Britian, but he slipped back home in time for the general election of 1918.

## 1918 General Election

The period of 1917/1918 was characterised by tensions in the IRB due to the divergence of opinion regarding support for the Rising. Additionally, it was felt in some quarters that Sinn Féin itself was a spent force due to similar divergences of opinion in its ranks. It fell to Éamon de Valera to pull the Sinn Féin party together, and in this he had a considerable measure of success. Prior to this, Arthur Griffith had voluntarily resigned the presidency of the party he himself had founded, in favour of de Valera. During this period O'Kelly was involved in an anti-conscription campaign to keep Irish people out of the British army. A proposal to impose conscription was made by the British Prime Minister, David Lloyd George, in March of 1918. Meanwhile, following the invention of a so called 'German Plot' by authorities in Dublin Castle, O'Kelly was one of the few leaders who managed to escape arrest and was able to keep working for Sinn Féin.

The year 1918 was an important one for O'Kelly in another way too. It was in that year that he married Mary Kate Ryan, a young lady from County Wexford.

The General Election campaign in 1918 was significant in that a number of factors now favoured Sinn Féin. Foremost was the effective collapse of the Irish Parliamentary party in Westminster due, partly, to their past failure to deliver on Home Rule. Nevertheless, Sinn Féin had to contend with some disadvantages too, not least the fact that the country was effectively under military rule. Their manifesto was drafted by O'Kelly and he was appointed Director of Organisation. In the end, they swept the boards in the election. Seventy-three candidates who fa-voured independence from Britain were elected, against only six Home Rule supporters (apart from Ulster, where Unionists held sway in the east-ern counties in particular). O'Kelly was elected by a sweeping majority for the College Green constituency in Dublin, and was then appointed chairman of the committee charged with responsibility for arrangements for the creation of Dáil Éireann (Irish Parliament). The Parliamentarians in Westminster, once so powerful under Charles Stewart Parnell, were now a spent force. Their cause was damaged further by the death of their leader John Redmond.

*Seán T. O'Kelly, Harry Boland and unidentified woman at*
*Kingsbridge Station in Dublin en route to Paris Peace Conference*

Twenty-seven Sinn Féin successful candidates (those who were not in jail because of the alleged 'German Plot') now met in Dublin in January 1919 and, refusing to take their seats in Westminster, declared Irish Independence and took the title of Dáil Éireann for their new parliament. With the setting up of the Dáil, O'Kelly was appointed Ceann Comhairle (Speaker). He was also made Chairman of the Foreign Relations Committee and was sent to the Peace Conference in Paris to lobby US President Woodrow Wilson and others to secure a hearing for international recognition. In this, however, he failed due to pressure placed on Wilson by Lloyd George.

In 1920 O'Kelly submitted his resignation from his various and onerous duties due to stress caused by his workload. On a visit to the Vatican he became seriously ill. He recovered and was urged by de Valera to continue his work. In Rome he had been granted an audience by Pope Benedict XV who wanted to be kept informed on political matters in Ireland. Later, in 1922, O'Kelly had a meeting with the new Pope, Pius XI.

Before the start of the Civil War, O'Kelly worked hard to preserve peace and unity. However, he took de Valera's side in the hostilities that

*Irish Free State army soldiers travelling by donkey cart*

followed and was arrested and jailed until Christmas 1923. In 1924 he was in America as envoy of the Republican anti-Treaty cause. On his return to Ireland he became immersed in the newly formed political party, founded by de Valera, called Fianna Fáil.

O'Kelly was elected to the Dáil in 1921, 1922, 1923 and twice more in the two elections held in 1927. His debating skills in the Dáil were recognised for their forthrightness. For example, in the Dáil in 1927, he responded to a proposal to elect W.T. Cosgrave as President of the Executive Council in a long dissertation a part of which was as follows:

*'... I am satisfied that on no conceivable ground that I can imagine should the Deputy (Cosgrave) who has been proposed be voted for or receive the votes of Deputies of this assembly. One would imagine that in proposing the Deputy for such a high position as President of the governing body of this country there would be advanced strong arguments and sound reasons why the particular Deputy should be chosen. It is very significant that the gentleman who proposed and seconded for this honour the Deputy – I do not know whether he sits for Kilkenny or Cork –'*

*(Interjection by an Ceann Comhairle: 'For Cork')*

*'It is, as I say, significant that neither one nor the other of them if they had good arguments to offer why their friend and colleague should be proposed as President, brought them forth ... I have arguments to bring forth, and I am not ashamed nor afraid to bring them forth, as to why the gentleman named should not be elected President ...The Deputy who has been nominated, to my knowledge, did a good deal in these early days to preach the gospel of Irish independence as Irish patriots know it, and to instil into young and old the necessity of standing faithfully by the old traditional gospel of Irish freedom. He did his share, as I say, and as I acknowledge, for some years to get that policy and that gospel understood and accepted by the people. To such an extent did that gospel which he preached, in company with others, get accepted at one time that those who stood for a different political*

*Irish Free State army soldiers firing artillery on the Four Courts, June 1922*

*ideal, the ideal of an Ireland subordinate to the British Empire, were swept out of political existence. He preached the gospel of Ireland independent, Ireland free, Ireland united, Ireland one nation, and that free and Gaelic – the gospel of Pearse, the gospel of independence as preached by Tone.*

*That is what he stood for then. If he stood for the same gospel now, or if there was anyone here offered to us as President who stood for that gospel, I would be the first to record my vote for him if he were fitted in other respects for the post. Primarily, on the grounds that the gentleman nominated does not stand for that gospel, I ask the Deputies not to vote for him ...*

*... One more word. If there is one particular item more than another in the last five years which seems to have brought a curse on our country it has been the partitioning of our ancient nation. There are some in this assembly who will remember that one of the main reasons why the party of the late Mr. John Redmond was driven out of power in 1918 by the party with which Deputy*

*Cosgrave was then associated, one of the main reasons why Sinn Féin got into political control, was because Sinn Féin preached that if the Redmond party were left in control they threatened to bring partition into operation in Ireland. Not alone did Deputy Cosgrave when he got into office and power, for that amongst other reasons, not threaten to bring partition into Ireland, but he brought it into full and complete operation for the first time in the history of our country ... If there were no other reason why the gentleman named should not be approved of and accepted in this Assembly, that one reason alone should suffice.'*

The vote in support of W.T. Cosgrave was won by 76 votes to 70.

The feisty nature of O'Kelly's debating skills is illustrated in the following verbal altercation. It also shows again the depth of bitterness festering as a result of the Civil War:

*The President (Cosgrave): 'I beg to acknowledge the very great honour conferred on me by the Dáil. I propose to carry out the duties of this office to the best of my ability, with the help of God. I would like to say, in answer to some of the speeches that have been made against my nomination, that from the strict point of view of Irish nationality, I yield to no man, in this House or outside it. That is a thing I would advise Deputy O'Kelly not to laugh at. Irish nationality is much more sacred than perhaps even he or his friends think.'*

*O'Kelly: 'You know a lot about it.'*

*The President: 'Whatever action I may have taken at any time during the last five years, I have taken it with the authority of the people of this country, with the authority of this Dáil.'*

*O'Kelly : 'You have not.'*

*The President: 'The Deputy's seat was vacant for five years. If he had a case to make against my administration, this Dáil was the place to make it, the first institution in this country.'*

O'Kelly: 'The seats of many are vacant. We know where their graves are.'

The President: 'And so do I.'

A Deputy: 'Kevin O'Higgins.'

An Ceann Comhairle (The Speaker): 'We will not advance any distance along this particular line.'

Mr Davin: 'The President started it.'

A Deputy: 'Take your President off it.'

An Ceann Comhairle: 'The Deputy must not make allusions to my President. I do not know who made the statement, but he must not make any such allusion.'

O'Kelly: 'You voted for him last time.'

An Ceann Comhairle: 'This is a serious matter. Will Deputy O'Kelly explain what he means?'

O'Kelly: 'You can explain it.'

Deputies: 'Chair, Chair.'

An Ceann Comhairle: 'This is a serious matter, and it may as well be settled at the outset. What does Deputy O'Kelly mean by saying that I voted for the President on the last occasion?'

O'Kelly: 'You can best explain yourself.'

An Ceann Comhairle: 'Will Deputy explain what he means?'

O'Kelly: 'You can best explain it.'

An Ceann Comhairle: 'If this Assembly is to be carried on any reasonable principle, one of the things that cannot be tolerated in it is any insinuation against the Chair, and if a Deputy, and, most of all, a responsible Deputy is of the opinion that the occupant of the Chair has now, or at any other time, behaved in an improper manner, it is his duty to put a motion before the House and make his case ...'

## Government Minister

Following Fianna Fáil's success in the General Election of 1932, O'Kelly was made Minister for Local Government. In this post he gained a reputation as a diligent and competent Minister. O'Kelly held this ministerial post until the outbreak of World War II when he held the Education portfolio for a short period.

In 1934 his wife died. Two years later he married Phyllis, the sister of his first wife. There were no children of the marriage.

Later, during the period of harsh war-time budgets, O'Kelly was made Minister for Finance (1939–1945) and, with the coming into effect of the 1937 Constitution, he took up the post of Tánaiste (Deputy Prime Minister). He held this latter position until 1945. The period of the Second World War was, economically, extremely severe in Ireland. The relationship with Britain was strained due to Ireland's declaration of neutrality in the war. Food and fuel rations were the order of the day.

In 1938, O'Kelly became the focus of attention when rumours began to spread in the Irish Parliament that he was being considered for the post of President of Ireland. The popular Lord Mayor of Dublin, Alfie Byrne, was also thought to be a possible candidate. In the event, the post went to Douglas Hyde. In 1945, however, the idea of O'Kelly becoming President of Ireland became a reality with the retirement of Douglas Hyde from the post.

## President of Ireland

The election for the Presidency was to be the first contested one. The *Irish Times* of 30 April 1945 reported:

> *'There is some talk about a compromise in candidates. We don't want any more of that. We are putting up Seán T. O'Kelly and we are going ahead with him,' said Mr G Boland, Minister for Justice, referring to the forthcoming Presidential election at a Fianna Fáil meeting in Roscommon yesterday. Mr Boland said that Dr O'Higgins and some representatives of Fine Gael had actually*

*said that in nominating Mr O'Kelly the Government was stand-
ing for the totalitarian system. 'Anything like the cheek of that I
never heard' declared Mr Boland. 'Dr O'Higgins started the Blue
Shirts, a movement that was the outward sign of all the totalitarian movements in Europe and they did all they could to bring that
movement into this country. It beats my comprehension to say that
we are standing for a totalitarian system. It is the very reverse.'*

O'Kelly was Deputy Leader of Fianna Fáil at that time and, in the end,
was nominated as its candidate. There were two other candidates for the
Presidency: Patrick MacCartan, an independent republican, and Fine Gael's
General Seán McEoin. In the first round of vote counting, O'Kelly did not
win sufficient votes to be elected outright, though he did win on the second
count. The fact that a second count was necessary was perhaps an indication
of a growing opposition to the de Valera-led Government of the day.

## Inauguration as President

Seán T. O'Kelly was inaugurated as the second President of Ireland in
Dublin Castle on 25 June 1945. In attendance were members of the Government, the Diplomatic Corps, Church representatives, the Judiciary, the
Army and the Civil Guard. Speaking after the Seal of Office had been presented to the new President, the Taoiseach, Éamon de Valera, paid tribute
to the new President in the following words:

*'... All of us congratulate you on the honour which your country
has done you. You are now our President, the first citizen of the
State, elected by the people of their own free will in accordance
with the democratic laws of the country. To you, therefore, are due
the respect and the authority which rightly belong to the person
lawfully chosen as Head of the State. You have surely earned the
high honour by all you have done over a period of many years to
secure the freedom of the nation and to save our mother tongue.
You are a worthy successor to the distinguished President who has
preceded you and to the chieftains who led and inspired this nation in the years gone by.'*

*President Seán T. O'Kelly and Mrs O'Kelly on the President's Inauguration Day*

The Taoiseach went on to convey to the President the good wishes of Douglas Hyde who was unable to be present on the occasion.

The President replied (in Irish):

> *'I thank you deeply for the kind words you have spoken. I thank all here for having come to show their goodwill towards me.... From my heart I am grateful to the people of Ireland, who have conferred upon me the highest honour in their power. It will always be my aim to be worthy of their trust. We ought, above all, on an occasion like this, to give thanks to Almighty God. It is He who has brought our community through bondage and to secure an honoured place amongst the peoples of the world. Without the help of His all-powerful hand it would not be in our power to elect either a government or a President. It is He who preserved us and set us free. May He be praised forever.... The message of my noble friend, Dr. Douglas Hyde, is a cause of joy for me. I thank him. I promise him that it will be a primary purpose of mine*

*while I am President, to put his teaching into effect and to follow*
*his example, especially with regard to the Irish language. May he*
*live long in our midst in happiness and honour.'*

## Presidential Duties

For someone who had been elected to Dáil Éireann on twelve occasions and held the high office of Tánaiste and two ministries between the years 1918 and 1945, it must have seemed somewhat restrictive to have found himself in the Presidency and, consequently, so far away from mainstream politics. Nevertheless, following in the tradition set by his predecessor in the post, the President carried out a wide range of duties in attending social and community functions and in receiving a variety of guests at Áras an Uachtaráin. He also attended many sporting events. His interest in sport was evidenced by his frequent attendance at race meetings; indeed, a couple of horses raced under Presidential colours. He was also to be seen at All Ireland (Gaelic football) games in Dublin's Croke Park and at rugby international matches in Lansdowne Road. He also attended on 'President's Day' at the annual Royal Dublin Society Horse Show. In December 1945, the President and Mrs O'Kelly attended the Gaeity Theatre, Dublin for the Dublin Grand Opera's production of *Rigoletto*. The exposure of O'Kelly in his role as President had the effect of enhancing his reputation among the general public as being friendly and approachable, whilst also holding to the dignity of his office.

The President was not, however, immune from criticism. On 9 March 1946, at a meeting of Kildare County Council, a question was raised as to whether Phyllis Ryan, otherwise known as Mrs Seán T. O'Kelly, was Analyst to the Council. The reply was that she still officially held the position. A Mr Henderson said:

> *'I think it is a disgrace to have the President's wife carrying on this*
> *job while her husband is getting £30,000 a year or thereabouts*
> *from the State. It is not very dignified, to say the least of it and no*
> *other State in the world would tolerate it.'*

47

The County Manager declared that Phyllis Ryan had been appointed and nominally she was Analyst still. All the analyses were done by her. The question of appointing a deputy or substitute for her had arisen and steps had been taken whereby deputies may be appointed.

Further criticism followed in May 1946 when a member of the GAA Wexford County Board said:

> 'I propose we do not agree to the President throwing in the ball. Anyone else attending foreign games would not be allowed to throw it in. If any of us attended a soccer match we would be suspended for five years.'

The criticism of his attending 'foreign games' did not impact greatly on the President, apparently, as it was reported on 4 June 1946 that:

> 'The President and Mrs O'Kelly visited College Park (sports grounds of Trinity College, Dublin) yesterday and watched play in the Trinity Week cricket match between Sir John Maffey's XI and Dublin University. They were met by Wing Commander A.V.R. Johnstone and Brigadier E. Woodhouse, air and military attachés.'

Following the conferring on the President in June 1946 of the Freedom of the Borough of Wexford, the President and his wife attended the Savoy Cinema, Dublin, for the first showing in Ireland of the RKO Radio film *The Bells of St. Mary's*.

Receiving guests at Áras an Uachtaráin was a constant feature of the President's role. For example, on 9 July 1947, more than 1,000 guests attended a reception hosted by the President and his wife in connection with the Rotunda Hospital's bicentenary celebrations.

It was known that President O'Kelly had a long-standing association with the Catholic Church in Ireland. In particular, he was a member of the Knights of Columbanus – in some ways a counter organisation to the Masonic Lodge.

*Group aboard the Drumm Train (battery operated) –*
*Seán T. O'Kelly is front right and Éamon de Valera is back left*

## Creation of a Republic

In September 1948, when Taoiseach John A. Costello was on an official visit to Canada, a reporter asked him about the possibility of Ireland leaving the British Commonwealth. Costello declared that they were indeed going to repeal the External Relations Act of 1936 and declare a Republic. The news took the British Government by surprise and, indeed, some of his own Ministers as well, although there had been some discussion about it earlier. Ireland left the Commonwealth on 18 April 1949 when the Republic of Ireland Act came into force. King George VI, who now no longer had 'King of Ireland' among his titles, sent a message of goodwill to President O'Kelly.

It is a matter of some legal debate as to who was Head of State in the period from 1937 (when the 1937 Constitution came into force) and 1949 when Ireland became a Republic. In practice, the President of Ireland, starting with President Douglas Hyde, was considered to all intents and purposes as being Head of State. Nevertheless, under the terms of the setting up of the Irish Free State, there existed certain formal connections with Britain by virtue of Ireland's membership of the British Commonwealth of Nations. One of these was the role of accrediting ambassadors which fell to be exercised by the 'King of Ireland'. It was of special significance, therefore, when President O'Kelly, in 1949, with the formal declaration of Ireland as a Republic, made a state visit to the Vatican where he met Pope Pius XII. This was the first visit abroad by an Irish President. It was in the aftermath of this visit that much publicity was given to a diplomatic faux pas made by the President in that he revealed to the press the Pope's private views on Communism. This, apparently, was a cause of strained relations between the Vatican and the Soviet Union.

The President continued his role of carrying out an array of formal and informal duties. In August, he formally opened the Military Tattoo and Exhibition at the Royal Dublin Society in Ballsbridge. In October, he attended the opening of the Oireachtas. In that month, too, he addressed the annual meeting of Comhdhail Náisiúnta na Gaedhilge. He said that the work which was done for the Irish language in the primary and secondary schools was good, but he was not sure that the same could be said of the universities. If all the universities and all the university students worked for the language in the way they should, there would be no danger that the language would die. If that work was not being done Gaels must work to see that Irish was used and that the spirit of Gaelicism was given a foremost place in the universities as well as in the schools.

In January 1949, it was reported that President O'Kelly had received the following letter from the Cardinal Archbishop of Munich thanking him for food gifts:

> *'Under Your Excellency's patronage, kind hearted Irish benefactors have recently sent, in addition to all their earlier gifts, a railway wagon load of tinned meat, to be distributed in my Archdiocese of Munich among the needy inhabitants of the ruined city of Munich.'*

The Cardinal offered sincere thanks on his own behalf and on behalf of the suffering citizens of Munich.

Later, in 1955, the President was awarded the Special Degree of the Grand Cross of the Order of Merit by the President of the Federal Republic of Germany, Dr. Theoder Heuss. This was as a mark of appreciation for assistance given by Ireland after the Second World War for the health and maintenance of German children.

On 18 July 1949, the new Belgian Minister to Ireland, Comte Ferdinand du Chastel de la Howarderie, presented his letters of credence to President O'Kelly at Áras an Uachtaráin. This was the first time that an accredited representative of a foreign Power presented his credentials to the President of Ireland.

On 9 October 1949, the President attended the final day of the Owen Roe O'Neill tercentenary commemoration celebrations and reaffirmed what he described as the nation's determination to do everything possible to end partition. The event was attended by about 75,000 people, including 35,000 from the North.

Before the end of the President's first term of office he attended a continuing round of social and sporting engagements as well as receiving the freedom of many cities around the country.

## Second Term of Office

The President's first term of office ended in 1952. There was some newspaper speculation that the former Taoiseach, John A. Costello, and General Seán McEoin would be candidates for the next term but, in the end, neither of them came forward and O'Kelly was re-elected for a second seven year term without the need for the holding of an election.

The President's second inauguration took place in Dublin Castle on 25 June 1952. The ceremony was short, but with the usual attendance of dignitaries from Church and state. A small number of Members of Parliament from Northern Ireland also attended. After the formal proceedings were over there was a deviation from the strict ceremonial programme when, on stepping down from the dais, the President paused to shake hands with both Protestant and Catholic Archbishops of Dublin.

## Renewal of Spirit

In August 1953, the President appealed for a revival of the spirit of Sinn Féin – the spirit of self-reliance.

> *'Long ago, the attitude of the young men of Ireland used to be expressed thus: "What can I do for my country? What can I do to help Ireland?" Nowadays, it seems to me, the attitude is: "What is the country going to do for me?" This seems to be the spirit of all classes. What benefit is my class or trade or profession going to derive from this measure or from that measure? What am I going to get out of it?'*

The President went on to say that the necessity for a virile national spirit was as necessary now as when they were fighting for their freedom. He hoped that he was wrong and that the heart and spirit of the people were as sound as ever they were.

Mrs O'Kelly was also very involved in carrying out many duties on behalf of her husband. In November 1953, she was guest of honour at the annual dinner of Wesley College Old Girls' Union. Prior to that, in June, she formally opened the Mendicity Institution's new premises at Island Street, Dublin.

The President was not without an adventurous streak in his personality as witnessed by this report in *Home Aviation History 1954*:

> *'A recent passenger aboard one of the two Viscounts in service with Aer Lingus was the President of the Republic of Ireland, Mr Seán T. O'Kelly. His Excellency, accompanied by his wife, flew for about three hours, covering 750 miles. During the flight Mr O'Kelly took over the controls and made two circuits of Galway City at a height of 1,000 feet.'*

This was prior to the first scheduled flight of one of the 48- seater Irish Viscounts made between Dublin and London on 5 April 1954.

Not content with this adventure, in January 1955, the whirling blades of a Bristol Sycamore helicopter created a lot of dust outside Áras an Uachtaráin when the plane went through its paces for the President. He became the first President to make a flight in a helicopter. The trip lasted for ten minutes and took in the area of the Phoenix Park. He was said to have enjoyed the experience greatly.

Whilst there was a great divide in Irish politics as a result of the Civil War, the bitterness that was left in its wake did not fester long in the President's persona. This can be illustrated by the fact that, although the role of the President is required to be 'above politics', he sponsored an attempt in 1957 by Deputy Tony Barry of Cork and Senator James Crosbie to bring Fianna Fáil and Fine Gael into an alliance, the purpose of which was to banish the scars of the Civil War. This piece of idealism came to naught, however, due to a lack of enthusiasm by the higher echelons of the respective political parties. Another illustration of the President's determination to heal past differences was at a dinner in December 1958 in Dublin's Shelbourne Hotel. The occasion was the celebration of the 10th anniversary of An Club Leabhar, the Gaelic Book Club. Mr Ernest Blythe, Managing Director of the Abbey Theatre, was presented with a portrait of himself painted by Séan O'Sullivan RHA to commemorate his 50 years in the Irish language movement. Blythe was a member of the Cosgrave Government during the Civil War and, therefore, an opponent of Seán T. O'Kelly. Speaking after the presentation, the President said that he was delighted to see the Gaelic world paying tribute to his friend, Ernest Blythe, a man who had devoted his whole life to the cause of Ireland. 'Ernest Blythe and I did not always agree on "all things", but no one can deny that he was at all times a patriot and a lover of Ireland ...'

Now into his new term of office, the President, once again, embarked on a busy schedule of official duties. He undertook State visits to France and to the United States of America. In the case of the latter, the purpose of the visit was to address a joint session of the US Congress on St. Patrick's Day in 1959. At a White House dinner marking the occasion, the US President Dwight D. Eisenhower said in reference to Ireland's neutrality in World War II:

> *'I pay again a tribute to this wonderful feeling of warm friend-ship that has never been broken between Ireland and ourselves*

*– and incidentally, Mr President, I have always wondered how you people can call yourselves neutral, you are in every fight there is – and maybe that's another reason we like you – but in any event … I … express the feelings of warm friendship that we know exists between your people and ours, and which we know shall never be broken.'*

In his response, President O'Kelly said:

*'The Irish Nation, which as you have so kindly said more than once, Mr President, is among the oldest on earth – it is one of these that has won its freedom in recent times. I thank God that it should have been given to me to witness, though still unfortunately for less than the entirety of our ancient land, the realisation of the dreams, and of the endeavours of many generations of Irishmen, and to have the privilege of playing some part myself … in that realisation.'*

In March 1956, the President unveiled a bust of Madame Markievicz in St. Stephen's Green. Another unveiling ceremony took place in September in Wexford when a statue of Commodore John Barry, father of the US Navy, was presented to the public.

In June of 1957, the President, in replying to the toast of 'The President of Ireland' at the Oliver Plunkett Union Dinner, recalled a statement made to him in private audience by Pope Benedict XV in May 1920: 'Ireland had every right to her independence. She has every right to fight for her independence but she should be careful of the methods used.'

On 7 August 1957, the *Irish Times* reported:

*'The President Mr O'Kelly will present a certificate of honorary citizenship to Sir Alfred Chester Beatty LL.d. DSc. at Áras an Uachtaráin today. The decision to grant honorary citizenship was taken by the Government last January as a token of honour to him "as being a person who in the opinion of the Government has rendered distinguished service to the Nation". The power to grant such an honour is vested in the President by Section 12 of the Irish Nationality and Citizenship Act 1956. Sir Chester, who will be*

*the first honorary citizen was born in New York city in 1875. His grandmother was born in Ireland.'*

Sir Alfred, a mining magnate, donated his collection of sacred texts, manuscripts, paintings and other art works from oriental and western religions to the nation. These are now housed in the Chester Beatty Library in Dublin Castle.

It was reported in October 1957 that the President's private residence in Roundwood, County Wicklow was destroyed by fire. The residence was a 240-year old mansion and had contained many valuable paintings and souvenirs of the 1916 Rising.

*Bust of President Seán T. O'Kelly*
*by Séamus Murphy, RHA*

In the course of his Presidency, O'Kelly was bestowed with many honours. Among them was the conferring on him of the Grand Cross of the Order of St. Gregory the Great by the Pope. The freedom of the City of Dublin was granted to him in 1953, and this was followed by the freedom of the Cities of Cork, Limerick, Waterford and Galway.

A hallmark of O'Kelly's Presidency was the fact that, notwithstanding his intimate involvement in politics in his earlier years, he transcended the political sphere in full as regards the discharging of his Presidential role. Although known to be somewhat quick-tempered at times, this was outweighed by his natural geniality. In summary, he was a popular President. Nothing illustrates this better, perhaps, than the fact that he was frequently referred by the citizens of the country simply as 'Seán T' rather than as 'the President'.

President O'Kelly left office on 24 June 1959 with the ending of his second term of duty. He retired to live in Roundwood, county Wicklow. He died on 23 November 1966, aged 84. He was survived by his wife, Phyllis. He was buried in Glasnevin Cemetery, Dublin, after a state funeral.

# Éamon de Valera

## Third President of Ireland (1959–1973)

### Family Background

Éamon de Valera was born in New York on 14 October 1882. The de Valera family were of Spanish stock, and their origins can be traced back many centuries. The original family was Galician but settled in Andalucia in the early twelfth century. Éamon de Valera was descended from Antonio de Valera, eighth son of Juan Jose Valera y Alcala-Gallano and Maria J Josefa Viana who resided in Seville around the end of the eighteenth century. Antonio de Valera married Marcedes Armenteros. They had only one son, also named Antonio, who emigrated to Cuba around 1840 where he met and married a Spanish lady. They had three children, but unfortunately the marriage did not last. In addition, two of the children died. Their surviving son, Vivian Juan, was born in Spain in 1853. Antonio left Cuba in 1879 and moved to the USA, taking Vivian, then 25 years of age, with him.

Vivian de Valera became friendly with a French family, the Girauds, and it was through them that he met the family's housekeeper, Catherine (Kate) Coll, who had emigrated from Bruree in County Limerick in October 1879. Vivian and Kate were married on 19 September 1881 in New York City. Kate gave birth to Éamon de Valera in October 1882 at a New York Children's Hospital located in Lexington Avenue between 51st and 52nd street. His first name was registered as 'George' but he was christened 'Edward' (Éamon). Later, in 1916, his mother had the name on the birth certificate changed to Edward as part of her endeavours to have him released, on the basis of his US citizenship, from Dartmoor Prison in England where he was incarcerated for activities against the British.

*De Valera's birth certificate, showing he was born in New York on 14 October 1882 – the doctor recorded de Valera's first name as George, which his mother later had amended to Edward*

Vivian developed bad health, possibly tuberculosis, and moved to the more conducive climate of Denver, Colorado in June 1884, leaving his wife in New York. He died in the Spring of 1885 but, due to poor local communications, Kate was not to learn of his passing until six months after the event, the news being brought to her by Frederick Hamilton, the best man at their wedding. Kate then put her son in the care of another Bruree immigrant, a Mrs Doyle, and went back to work again.

Some historians have suggested that Éamon de Valera's parents were not married at the time of his birth. This may have stemmed from the fact that the Nursing and Child's Hospital catered for 'destitute' children. However, this was only a secondary service of the hospital. The primary objectives of the hospital, as set out in its charter, were 'for the maintenance and care of women and children and the care of lying in women and their infants'. There was nothing to indicate that the de Valera family was unable to pay the necessary maternity costs as Vivian was employed at the time of his child's birth. In addition, the admission records show that Kate de Valera was admitted as 'Mrs Kate de Valero (the final letter being a typographical error). The birth certificate of 'George' de Valera shows that Kate's husband was named Vivian and that he was father of the child. His occupation was given as an artist, his birthplace Spain and his age as 28.

## The Young de Valera

In Terry de Valera's book, *A Memoir*, he states that his grandmother, Kate, confirmed that she and Vivian de Valera were married in New York city and not in Greensville, New Jersey, as previously supposed by some historians. The best man was Frederick Hamilton and the bridesmaid was Kitty Brady. The officiating priest was Father Patrick Hennessy, a native of County Limerick. Kate de Valera, after the death of her husband, found herself alone and with little means of support. She decided, therefore, that the child should be sent to Ireland to be raised by his uncle and other relatives. Kate's brother was in the USA at this time and about to return to Ireland and so was entrusted with the task of taking the child to Ireland. The young Éamon de Valera arrived in Ireland in 1885. He was looked after by Kate's brother and by his grandparents. In the following year, Kate made a visit to Ireland to see her son.

In May of 1888, Kate married a Charles Wheelwright in the USA. In that same month, at the age of six, Éamon started school at the local national school in Bruree. In 1896, at his own request, he was sent to the Christian Brothers School in Charleville, a walk of seven miles. Later still he won a scholarship to the prestigious Blackrock College in Dublin. Here his natural interest in mathematics took root. Highly successful in his final examination, he won scholarships which opened the way for him to attend University College, Blackrock in Dublin. The college was affiliated to Newman's Catholic University but was not recognised by the Royal University. In addition to his studies, he immersed himself in all the usual facets of university life – attending debates, playing rugby and showing some class in middle distance running. The funds afforded by his scholarships did not cover the full cost of college fees, but he was allowed to make up the difference by teaching without payment. In 1903, he got a full-time teaching job in Rockwell College, near Cashel, County Tipperary. Rockwell College, run by the Holy Ghost Fathers, was a sister college of Blackrock College. In addition to de Valera's teaching ability, his prowess on the rugby pitch stood him in good stead in gaining the respect of peers and pupils alike.

In was in Rockwell College that a fellow teacher was to dub him 'Dev', a name that was to stay with him all his life and, indeed, afterwards.

De Valera continued to study for his university degree during his teaching period, availing of the assistance of tutors. He was disappointed in 1904 when he obtained only a pass degree.

After a brief job in Belvedere College in Dublin, he was appointed in 1906 as Professor of Mathematics in the training College of Our Lady of Mercy, Carysford Avenue, in Blackrock, close to his old college. He continued his own studies by attending lectures in mathematics at the newly founded National University of Ireland and at Trinity College Dublin. He was disappointed in being unsuccessful in obtaining a post in any of the main constituent colleges of the National University, but he did land a temporary part-time appointment as a lecturer in mathematics and mathematical physics in St.Patrick's College in Maynooth in County Kildare – a college mainly for students studying for the priesthood.

## Marriage

The year 1908 was a significant one in the life of young de Valera. It was in this year that he joined the Ard Chraomh (main branch) of the Gaelic League to study the Irish language. One of his teachers was Sinéad Flanagan, a primary school teacher by profession. They fell in love and on 8 January 1910 were married in St. Paul's Church on Arran Quay in Dublin. The wedding was a quiet affair with only family and close friends invited. Afterwards they had a short honeymoon in Woodenbridge in County Wicklow. They would go on to become the proud parents of seven children: Vivian, Máirín, Éamonn, Brian, Ruairí, Eimer and Terry. Brian de Valera was killed in a horse riding accident in the Phoenix Park in Dublin in 1936.

## Early Politics

De Valera continued his Irish language studies and eventually became fluent, thereby sealing what was to become a lifelong love of Irish and an interest in its propagation. Meanwhile, on the political front, the Home Rule for Ireland Bill in Westminster brought a threatened backlash from the Unionists in north-east Ulster. This manifested itself in the formation and arming, with British blessing, of the Ulster Volunteers. The emergence of the Volunteers and their underpinning by the English Conservative Party convinced de Valera, not engaged in politics up to then, that Home Rule would be lost without a counterbalancing military response from nationalists. The formation of the Irish Volunteers was established with this aim in view, and de Valera decided that he should join. He did so in November of 1913. The Irish Volunteers were, unbeknownst to most, infiltrated heavily by the IRB (Irish Republican Brotherhood) – a secret society dedicated to regaining freedom from Britain. De Valera's involvement in the Irish Volunteers was an active one and it was not long before he was promoted to the position of Squad Leader and then to Section Commander. Later, he was elected to the post of Second Lieutenant. On the foundation of the Donnybrook Company he was appointed Captain. Training and the use of weapons were his forte.

*De Valera in uniform*

## Irish Volunteers

In 1914 there was a split in the Irish Volunteers between the supporters of the Irish Parliamentary Party at Westminster, headed by John Redmond, on the one side, and the original founders of the Volunteers on the other. This was caused by Redmond's call for support of Britain in World War I – a call made despite the fact that, although the Home Rule Bill had been converted into law, it had been suspended by another act until the end of the war. During this period, drilling and training of the Donnybrook Company continued, albeit with reduced numbers due to the split.

## The 1916 Rising

In early March 1915, de Valera was informed by Patrick Pearse that he was to be made a Battalion Commandant. At a meeting in the middle of that same month, the possibility of an armed rising was discussed. The involvement of the IRB was of some concern to de Valera because he did not approve of secret societies. Nevertheless, he was persuaded by Thomas MacDonagh to join it on the basis that he would become privy to confidential information not otherwise available to him. As a result, de Valera took full part in the preparations for the 1916 Rising. He knew in advance

*1916 Rising – Abbey Street corner and DBC Building shelled*

which part of Dublin city would fall under his responsibility and he made it his business to reconnoitre it fully.

Mobilisation for Easter Sunday morning was agreed. Eoin MacNeill, President of the Irish Volunteers and, therefore, nominally at least, its leader, got to hear of the plans from which he had been excluded up to then. He considered the plans doomed to failure and, consequently, countermanded the mobilisation order. This caused much chaos. However, at a meeting in Liberty Hall in Dublin on Easter Sunday, attended by Pearse, Connolly, Clarke, MacDonagh, MacDermott, Kent and Plunkett, it was decided that 'we would be a disgrace to our generation' not to go ahead with the Rising. And go ahead it did, on the following day, Easter Monday 1916.

For his part, de Valera concentrated his men (their numbers were reduced as a result of MacNeill's countermand) in defence of three bridges over the Grand Canal, namely at Ringsend, Grand Canal Street and Lower Mount Street. The railway route into the city centre ran through this area and it was overlooked by Boland's Bakery in which de Valera was stationed. In fact, most of the action took place on nearby Northumberland Road. Here a contingent of Sherwood Foresters, numbering somewhere between 500 and 1,000, were held at bay for nine hours and suffered severe losses at the hands of only fourteen Irish Volunteers.

Sniping around Boland's Bakery continued during the week but an expected artillery assault on the bakery did not materialise. Overall, however, the Volunteers were outnumbered by about twenty to one, not to mention the significant difference in armory (there were no machine guns in the entire Republican force). By Saturday of that week, Pearse and Connolly and their supporters were forced to evacuate the General Post Office in the heart of the city, the very hub of the Rising. In the afternoon, Pearse signed an order for submission to all commandants. It ran as follows:

> *'In order to prevent the further slaughter of Dublin's citizens and in the hope of saving lives of our followers now surrounded and hopelessly outnumbered … the Commandants of the various districts in the City and County, will order their commands to lay down arms.'*

De Valera received his copy of the order the following morning. He was despondent, feeling that the rising had been a failure. He despaired, too, at the acts of some Dublin citizens rushing out to give cups of tea to the British soldiers while his own men received a hostile reception from them. De Valera was held in Richmond Barracks in west Dublin pending court martial proceedings. He fully expected and prepared himself for the same fate as befell Pearse, MacDonagh and Clarke the next day, namely, execution. Among those held in Richmond Barracks with de Valera was Seán T. O'Kelly, later to become the second President of Ireland.

De Valera was court martialled on 8 May 1916 and transferred to Kilmainham Jail where he awaited his execution. His wife had contacted the American Consul a few days earlier to seek avoidance of execution on the basis of his American citizenship. Indeed, representations were made on this matter to the British Under Secretary but, in the end, the decision not to carry out his execution was put down more to British recognition of the feelings of revulsion, which were now beginning to pervade Irish public opinion in the aftermath of the execution of all of the signatories of the Irish Proclamation of Independence. This applied not least in the case of James Connolly, who was so badly injured that he had to be strapped to a chair for his execution. Éamon de Valera and another republican, Thomas Ashe, were reprieved on the same day. It was thought by some historians that de Valera's reprieve was due to his being an American citizen. Certainly de Valera himself did not believe that his place of birth had any influence on this decision, but rather was due to public opinion.

In July of 1917, following his release from Lewes Jail in Britain, de Valera obtained almost double the number of votes in a by-election compared to his opponent from the Irish Parliamentary Party, and was elected a Member of Parliament (MP) for East Clare as a Sinn Féin candidate. In that same year he was also made President of Sinn Féin and of the Irish Volunteers.

## General Election, 1918

A general election was called in Westminster on 1918. Irish national feeling had been stirred by the Rising and convincing by-election victories by Sinn Féin ensued. In addition, the Irish Parliamentary Party at Westminster was seen as being less relevant to Ireland's nationalists' aspirations. Sinn Féin won a sweeping victory, capturing nearly three-quarters of all the Irish seats. Successful candidates, apart from those still in English jails, met in Dublin as Dáil Éireann (Irish Parliament) and declared a sovereign independent Irish Republic. In May 1918, de Valera was jailed again, as were other prominent members of Sinn Féin, as a result of a so-called 'German Plot'. This arose from a British Cabinet decision to instruct the Viceroy, Lord French, to investigate any possible Sinn Féin links with Germany. This, in turn, was initiated by the arrest of a member of Roger Casement's Irish Brigade on the Clare coast in 1916. De Valera remained in Lincoln Jail until his escape in February 1919.

*Éamon de Valera, Michael Collins and Harry Boland at the second session of the first Dáil Éireann, Mansion House, Dublin, 1 April 1919*

## The United States

In June of 1919, de Valera visited the United States of America. The principal reasons for the visit were as follows:

- To ask for official recognition of the independence of the Irish Republic

- To try to float an external loan for Ireland, and

- To plead with the American people that 'notwithstanding Article 10 of the covenant of the League of Nations' (undertaking to preserve the existing borders of member states) the US was not, in fact, pledging itself to maintain Ireland as an integral part of British territory.

De Valera was greeted effectively as a 'head of state' at his innumerable meetings on both the east and west coasts of the USA. On 17 January 1920, he was granted the freedom of New York. His visit was not without controversy, however, as there emerged a split – a characteristic of Irish politics – in Irish/American support. This division was between de Valera, on the one hand, and local Irish/American leaders John Devoy and Judge Cohalan on the other. In particular, there was a clash of personalities between Colahan and de Valera, the former believing that his hold on Irish/American sentiment was being intruded upon by the latter. A 'truce' was agreed but distrust between them remained and had a detrimental impact on de Valera's efforts to achieve the aims of his campaign. De Valera tried to use the Democratic and Republican conventions to declare recognition for Irish independence, but failed. In the case of the Republican convention, the failure was as a result of his efforts being undermined by Colahan, although de Valera did muster some degree of support.

## War of Independence

Shortly after the end of World War I, the concept of partition of Ireland gathered support in British Government circles, principally because by this method they could satisfy the demands of Northern Unionists who adamantly opposed home rule for Ireland. This culminated in a guerrilla war – the War of Independence – between supporters of Sinn Féin on the one side and British forces on the other. Republican Volunteers under Dan Breen ambushed and shot dead two members of the Royal Irish Constabulary (RIC) in Tipperary, and this was the start of a war that was to last for two years.

In the midst of this activity, the British Government enacted the Government of Ireland Act in 1920, 'creating' two states. 'Northern Ireland' was formed by allocating to it six counties (the most Unionist-dominated counties) of the nine counties of the province of Ulster. The remaining twenty-six counties were to comprise 'Southern Ireland'. The artificial nature of this title resulted in the north coast of County Donegal, the most northerly part of the island of Ireland, being in 'Southern Ireland'.

## Truce

On his return to Ireland in December 1920, de Valera kept a low profile and managed to avoid arrest. In May of 1921, however, he was arrested by British soldiers and imprisoned in Portobello Barracks in Dublin. He was detained there for about three months. He was then released, however, apparently because the British Government thought that by doing so they could sue for peace. They endeavoured to do this through the good offices of General Smuts acting as 'go-between'. The General was unable to convince de Valera that dominion status was in Ireland's interests. De Valera's view on a possible truce proposal was that 'any settlement on this basis would be impermanent and would cause great problems later'. Nevertheless, a meeting was arranged for 14 July 1921 between de Valera and British Prime Minister Lloyd George. Michael Collins was excluded at this stage because de Valera felt that a resumption of hostilities was on the cards and, for security reasons, he did not want Collins's face to be widely known. The two leaders met alone but were unable to come to an agreement – Lloyd George pushing for Commonwealth status and de Valera seeking independence.

## Anglo Irish Treaty

The hostilities of the War of Independence continued at significant cost to both sides until July 1921 when a truce was signed. Under the terms of a proposed treaty, twenty-six of the thirty-two counties were to be given dominion status with its own army and navy and control of its own domestic and foreign affairs. However, the new 'Irish Free State' was to remain within membership of the British Commonwealth and members of the Irish Parliament would have to take an oath of allegiance to the King of England. De Valera had not attended the treaty negotiations but had sent Michael Collins to head the Irish delegation. The reasoning behind de Valera's decision not to attend personally became a matter of contention afterwards. However, it seems he considered it important to have a fall back position, and to remain untainted by the negotiations in the event of their breakdown.

The pressure on the Irish delegation was considerable with the threat of 'immediate and terrible war' by Lloyd George being held over them if they did not settle. For his part, Collins believed that they had got all that it was possible to get and that it was a good stepping stone to the eventual establishment of an Irish Republic. De Valera was furious with the terms agreed. He contended that the delegation was under instruction to report to Dublin before agreeing to anything. Indeed, the instructions to the delegation members included the following:

> '... before decisions are finally reached on the main questions that a dispatch notifying the intention of making these decisions will be sent to the members of the cabinet in Dublin and that a reply will be awaited by the plenipotentiaries before the final decision is made... It is also understood that the complete text of the draft treaty about to be signed will be similarly submitted to Dublin and reply awaited.'

From de Valera's perspective, the Treaty conditions as a whole were unacceptable. Whilst some form of 'external association' with the Commonwealth might have been possible, what was now proposed was not, nor was the taking of an oath to the King. The treaty was put to the cabinet. It was supported by Collins, Arthur Griffith, Robert Barton, and W.T. Cosgrave. It was opposed by de Valera, Cathal Brugha and Austin Stack. On his return from London, Collins had called a meeting of the IRB and they sided with him on the treaty. The Dáil finally ratified the treaty by a small majority (64 to 57). Sensing that he was losing control of Parliament, de Valera tendered his resignation from the Dáil on 6 January 1922.

## Civil War

In a general election held in the Free State in June 1922, the electorate effectively accepted the treaty by returning a majority of members who were in favour of it. There were 58 pro-treaty Sinn Féin members, 36 anti-treaty Sinn Féin members, and 35 others (Labour, farmers and Independents) all of whom were committed, to some extent, to accepting the treaty.

In the tragic civil war that followed, former colleagues in arms against the British now faced each other. The Free State government was led by W.T. Cosgrave on the pro-treaty side. De Valera led the Republican side which considered the treaty a sell-out. The position was exacerbated by the action of the Unionists in the north-east of the country, where the minority Catholic population was subjected to a reign of terror by local 'B Special' police. Meanwhile, in the Free State, unlike previously, the anti-treaty forces were less able to rely on local support for aid and protection except in Republican areas and, consequently, their forces were more scattered. In addition, the Free State army was better armed – many arms having been purchased from the British Government.

Devastating news to both sides was the sudden death in August 1922 of the founder of Sinn Féin, Arthur Griffith, who had accepted the pro-treaty side. A short while later, the shooting dead by Republican forces of the leader of the Free State forces, Michael Collins, was an even more devastating event. An Emergency Powers Bill introduced by the Cosgrave government resulted in the execution of Republican prisoners. The effect of these events was traumatic for both sides. However, the result was a decision by de Valera, in May of 1923,

*Michael Collins in uniform*

backed by Republican leaders, to 'dump arms', thereby bringing the Civil War to an end but leaving a legacy of entrenched bitterness on both sides. It also marked the beginning of the acceptance by de Valera of exclusively democratic means to achieve his political aims. Prior to this, the Free State Government formally came into being on 6 December 1922, a year after the signing of the Treaty.

## General Elections

De Valera was arrested by Free State soldiers in August of 1923 while electioneering in Ennis, County Clare. Although ensconced in Arbour Hill jail,
he headed the poll. He was released in July of the following year. He stayed
out of the Dáil, claiming it to be illegal and objecting to the requirement
to take an Oath of Allegiance to the British Monarch. During this period
de Valera founded a new political party, Fianna Fáil – a party dedicated to
pursuing a political way forward instead of a military one. Meanwhile, the
Free State Government suffered on two fronts. Firstly, a small number of
its members left to form a new party called Clann Éireann, and secondly,
the work of the Boundary Commission, giving effect to the formal partitioning of the country, lost them some further support.

*De Valera being arrested in Ennis, County Clare*

A general election in June of 1927 saw W.T. Cosgrave's Cumann na
nGeadheal Party drop from 63 seats to 47 (including that of the Ceann
Comhairle). De Valera's Fianna Fáil won 44 seats. Sinn Féin dropped from
25 seats to five and Independents gained two seats, one of whom immedi-

ately joined Fianna Fáil. The overall outcome, taking into account the Labour Party and others, was a return to power of the Cosgrave government. A further election was called in September of that year which resulted in healthy gains for both main parties and a consolidation of the Cosgrave Government's position.

De Valera now decided to engage more formally in the politics of the Free State. This was probably prompted, at least partially, by the killing by the IRA of Kevin O'Higgins, Minister for Home Affairs. However, he was now presented with a dilemma: having resolutely refused to accept the Oath of Allegiance in the past he could not now enter the Dáil without doing so. He was forced, at least to some extent, to swallow his pride. This entailed his signing the book containing the Oath although he did not take the oath orally. He informed the Clerk of the Dail:

> *'I want you to understand that I am not taking any oath nor giving any promise of faithfulness to the King of England or to any power outside the people of Ireland. I am putting my name here merely as a formality to get the permission necessary to enter amongst the other Teachtai [members of Parliament] that were elected by the people of Ireland and I wish you to know that no other meaning is to be attached to what I am doing.'*

In addition, de Valera removed the bible which was resting on top of the book and deposited it at the far side of the room. Thus was the Fianna Fáil abstentionist policy ended. On 12 August 1927, the elected members of Fianna Fáil took their seats in Leinster House. Despite this democratic move, the IRA continued to drill and was militarily active, albeit at a much reduced level.

A General Election was called in June of 1932. This proved to be a crucial one for Fianna Fáil as theirs was the only party to gain seats (15), giving them a total of 72 seats and making them the largest party in the Dáil. Cumann na nGaedhael, led by Cosgrave, lost a vital five seats. They were not helped by the impact of the economic depression of the early 1930s. De Valera was thus swept to power with the help of the Labour Party. He became President of the Executive Council of the Irish Free State, a State he had previously so strenuously opposed. He then set about pursuing the Republican agenda by abolishing the Oath of Allegiance, reducing the role of the Governor General to a meaningless one, and suspending the payment of land annuities and other payments to the British Exchequer. The British Government retaliated by imposing customs duties on Irish goods entering the UK. Thus began what became known as the 'Economic War', which was set against the background of the world-wide depression of the early 1930s. This caused considerable damage to an already frail economic situation in Ireland. A general election in 1933 gave Fianna Fáil an overall majority and they therefore no longer needed the Labour Party support to govern.

## A New Constitution

With the establishment of the Irish Free State came the 'Constitution of the Irish Free state Act 1922'. This was shaped by the terms of the 1921 Anglo-Irish Treaty. De Valera expressed his dissatisfaction of the terms of the Constitution as follows:

> 'Let it be made clear that we yield no willing assent to any form or symbol that is out of keeping with Ireland's right as a sovereign nation. Let us remove these forms one by one, so that this State that we control may be a Republic in fact, and that, when the time comes, the proclaiming of the Republic may involve no more than a ceremony, the formal confirmation of a status already attained.'

He introduced a new Constitution for the country in 1937. In his book *A Memoir*, Terry de Valera makes reference to the fact that the new Constitution was drafted by de Valera himself using a pen with a very large nib which was necessary because of his poor eye sight.

Significantly, de Valera saw the need for a new republican constitution to retain a link with the British Commonwealth in the form of an external association along the lines suggested by him as far back as 1921. Thus the amended Constitution retained the clause which stated that the Irish Free

State was a co-equal member of the British Commonwealth. While the new Constitution had no place for the British King in it, neither did it declare the country a republic. It seems that this omission was deliberate on de Valera's part, perhaps taking the pragmatic view that to push for a formal republic at that stage would further damage the economic trade situation with the UK. Consequently, the use of 'Poblacht na h-Éireann' (Republic of Ireland) was rejected by de Valera and the designation 'Éire' was settled on. Other essential elements of the new Constitution were the creation of the role of 'President of Ireland' to replace the British King and Crown (together with the post of Irish Governor General), and a declaration that the Irish language was the official language of the nation. Following discussions with religious leaders of the Catholic and Protestant churches, the proposed Constitution included the following wording:

*De Valera and Seán T. O'Kelly (to de Valera's left) processing behind Papal Nuncio, Most Rev. Pascal Robinson OFM at the Eucharistic Congress, Dublin, 1932*

> *The State recognises the special position of the Holy Catholic Apostolic and Roman church as the guardian of the faith professed by the great majority of the citizens. The State also recognises the Church of Ireland, the Presbyterian Church in Ireland the Methodist in Ireland, the Religious Society of friends in Ireland as well as the Jewish Congregations and other religious denominations existing in Ireland at the date of the coming into operation of this constitution.*

De Valera was careful not to propose that the Catholic Church be considered the 'established church'.

Debate in the Dáil on the proposed Constitution saw opposition in two principal areas, namely, the rights of women and the powers of the President. In the former case, there was a fear that women's rights were being less recognised compared to the 1922 Constitution; in the latter, there was some concern on the opposition benches that de Valera was preparing a later presidential role for himself, one that would give him near dictatorial powers. The Constitution was approved by the Dáil on 14 June 1937, and following the referendum (685,050 in favour, 526,945 against), was brought into force on 29 December 1937.

## Negotiations

In 1938, protracted negotiations between Britain and Ireland took place on the following main points:

- The reunification of Ireland,
- The handing back of control of Irish ports to the Irish government (ceded to Britain under the treaty) under a 'defence agreement', and
- The ending of the placing of special duties by the British Government on Irish exports to Britain (imposed for the non-payment of annuities by the Irish government).

Despite an excellent working relationship between de Valera and Britain's Prime Minister, Neville Chamberlain, negotiations soon broke down. However, by March 1938, an agreed text of an Anglo-Irish Agreement was published. In it, the ports were to be returned to Irish control, a British proposed 'defence agreement' being omitted. Additionally, the financial dispute regarding annuities was to be ended by the payment to the British Government of a once-off amount of 10 million pounds sterling. There was, however, no agreement on the thorny matter of partition.

## League of Nations (Forerunner of the United Nations)

At the behest of the Cosgrave government, Ireland joined the League of Nations in 1923.

As early as 1930 the Free State was elected to the Council of the League and de Valera represented Ireland at its meetings. His international reputation was enhanced in 1932 when he made his first appearance in Geneva as President of the League. He made a significant speech in which he criticised Japan for attacking the territory of China, which he stated was in breach of the 'covenant of the League'. He continued: 'No state is powerful enough to stand for long against the League if the governments in the League and their peoples are determined that the Covenant shall be upheld.' His speech was widely acclaimed.

In September of 1938, the Munich Agreement was finalised and war, for the moment, was averted. Speaking as President at the closing session of the League, and referring to German pressure on Czechoslovakia, de Valera spoke of the need for all to adhere to the principles of the League as a vehicle for peace.

## Neutrality

De Valera's activities in the League of Nations also served to increase his reputation at home. This was no disadvantage in the General Election of 1938, which resulted in Fianna Fáil winning 77 of the 138 seats.

In an effort to better inform British public opinion about the evils of partition, de Valera set up an Irish Anti-Partition League. He proposed what was termed a single all Ireland Parliament elected under a proportional representation system. He tried to entice the northern Unionists by offering them a guarantee of fair play and acceptance of their consent to the transfer to the all-Ireland Parliament of the powers now reserved to the parliament at Westminster. However, a bombing campaign in England in 1939 by the IRA put paid to any progress on this front. In an effort to thwart the IRA, a force over which he now had no control, de Valera introduced an Offences Against the State Act. The commencement of World War II, however, was the real reason there was no further progress in Anglo-Irish relations. This was especially so given Ireland's neutral position in the war. On 1 April 1939, de Valera wrote to Chamberlain saying that 'a free, united Ireland would have every interest in wishing Britain to be strong, but when Britain's strength appears to be used to maintain the division of our island, no such considerations can have any force'.

*De Valera chatting with guests at a reception for the French Legation*

De Valera's attitude towards neutrality was based on the premise that small nations had not been consulted beforehand about the necessity for the war. There is little doubt, however, that had the decision to go to war been decided upon by the League of Nations, de Valera would have felt honour bound to support the Allies. When sounded out by Dr Edouard Hempel, the German Minister in Ireland, regarding Ireland's attitude to the war, de Valera informed him that Ireland would be neutral and warned against any violations of Ireland's territorial waters by either Germany or Britain. Although he was acutely aware of the need to maintain trade links with Britain, he considered, nevertheless, that the problem of the partition of the country was good enough reason to stay out of the war. In addition, he felt that Irish public opinion was solidly behind this strategy. De Valera sought formal recognition by Britain of Ireland's neutrality, but this was not forthcoming. Nevertheless, it was accepted by the Irish Government that British surface craft would pursue hostile submarines in Irish waters and that UK aircraft would overfly the headlands of Éire. And, in fact, on these matters a blind eye was turned by the Irish.

In 1940, Winston Churchill replaced Neville Chamberlain as Prime Minister of Britain. Churchill made it clear that he was unhappy about not having access to Irish ports. However the Irish Government was un-yielding and confirmed its determination to resist invasion no matter from which quarter it might come.

In mid-1940 Britain came forward with proposals which included the following:

- A declaration to be issued by the UK government forthwith accepting the principle of a united Ireland.
- A joint body, including representatives of the Government of Éire and the Government of Northern Ireland, to be set up at once to work out the constitutional and other practical details of the Union of Ireland. The UK government to give such assistance towards the work of this body as might be desired.
- A Joint Defence Council representative of Éire and Northern Ireland to be set up immediately.

- Éire to enter the war on the side of the UK and her allies forthwith, and for the purposes of the defence of Éire, the Government to invite British naval vessels to have the use of ports in Éire, and British troops and aeroplanes to cooperate with the Éire forces and to be stationed in such positions in Éire as may be agreed between the two governments.

It was stated that the proposals would be submitted to the Northern Ireland Government for their assent as regards the use of ports which affected them. This was a point which indicated to de Valera that the matter of dealing with partition was unlikely to be progressed seriously. In addition, de Valera was aware that in 1914 the Leader of the Irish Party in Westminster, John Redmond, had received similar promises from Britain only to have them reneged upon as soon as large numbers of Irishmen had joined the British forces in 'defence of small nations'. He saw a similar situation arising in 1940. On the proposals he commented:

> *'The plan would commit us to an immediate abandonment of our neutrality. On the other hand, it gives no guarantee that, in the end, we would have a united Ireland unless concessions were made to Lord Craigavon opposed to the sentiments and aspirations of the great majority of the Irish people.'*

Following criticism of Ireland's neutral position by Churchill, de Valera responded:

> *'We have chosen the policy of neutrality in this war because we believed that it was the right policy for our people... There can be no question of the handing over of these ports so long as this State remains neutral. There can be no question of leasing these ports. They are ours. They are within our sovereignty and there can be no question, as long as we remain neutral, of handing them over on any conditions whatsoever. Any attempt to bring pressure to bear on us by any side – by any of the belligerents – by Britain – could only lead to bloodshed.... I want to say to our people that we may be – I hope not – facing a grave crisis. If we are to face it,*

*then we shall do it, anyhow, knowing that our cause is right and just and that, if we have to die for it, we shall be dying in that good cause.'*

At this time the USA was still neutral but it did not stop Gray, the American Minister to Ireland, endeavouring to put pressure on de Valera to give the ports over to Britain. So annoyed was Churchill by de Valera's unwillingness to do so that he withdrew shipping services between Britain and Ireland with the intention of causing the maximum damage to Ireland's economy (Ireland had no merchant navy of her own). In response, de Valera drew up a plan of self-sufficiency. Under this scheme wheat production increased from 21,000 acres in 1932 to 220,000 acres in 1939. However, rationing had to be introduced for many commodities. Eventually, Irish Shipping Ltd was established by the Government and a small fleet of ships acquired. With these ships, supplies were brought to Ireland despite the German blockade.

Conscription was proposed in the six counties of Northern Ireland. De Valera objected strongly to this on the basis that it would mean that nationalists would have to fight for a freedom which they themselves had been denied. Churchill was furious about de Valera's objections but saw the problems it might stir up and dropped the matter.

The bombing of Pearl Harbour by the Japanese in 1941 brought about a changed scenario. It was clear that the USA would now come into the war on the side of Britain. Up to this, Churchill's efforts to get the USA to enter the war had been unsuccessful.

On 8 December 1941, de Valera received a note from Churchill marked personal and secret. It read:

*'Now is your chance. Now or never. "A nation once again." Am very ready to meet you at any time.'*

The tone of the note seemed unusual to say the least, and it was not clear to de Valera what was meant by it. De Valera answered by suggesting that a visit from Lord Cranborne would be best towards a better understanding, at least of the Irish position. In the end it was clear that Britain was not prepared to yield on the matter of partition, and consequently there was no move from neutrality on the Irish side.

A general election was called in the summer of 1943. Fianna Fáil won 67 seats, a loss of 10. Fine Gael (formerly Clann na nGaedheal) also lost seats, a drop from 45 seats to 32, but gains by Labour and the Clann na Talmhan Party resulted in de Valera being elected Taoiseach, albeit of a minority government. Meanwhile, Gray was becoming ever more anti-Irish and he persuaded the USA and Britain to seek the removal of German and Japanese diplomats from Ireland. De Valera refused and sought assurances from the USA that Roosevelt's earlier pledge on this point still stood, namely that de Valera's refusal would not result in the invasion of Ireland.

On 9 May 1944, the Government was defeated on a transport bill and de Valera resigned. In the ensuing election, Fianna Fáil won 76 seats, 14 more than the combined opposition, and de Valera was again Taoiseach.

On 12 April 1945, Franklin Roosevelt died. De Valera moved the adjournment of the Dáil as a mark of respect. On 30th of that same month Hitler died. De Valera paid a formal call of condolence on the German Minister. This was, as expected, very unpopular with Britain and her allies. De Valera's reasoning in doing so was sct out in a letter to a Washington colleague (Mr Bob Brennan):

> 'I have noted that my call on the German Minister on the announcement of Hitler's death was played up to the utmost. I expected this. I could have had a diplomatic illness but, as you know, I would scorn that sort of thing.... So long as we retained our diplomatic relations with Germany, to have failed to call upon the German representative would have been an act of unpardonable discourtesy to the German nation and to Dr Hempel himself. During the whole of the war Dr Hempel's conduct was irreproachable. He was always friendly and invariably correct – in marked contrast to Gray. I certainly was not going to add to his humiliation in the hour of defeat.'

De Valera acted according to his lights as indeed he had done when, earlier, he refused the German offer of a deal on partition when victory for them seemed certain in 1940.

## Churchill's Attack/De Valera's Response

Churchill made a final attack on de Valera when making his victory speech after the war was over.

> *'Had it been necessary we should have been forced to come to close quarters with Mr de Valera. With a restraint and poise to which, I venture to say, history will find few parellels, His Majesty's Government never laid a violent hand upon them, though at times it would have been quite easy and quite natural, and we left the de Valera government to frolic with the Germans and later with the Japanese representatives to their hearts' content.'*

De Valera's reply was awaited in Ireland with great expectation. He delivered it on Irish radio. In it he thanked God for the ending of the war which had devastated Europe and from which Ireland had been spared. He thanked all who had contributed to the saving of the nation, especially the defence forces and the political parties. He warned of the tough economic situation which the nation now faced, but also for the need for Ireland to look to the needs of nations less fortunate than ourselves. In direct response to Churchill, he said:

> *'Mr Churchill makes it clear that in certain circumstances, he would have violated our neutrality and that he would justify his action by Britain's necessity. It seems strange to me that Mr Churchill does not see that this, if accepted, would mean that Britain's necessity would become a moral code and that, when this necessity became sufficiently great, other people's rights were not to count. It is quite true that other great powers believe in the same code – in their own regard – and have behaved in accordance with it. That is precisely why we have the disastrous succession of wars, World War I and World War II and should it be World War III?'*

*Éamon de Valera with Mr Oscar Traynor and Mr T. Leydon*
*boarding an Irish Air Lines aircraft*

He went on to mention partition and its impact on Anglo-Irish relations, and referred to Churchill's pride in Britain's stance after the fall of France.

> 'Could he not find in his heart the generosity to acknowledge that there is a small nation that stood alone not for one year or two, but for several hundred years against aggression; that endured spoilations, was clubbed many times into insensibility, but that each time on returning consciousness took up the fight anew; a small nation that could never be got to accept defeat and has never surrendered his soul?'

De Valera's speech was warmly and enthusiastically received in his native country. The aftermath of the war saw a concentration on the severe economic situation in the country. It saw, too, the emergence of a new political party, Clann na Poblachta, headed by Sean MacBride, a former chief of staff of the IRA.

A debate on the status of Éire drew these words from de Valera:

*'We are an independent Republic associated as a matter of our external policy with the states of the British Commomwealth.'*

This point referred to the External Relations Act (though not in the Irish Constitution) under which the King was permitted and authorised to act in matters such as the appointment of diplomatic and consular representatives on the advice of the Irish Government, as he did for other Commonwealth countries.

## General Election, 1948

A general election held in 1948 resulted in Fine Gael's John A. Costello being elected Taoiseach. It was not long after his appointment that Costello introduced a repeal of the External Relations Act and Ireland was declared a 'republic'. It was somewhat of a surprise that this important step was taken by Fine Gael rather then the more 'republican' Fianna Fáil party. The decision was, of course, welcomed by de Valera. In 1951, de Valera was once again elected Taoiseach, this time with the support of Independents. He was now 69 years of age and his lifelong problem of troublesome eyesight resulted in him attending specialists in Dublin and London. An operation in Dublin, and additional ones later, nonetheless left him with greatly impaired sight.

In 1954, Fianna Fáil lost four seats and this was enough to see de Valera once again in the role of Leader of the Opposition. At this time there was a revival of IRA activity in Northern Ireland. This took the form of cross border raids from the Republic's side, but in 1962 they ceased their activities.

## The Presidency

The General Election of 1957 gave Fianna Fáil an overall majority and saw de Valera, now in his 75th year, elected Taoiseach once again. His last major political activity was to promote an abolition of the proportional representation voting system on the basis that it led to weak governments. However the Bill was defeated in the Seanad by one vote and so it was

*Taoiseach Éamon de Valera with the Minister for Defence, Frank Aiken*

decided to put the matter to a referendum. It was also decided to hold the election for the Presidency on the same date as the post was about to become vacant. In mid-January 1959, de Valera informed the Fianna Fáil Parliamentary Party of his intention to retire. In doing so he said that, in the light of the completion of the maximum two terms of the office of President by Seán T. O'Kelly, he had been approached by some members of the party asking him to allow his name to be put forward for the position of President of Ireland.

De Valera's opponent for the Presidency was General Sean MacEoin. The election was won by de Valera but the proposed change to the voting system for the Dáil, held at the same time, was defeated. Fianna Fáil's Sean Lemass was elected Taoiseach.

The inauguration of Éamon de Valera as President took place in Dublin Castle on 25 June 1959. He was 77 years of age. It is generally considered that he carried out his Presidential duties in an exemplary way. During his period of duty he consulted the Council of State twice as to whether proposed legislation needed to be referred to the Supreme Court to test its constitutionality. In the first instance, an Electoral Bill was considered by the court as being in line with the Constitution and de Valera therefore duly signed it into law.

In the second case, a proposed Bill in 1967 contained certain provisions of entry and arrest being granted to Revenue Officers under the Income Tax Bill. De Valera was unsure about the constitutionality of the proposals and called on the Council of State to examine the Bill. The result was that it was decided not to refer the Bill to the Supreme Court but, instead, an Income Tax Amendment Bill was passed immediately by both houses of the legislature. This repealed the repugnant section of the original Bill. The President

*President de Valera greeting US President John F. Kennedy on his arrival at Dublin at the start of his visit to Ireland in June 1963*

signed the Income Tax Bill first and the amending Bill immediately afterwards. This meant there was no need to refer the original Bill to the Supreme Court.

Public duties included holding receptions for important visitors including those on State visits. Visitors included Presidents from India, Pakistan and Zambia. A visit from Prince Rainier and Princess Grace of Monaco was especially high profile because of the Princess's Irish connections. King Baudouin and Queen Fabiola of Belgium and U Thant, the Secretary General of the United Nations, were also visitors to Áras an Uachtaráin.

*Princess Grace, President de Valera and Princess Caroline*

The visit of John Fitzgerald Kennedy, the President of the United States of America, was an especially striking one and received widespread publicity both here and in the USA. It certainly was not detrimental in underpinning support for the US Democratic Party among the 40 million or so Irish Americans in the USA. Kennedy made it clear that he was greatly impressed by both de Valera and his wife, Sinéad. Another high profile visitor was the former President of France, Charles de Gaulle. It was reputed that he, too, got on extremely well with de Valera.

In general, although de Valera was perceived in some quarters to be of a somewhat austere character, it is clear that the various visitors to Áras an Uachtaráin were warmly received. It seems, too, that the hospitality offered by him was equally offered to countless 'ordinary' visitors. His visits abroad included one to the Vatican for the Coronation of Pope Paul VI.

When President Kennedy was assassinated, de Valera, although then 81 years old, insisted on travelling to Washington for the funeral.

In 1964, President de Valera accepted an invitation to address the US Congress. The President's sight had deteriorated so much that he was unable to read a script. However, it did not deter him and he spoke confidentally without notes for 25 minutes. In reference to Kennedy's visit to Ireland, he spoke in the following terms:

> *'He was welcomed not merely because he was of Irish blood, not merely because of his personal charm and his great qualities of heart and mind, not even because of the great leadership which he was giving to the world in critical moments; but he was honoured because he was regarded by our people as a symbol of this great Nation. Because he was elected President of this great people.'*

On the topic of partition he said:

> *'When I was addressing you here in 1919 and 1920, our ancient Ireland was undivided. Since then it has been divided by cruel partition. I salute here in prospect the representative of Ireland who will be able, with full heart, joyfully to announce to you that our severed country has been re-united and that the last source of enmity between the British and Irish peoples has disappeared and that at last we can be truly friends.'*

During de Valera's political life there was, understandably, a significant rift between him and W.T. Cosgrave due to differences between them over the Treaty of 1921 with Britain. During de Valera's presidency, however, Cosgrave accepted an invitation to a function in Áras an Uachtaráin in the course of which both men were observed standing together and chatting in an obviously friendly way. The subject matter of their discussions was, alas, never disclosed.

Another notable historical event took place in the political arena during the Presidency of de Valera, namely, the return to Ireland of the remains of the 1916 leader, Roger Casement. After much pressure was exerted on Prime Minister Harold Wilson, consent to the return of Casement's remains was agreed. He had been executed in Pentonville Jail on 3 August 1916 and buried there. Casement had left explicit instructions that he was to be buried in his native County Antrim at Murlough Bay. But because Murlough was in the now designated Northern Ireland area, it was not considered politically expedient to adhere to this request. Instead, Casement was given a state funeral in Dublin and his remains finally laid to rest in Glasnevin Cemetery in 1965. The weather on the day was bad, but against the advice of his doctor, de Valera insisted on attending the graveside.

In 1966, de Valera attended commemorations for the fiftieth anniversary of the 1916 Rising. At the General Post Office in Dublin he paid tribute to the men and women of the rising. He spoke about:

A sketch of de Valera, 'The Chief', by Dr W. King, made on the inside of a cigarette packet

> '... political freedom alone not being the ultimate goal but the building up of the Community in which an ever increasing number of members, relieved from the pressure of exacting economic demands, would be free to devote themselves more and more to the mind and spirit and so be able to have a full life. The nation could then become again, as it was for centuries in the past, a great intellectual and missionary centre from which would go forth the satisfying saving truths of Devine revelation as well as the fruits of the ripest secular knowledge.'

In relation to the Irish language, the President said:

*'Our national language has a vital role. Language is the chief characteristic of nationhood – the embodiment, as it were, of the nation's personality and the closest bond between its people. The people of Denmark, Holland, Norway, for example, learn and know well one or more other languages, as we should of course for the sake of world communication, commerce, and for cultural purposes; but they would never abandon their native language which enshrines all the memories of their past.'*

On the occasion of the jubilee of the founding of the first Dáil, de Valera exercised his prerogative under the Constitution to address a joint meeting of the Dáil and Seanad. He did so on 21 January 1969, exactly fifty years after the first meeting of the Dáil. The Mansion House was the venue, also matching the venue of the first Dáil meeting. He spoke about the need not only to retain the characteristics and culture of the ancient nation, but to blend this with international co-operation for the benefit of all mankind. The heroes of the past had enabled us to take our place among the nations of the world.

Despite his failing health and busy schedule, de Valera found time to engage in his favourite pastime – mathematics. He subscribed to foremost mathematical journals and carried on correspondence with eminent mathematicians. Two other overriding interests remained, namely, the Irish language and the partition of the country. He considered that the former was the more critical believing that partition would not last.

President de Valera's first seven-year term of office ended in 1966. Under the terms of the Constitution he was eligible to stand for a second and final term. De Valera, at the age of 84, allowed his name to go forward once again as Fianna Fáil's candidate. Fine Gael proposed T.F. O'Higgins (a nephew of Kevin O'Higgins, the Free State Vice President assassinated in 1927). De Valera won by a small majority. He declared: 'It is better to win by a short head than to lose by it.' In his inaugural speech he again took up the matters of the unity of the country and the preservation of the national language.

*President de Valera, Chancellor of University College Dublin, after presentation
of an honorary doctorate to writer Bryan MacMahon*

The great paradox of de Valera's life was that he was a great revolutionary and a great constitutionalist, though some may argue that he was converted to constitutionality only when he had had his way on the revolutionary front. It could also be claimed that he took the constitutional course only when his side in the Civil War failed. He once contended that 'when I want to know what the people of Ireland want I examine my own heart'. In more modern times some commentators have taken issue with this assertion. However, forty years of leadership might give some weight to the claim.

## Death of 'Dev'

In June 1973, Éamon de Valera retired after 14 years as President. On 29 August 1975, he died at the age of 92, his beloved wife Sinéad having passed away eight months previously.

The remains of Mr de Valera lay in state in St. Patrick's Hall in Dublin Castle for two days. Thousands of citizens attended to pay their respects and the queues stretched right around the Castle. The State Funeral took place on 3 September. At Glasn-evin Cemetary in Dublin a guard of honour of old IRA members was assembled. Four Irish Army jeeps laden with flowers in the national colours of green white and orange were part of the cor-tege, and their contents were added to the hundreds of wreaths already in place. A 21 gun salute was fired by the 2nd Field Artil-lery Regiment, McKee Barracks.

Éamon de Valera was laid to rest beside his wife in a modest grave.

*Bust of President Éamon de Valera by Séamus Murphy RHA*

# Erskine Childers

## Fourth President of Ireland (1973–1974)

### Family Background

Erskine Hamilton Childers was born in London on 11 December 1905. His family, of Protestant background, was financially well off and enjoyed an upper class lifestyle. His father, Robert Erskine Childers, had also been London-born but, because of the early demise of both of his parents, was brought up by an aunt and uncle of the Barton family (his mother's side of the family) in County Wicklow.

In 1895, Robert Childers took up the post of Clerk of the British House of Commons. He later resigned this post with the aim of getting himself elected to parliament as a Liberal Party candidate, however he failed to secure a nomination. He served with the British Forces in the Boer War (1899) and, following active service in World War I with the Royal Air Force, was awarded a DSO (Distinguished Service Order) in 1917. Before that, in 1903, he had published a novel entitled *The Riddle of the Sands* which was widely acclaimed. Although the subject matter was primarily a yachting adventure story, it was fashioned as a warning about the possibility of a German invasion of Britain.

Erskine Childers's mother was Mary Alden Osgood, affectionately known as Molly. She was born in Boston. During a visit to Boston in 1903 by the Honourable Artillery Company of London, Robert Childers, then the author of two books about the regiment, met his future wife. They were married in Boston on 4 January 1904 after which they returned to settle in London.

## Introduction to Nationalism

The 1916 Rising in Dublin was initially regarded by Robert Childers as a mistake but, through his visits back to the Barton household in Ireland, and especially through his closeness to his cousin, Robert Barton, his opinion gradually changed. It was through his cousin that he met Éamon de Valera and Michael Collins, and no doubt they, too, had an influence on his becoming sympathetic to the Irish political cause, especially to the idea of the establishment of an Irish Republic. To take such a view could not have been easy for such an 'establishment' figure. There is little doubt that he was considered a 'turncoat' by his friends in London society for taking this line. His belief in Ireland's cause manifested itself very clearly in July 1914, when he sailed his yacht, the Asgard, into Howth harbour on the outskirts of Dublin city with a cargo of arms from Germany for the Irish Volunteers. In 1921, he was elected to Dáil Éireann as a Sinn Féin member for County Wicklow, and in that same year was selected as Secretary to the Irish delegation in London for truce negotiations.

When the emerging Treaty was rejected by de Valera, Robert Childers took the Republican side in the ensuing Civil War. Captured by the Pro-treaty forces he was executed by the Cosgrave Government on 24 November 1922 for possession of a small colt revolver (which apparently he had been given by Michael Collins). Erskine Childers was allowed to visit his father in Portobello Barracks in Dublin before his execution. He was instructed by his father always to do all he could to reconcile British and Irish interests, and to tell those who had signed his death warrant that he forgave them. As evidence of his sincerity on this point, Robert Childers shook

*Robert Erskine Childers*

hands with the members of the firing squad at Beggars Bush Barracks. He was later described by Winston Churchill as a murderous renegade, and by de Valera as a prince among men.

## Erskine's Early Years

The political influence of Robert on his son, Erskine, was no doubt significant. Erskine also developed a love of Ireland through spending so much of his school holiday time in the Barton home, Glendalough House, in Laragh, County Wicklow. Here he loved to roam the countryside with his father. His parents also had an enduring influence on him in the areas of art, music and poetry.

Erskine Childers's early education was undertaken as a border at Gresham's School in north Norfolk, commencing in May 1918. The school was a public one (that is to say a private school). In the summer of 1922, while still a schoolboy, he met a 23 year old American girl whom his grandmother had befriended en route from the USA to Dublin. His grandmother was travelling to visit her now widowed daughter (Erskine's mother). The girl's name was Ruth Ellen Dow. She and Erskine struck up an immediate rapport and corresponded regularly, he from school, she from the London Savoy Hotel where she was staying. Ruth visited Erskine's mother, Molly, in Dublin and was intrigued by the political situation in Ireland and also by the influence of the Catholic Church there. It was a far cry from her experience of her Congregational Church in the USA. She even became engaged in publicity work for Sinn Féin during her short stay in Dublin.

Meanwhile, correspondence between Erskine and Ruth continued apace and it cemented their common interest on a wide range of topics. Erskine was not pleased, however, by her new-found interest in the Catholic Church. He had reservations, too, about the Anglican Church and informed his mother that he could not in conscience take Communion as he did not believe in the tenets of the Creed as set out in the 39 Articles (the basic summary of belief of the Church of England).

## First Politics

The first formal political act by Erskine Childers took the form of an address at a rally in O'Connell Street in Dublin on 19 August 1923. It was a protest meeting against the arrest of Éamon de Valera by the Free State Government. Influenced, no doubt, by his late father's political ideals, he spoke in terms that would sound unusual in today's modern Ireland:

> *'I shall fight tooth and nail against industrialising Ireland. Let her remain poor but let us never become complex. The people are simple and spiritual. That word "prosperity", ugh! I shall not mind living in poverty if we can be simple... If we cannot live in prosperity, on agriculture, then let us be poor.'*

How this speech was received by the already poor onlookers was not recorded, nor were the opinions of Irish capitalists. The speech itself was, however, noted by the British press and the ensuing publicity reached the ears of Erskine's headmaster who, supportive of his pupil up to now, bowed to pressure and told him that he must leave the school. He did so in July 1924. This meant that he forfeited the chance of applying for a scholarship to Cambridge University, although he was later to sit the entrance exam successfully. In October 1924 he entered Cambridge to study history.

## Marriage

Erskine's relationship with Ruth continued and indeed even the possibility of marriage was discussed. It was not a practical proposition given that he was six years her junior and still at university. Additionally, any such marriage was opposed by Erskine's grandmother, Mrs Osgood. Erskine's mother felt duty bound to take her mother's side. Ruth returned to the USA for health reasons and during that time his grandmother's attitude softened. When Ruth had recovered from her illness she and Erskine were married. The ceremony took place at Exeter, New Hampshire, on 26 September1925. Erskine was only 19 years of age.

The married couple returned to England and Erskine continued with his studies. They were interrupted, however, when Ruth became pregnant. As a consequence he had to forego the Easter 1927 term. A baby daughter, Ruth Ellen, was born in Dublin after which Erskine returned to his studies and graduated in June 1928 with a Bachelor of Arts degree.

After university, Erskine took up a job as a travel courier with an American travel company, Drake Travel, in Paris. By early autumn of 1928 he had found an apartment there. Later in that same year, however, Ruth returned to Dublin for the birth of their second child, a son, Erskine Barton Childers. The intense pressure of business in Paris precluded Erskine from going to Dublin to see his new son until later. By 1930, business had turned bad because of the recession affecting both USA and Europe. His mother agreed, therefore, to check out possible job opportunities in Dublin. A third child, Roderick Winthrop, was born in Paris in June 1931. Business, however, continued to decline and the rest of Erskine's family now moved to the USA.

## Back in Ireland

In Ireland, Éamon de Valera decided to set up a newspaper that would be friendly to the Republican side of the political divide. As a result, the *Irish Press* newspaper came into being, commencing business in September of 1931. Childers returned to Dublin for a few days and met de Valera. De Valera told him that as soon as the problem of the Oath of Allegiance had been resolved, and Fianna Fáil members were enabled to take their seats in the Dáil, Childers's presence in the Parliament would be needed. He was further told that a suitable seat would be identified for him. Meanwhile, Childers was offered the post of Assistant Advertisement Manager with the *Irish Press* which he was happy to accept. He was equally happy to be back, once again, in Ireland.

In February 1932, Fianna Fáil took power winning 72 of the 153 Dáil seats and engaging the support of Labour and the then Independent deputy (later Fine Gael) James Dillon. The Cosgrave government was no longer in power. Childers worked hard for the Fianna Fáil party. While happy to be back in Ireland, the matter of integration with the Irish people was not easy for the Childers family. Both Erskine and Ruth had been educated outside Ireland. Ruth had no Irish roots and Erskine's were limited to those originating from his Irish grandmother (Anne Barton) and, even then, she was of Anglo Irish stock. Nevertheless, gradually they forged a place for themselves in society, especially in the artistic world. Micheal MacLiammoir and Hilton Edwards of theatrical fame were regular dinner guests, as were members of the newly formed diplomatic corps.

In 1935, Childers became secretary of the National Agricultural and Industrial Development Association and immersed himself fully in the business of promoting Irish goods – a far cry from his 'anti-industrial' outpourings in his maiden political speech on O'Connell Street in 1923.

In November 1937 Erskine's wife gave birth to twin girls, Carainn and Margaret.

## Citizenship

De Valera introduced a new Constitution for the country which was approved by the Dáil on 14 June 1937. A referendum was held in conjunction with a general election on 1 July 1937 and the new Constitution came into force on 29 December 1937. The provisions of the Constitution called for the institution of a Senate or Seanad (an Upper House). The composition of the chamber was 43 elected members, six university representatives, and 11 nominees of the Taoiseach. De Valera selected Childers as one of his nominees, but the legal advisor to the Government said that this was not appropriate because Childers was not actually an Irish citizen. This came as a complete shock to Childers as he always considered himself Irish. His father had claimed Irish citizenship through a statement issued by him in November 1922, shortly before his execution. Robert Childers had based his claim on the fact that his mother (Anna Barton) was born in County Wicklow. However, it transpired that in order for his claim to citizenship to hold good he would have to have been alive on 6 December 1922 when the Free State came into being. Erskine, however, qualified later when a Nationality and Citizenship Act came into being. He was declared an Irish citizen on 2 March 1938.

## Election to Dáil Éireann

Following a defeat in the Dáil on a motion regarding a Civil Service pay claim, de Valera called a general election in June 1938. Childers was asked to run in the newly created constituency of Athlone/Longford. He was unfamiliar with the area, and in fact had had his eye on a possible Wicklow seat. Nevertheless, he was happy to take up the challenge. He won the second of two Fianna Fáil seats. However, the first candidate to be declared elected after the vote counting was Fine Gael's General Sean MacEoin.

## The Emergency

Under an Anglo-Irish agreement with Britain, the Irish ports, held under British sovereignty, were returned to Irish control. The main political focus in Ireland was then concentrated on partition. Childers undertook a series of speaking engagements in the north to try to win over Unionist opinion. In his book *Erskine Childers: President of Ireland*, John Young described Childers's opinion of the Second World War in the following terms: 'Privately his wholehearted sympathy lay with Britain and her allies yet he understood and supported the policy of Irish neutrality and ceased to comment publicly on the Nazi regime.' In November 1938, Childers supported a motion in a Trinity College Historical Society debate entitled 'That this House has confidence in Mr Chamberlain's Foreign Policy'. In the course of his speech he denounced Nazism and described Hitler's book *Mein Kampf* as detestable.

Childers was appointed secretary of the Federation of Irish Manufacturers in 1939, an organisation whose aims were to advance Irish industry. Later, non-manufacturing business was included with the aim of promoting exports. The federation later became the Confederation of Irish Industry.

In the context of his Dáil membership, Childers was unique given his background of an English public school and Cambridge University education. Additionally, his later career in Paris was also somewhat novel, though the experience gained by him there no doubt stood him in good stead in his political career. Futhermore, he was the only Protestant on the Government side and did not speak any Irish in a party which was dedicated to the revival of the language. His mother encouraged him to learn Irish but he refused claiming that it would be false. Despite de Valera's dedication to the Irish language, he in no way held it against Childers that he had virtually no knowledge of it.

Childers visited his local constituency as often as possible but this was not easy in the 'Emergency' period, as World War II was referred to in the Irish Free State. Trains were few and petrol for transport by car was greatly restricted. However, this did not prevent him coming to know the local needs and dealing with them with the utmost dedication. He also had great foresight in that he drew up a planning paper for the post-war period. In it he considered that aviation travel would have an ever increasing impact, especially in the area of international trade. He considered that increasing non-UK trade was critical for Ireland as a free nation. Addressing the Irish Red Cross in Rathmines Town Hall on 8 May 1945 (VE Day), he said that Ireland's destiny was inextricably linked with that of Europe and that the preservation of European civilisation would have a significant impact on Ireland.

## Ups and Downs

In general elections held in 1943 and 1944, Childers held his seat and in March 1944 he was appointed Parliamentary Secretary to the Minister for Local Government and Public Health. Following two by-election wins by the new Clann Na Poblachta party under the leadership of Seán Mac Bride (son of the 1916 patriot Major John MacBride and his famous wife, Maud Gonne MacBride), de Valera called a general election in February 1948. Fianna Fáil lost the election and the result was a coalition of Fine Gael and Labour in a new inter-party Government with Fine Gael's John A. Costello as Taoiseach.

Childers now found himself out of a job. He took up a post as Dublin Manager of the British-based Blackwood Hodge company, an engineering concern. On the social front he continued to attend gatherings and meetings of political and theatrical interest. It was noticeable, however, that Ruth was not enamoured with these activities and avoided participation whenever possible. She did, however, help and encourage him in fulfilling his political ambitions. Despite this, it seemed that their relationship was no longer especially close. Sadly, she contracted cancer and died in Portobello Hospital in Dublin on 12 March 1950, leaving Childers a widower at the age of forty-four.

## Government Minister

Fianna Fáil won their way back to power in 1951 and Childers was appointed Minister for Posts and Telegraphs. He was the youngest member of the cabinet. The new post kept him very busy and he approached his work with his usual dedication. On the domestic front he was now effectively alone. Erskine Barton was married in Australia, Ruth was married in Yorkshire, Rory was studying in Trinity College Dublin, and the twins were at school in Hertfordshire in England.

## Romance Again

In 1952 Childers met Margaret Dudley, known as Rita. She was reared in Ballsbridge in Dublin. She worked in the Welfare Department of St. John's Ambulance Brigade and was responsibile for running dining rooms for expectant mothers who were suffering from malnutrition. Later she became Assistant Press Attaché at the British Embassy in Dublin. It was in this capacity that she met Childers. They forged a close bond and it resulted in their becoming engaged in that same year. Their proposed marriage

*Erskine and Rita Childers on their wedding day in Paris, 16 September 1952*

*Erskine and Rita Childers leaving the church on their wedding day*

raised some difficulties in that Rita, being a Catholic, would be marrying a non-Catholic, a situation then greatly frowned upon in the Catholic Church and not greatly encouraged in the Protestant one either. It meant that when permission for the 'mixed' marriage was forthcoming from the Catholic Church, it was on the basis that the ceremony could take place only in a sacristy or private chapel, a Nuptial Mass being out of the question. The couple decided, therefore, to marry in Paris and did so on 16 September 1952 at St. Joseph's Catholic Church on Avenue Hoche, with a full Nuptial Mass.

Rita readily took on the responsibility of her married state involving, as it did, being mother to her newly acquired five children. This necessitated her giving up her job in the Attaché's office.

In his position as Minister for Posts and Telegraphs Childers put a lot of effort into moving Irish radio away from its civil service attachment towards an independent statutory body. He also pushed for the introduction of a national television service, with a planned emphasis on cultural matters.

In May 1954, the Fianna Fáil government was once again out of power and Childers had to find new employment. He took up the post of Managing Director of PYE Telecommunications in Ireland. The period out of government gave him the opportunity to enjoy his family life even more. This was greatly enhanced by the arrival of a new baby daughter, Nessa, born in 1956.

## Harsh Times

The 1950s were characterised by a serious decline in the economic climate in Ireland with approximately 500,000 people emigrating in the decade.

In the general election of 1957, Childers was re-elected, though marginally out-polled by Sinn Féin's abstentionist candidate, Ruairi Ó Brádaigh. For the first time Fianna Fáil won an overall majority. Childers was appointed Minister for Lands, Forestry and Fisheries, a position he was to occupy until 1959. Before this, in 1958, a programme of economic expansion, based on a paper prepared by Dr Ken Whitaker, Secretary of the Department of Finance, was introduced. This was to be the forerunner of a significant period of economic activity under the careful watch of Dr Whitaker. Immediately prior to this, de Valera stepped down as Taoiseach and was nominated as President of Ireland, and was duly elected.

With Sean Lemass now in place as Taoiseach, Childers was appointed Minister in a newly created Department of Transport and Power. In this role he created a 'first' in appointing a woman, Thekla Beere, to the post of Permanent Secretary. In his new post Childers was responsible for semi-state companies such as the Electricity Supply Board, Aer Lingus, Bord Na Mona, Irish Shipping, Córas Iompair Éireann and the Shannon Free Airport Development Company.

In 1961, Childers was imposed by Fianna Fáil headquarters as an 'agreed' candidate for Monaghan. The local Fianna Fáil deputy, Dr Francis Ward, was greatly annoyed by this action and contested the election as an independent but was unsuccessful. The local, diminishing Protestant population supported Childers and helped him to gain the seat. Childers was more than happy to add the brief of Tourism to the Ministry of Transport and Power, it being a topic close to his heart by virtue of his practical experience of the business during his sojourn in Paris. In promoting tourism he pushed for the purchase by the Government of the British and Irish Steam Packet Company and its modernisation by the introduction of car ferry facilities and also 'roll on/roll off' freight services. He also promoted the idea of farmhouse accommodation and the development of forestry for tourism by the creation of nature trails and so on.

The Government, guided by Whitaker, gained success in the expansion of trade, especially foreign trade. In 1961, an application for membership of the European Economic Community was sought although unsuccessfully at this stage. Childers was eager for Irish membership which he considered would eventually lead to re-unification of the country. He was involved in a number of cross-border initiatives in the wake of a much publicised meeting between Lemass and the North's leader, Captain Terence O'Neill in January 1965. Childers's meetings included one with the North's Minister of Commerce, Brian Faulkner, who was later to become Northern Premier.

In 1966, Seán Lemass stepped down both as Taoiseach and Leader of Fianna Fáil. There followed a significant battle between George Colley and Charles Haughey in a contest for the leadership. In the end, a compromise candidate, Jack Lynch, was elected. Despite Childers's high profile in government and his widely admired dedication to his work, he was still considered somewhat of an outsider by the other members of the government. He was slow to take sides in any disagreements and never fell into one faction against another. In the end, however, on the question of a replacement for Lemass, he joined the majority in voting for Jack Lynch, and under him was appointed Minister for Posts and Telegraphs.

## Northern Troubles

Towards the latter half of the 1960s the political situation in the six counties of Northern Ireland worsened. It was exacerbated by the brutal way the Royal Ulster Constabulary (RUC) put down a civil rights march. This had a very unsettling effect on the nationalist sector generally and was a significant factor in breathing life back into a practically defunct IRA.

In 1969, Jack Lynch won Fianna Fáil's fourth election in a row. In addition to being handed responsibility for the Department of Health, Childers was also made Tánaiste (Deputy Prime Minister). With ongoing tension in the North, Childers's cabinet colleague, Dr Paddy Hillery, warned his counterpart in the British Government, Michael Stewart, that to allow a Protestant Apprentice Boys march around the walls of Derry city would be very dangerous. Nothing was done to stop it, however, and the street violence which

*Erskine Childers and Brian Faulkner, Stormont Minister of Commerce, signing an Electricity Power Link Agreement in Belfast, October 1967*

followed in its wake caused huge tension on both sides of the border. It also caused a split in the Irish Government as to the best way to approach the volatile position in the North. Neil Blaney, Kevin Boland and Charles Haughey pushed for firm action, while Childers, George Colley and Paddy Hillery opted for a softer line. For his part, Lynch made a call for the introduction of a UN peacekeeping force. The British refused to consider this, deeming the situation to be 'an internal domestic matter' and therefore outside the remit of the UN. They also significantly increased the number of British troops in the North. The split in the approach by the Irish cabinet resulted in Boland indicating orally his intention to resign, but apparently he withdrew it after intervention by de Valera. There seems to have been little comment at the time about Presidential involvement in political matters.

## Arms and the Men

A scheme to import arms into the Republic for the revitalised IRA became public knowledge, and it was thought that Blaney, Haughey and others had known of this plan and perhaps even had a hand in facilitating it. The leader of the opposition, Liam Cosgrave, advised Lynch of their apparent involvement and, as a result, Lynch sacked both Blaney and Haughey. Boland resigned in sympathy. Later Haughey and Boland were to be cleared by the courts of all charges but the whole matter had a very unsettling impact on the Government. Indeed, there was a concern that events surrounding the North might cause the Government to fall. Childers appeared on a current affairs television programme and his demeanour had a calming effect on the matter. Nevertheless, a motion of 'no confidence' in the Government was proposed by the opposition. Speaking against the motion, Childers said that no one could remain a member of Fianna Fáil if they engaged either directly or indirectly in armed activity in the North.

*Kevin Batt, Erskine Childers, Tánaiste and Minister for Health, and Dr Maurice O'Connell at meeting in the Gresham Hotel*

In 1970 the American magazine *Newsweek* named Childers as 'Minister of the Year'. The introduction of internment in the North in August 1971, and the dreadful events of Bloody Sunday, served to ensure that the northern situation was perpetually to the fore.

Childers, meanwhile, got on with his work in the Health Ministry. Expenditure on health increased significantly and eight new regional health boards were set up.

## EEC Membership

Although the Government was tussling with northern problems, attention was being directed once again to Ireland's wish to join the EEC. France's President Charles de Gaulle had retired (he had blocked Britain's entry) and a more favourable climate now existed for possible new entrants. Childers was, of course, in favour of this. On Northern matters he continued to speak out against violence from any quarter. On this topic, and on others, he was engaged with events covered extensively by the media which resulted in his gaining increased public prominence.

On 22 January 1972, Ireland signed a Treaty of Accession to the EEC in Brussels. The necessary referendum required under the Constitution was held on 10 May in that same year and was passed by a majority of about five to one. Childers's name was talked about as a possible candidate for the post of Ireland's first Commissioner in Brussels, but ultimately the job was given to Patrick Hillery, Ireland's Minister for External Affairs, who had the main responsibility for negotiating the accession conditions.

## President of Ireland

With de Valera's time as President of Ireland due to come to an end in 1973, a number of names were discussed as a possible successor. Those being considered were Jack Lynch, Childers, Frank Aiken and Michael Yeats, son of W.B. Yeats. Lynch declined to go forward and Childers was not at all keen on the post as he considered he still had much to do as a Minister and wanted to remain at the very heart of political power. Meanwhile,

Fine Gael proposed Tom O'Higgins who had lost by only a narrow margin to de Valera in the previous election in 1966. On 28 February 1973, Jack Lynch called a surprise election and Childers immediately set about preparing to contest his Monaghan constituency for the fourth time. Not only was he successful himself, but with great party support a second Fianna Fáil candidate was elected as well. Notwithstanding this, the party lost out overall and a new coalition government of Fine Gael and Labour came into power with Liam Cosgrave appointed Taoiseach.

Focus now returned to the Presidency and although Childers had informed the media that he was not interested in running, he was approached by Lynch who asked him to change his mind. Lynch emphasised the prestige for the party of a strong Fianna Fáil candidate, especially in the light of their losing the general election. Childers finally agreed and his candidature was announced on 6 April 1973. The presidential election date was set for 30 May 1973.

Childers made it clear from the very start of his election campaign that he saw a much expanded role for the Presidency with special emphasis on reconciliation on Northern matters and recognition for, and interest in, the youth of the country. His rival for the post was a very strong candidate, Tom O'Higgins. The O'Higgins family had a firm political pedigree going back to the foundation of the State. His father had been a Dáil deputy for 25 years and a former Minister. He himself was well known in legal circles as a successful barrister and had been Minister for Health in the period 1954–1957. In addition, he had gained confidence by his good electoral showing in the Presidential race in 1966.

A full and vigorous campaign was embarked upon by both candidates. Fianna Fáil arranged for Childers to visit the entire country on a county by county basis. This was undertaken in a bus decorated for the occasion in an especially eye-catching way. The opposition made a score against Childers by pointing out that he spoke no Irish. His own party played down that point and also the fact that he had been born and educated in England. In the end, however, Childers won 52 per cent of the vote, an equivalent majority of 48,000 votes.

## Inauguration

Childers's electoral success was widely reported at home and abroad. Outside Ireland much was made of the fact that Childers was a Protestant, although on the domestic front that was not an issue. He received messages of congratulations from Queen Elizabeth, President Nixon, President Podgormy and President Pompidou.

An inter-denominational service was held in the Protestant St. Patrick's Cathedral in Dublin on 25 June 1973 prior to Childers's inauguration. Attendance included the outgoing President de Valera, the Catholic Primate of All Ireland, Cardinal Conway, and the Catholic Archbishop of Dublin, Archbishop Ryan, together with the Apostolic Nuncio. The service was conducted by the Protestant Archbishop of Dublin, Dean Griffin. Also represented were the Presbyterian Church, the Methodist Church, the Salvation Army and the Society of Friends.

*Receiving Freedom of the City of Sligo, September 1974*

Later, in the historical St Patrick's Hall in Dublin Castle, the Taoiseach, Liam Cosgrave, announced the election of Erskine Hamilton Childers to the post of President of Ireland. Childers made the Declaration of Office, in Irish, and was presented with his seal of office by the Chief Justice, Mr William O'Brien FitzGerald.

Long before he was elected President, going back to the time of the Presidency of Seán T. O'Kelly, Childers had spoken about how he saw the role of the Presidency. He considered that the President was elected as a symbol of all that was best in an Irish person. The role of the Presidency should act as a reminder to the citizens of the country that they should consider their duties as citizens instead of themselves. The President should act as a protector of the citizens against any possible wrongdoing of the Seanad or Dáil. And he should act as the nation's chief host to foreign dignitaries.

*First meeting between an Irish Head of State and a member of the British*
*royal family, Summerhill College, Sligo, 1974 (l-r Bernard McDonagh,*
*President Childers, Mrs Childers, Lord Mountbatten)*

*President and Mrs Childers at an art exhibition with two unnamed people*

Now elected, Childers saw the role of President not only as a leader outside politics but as a focal point for discussion by those of differing views on the North. The post was not without its practical difficulties, however. The household budget was meagre and this made difficult the upkeep of the 94 roomed mansion that was Áras an Uachtaráin. In any event, he got on with the job.

## Routine

President Childers's normal day started at 7.30 a.m. with prayers in the Presidential chapel. The Presidential chaplain was Canon E.M. Neill, Rector of St. Brigids Church in nearby Castleknock.

Routine duties included dealing with a considerable volume of correspondence, some of which had to be re-directed to an appropriate Government department when the subject matter was outside his brief. He was required to examine and, if he found them to be in order, sign Bills sent to him by the Government. He also had to study Dáil and Seanad reports to keep himself briefed on current affairs.

In the afternoons he would make outside trips. Evenings were reserved in the main for his own private time except when he hosted formal dinners at Áras an Uachtaráin, which he undertook about four times a month. Time had to be set aside, too, for monthly briefings by Taoiseach Liam Cosgrave. These updates on the processing of government business were somewhat frustrating for Childers separated, as he now was, from having any real influence on the political matters of the day.

In the early stages of his Presidency, Childers gave an interview to an American radio station on the topic of Northern Ireland. He said that violence had postponed the prospects for re-unification and that co-operation between all parties in the North was necessary before re-unification could become a reality. He added that, meanwhile, British troops should remain in the North to avert further sectarian violence. He further offered to mediate in the conflict and warned against fundraising in the USA being possibly used for the illegal purchase of arms. Although nothing he said would have been far from the views of the government of the day, he nevertheless received a rap on the knuckles by being reminded that all scripts should be submitted to the Government in advance for vetting.

President Childers received many northern groups in Áras an Uachtaráin; he was also host to Lord O'Neill (Northern Premier in 1963-1969) on two occasions. Additionally, the President was engaged in the opening of local museums, tree plantings, unveiling of plaques and hosting musical recitals. He was also more than willing to lend his support to the Wexford Festival of Grand Opera and the Killarney Bach Festival. In summary, his schedule was a busy one as evidenced by the fact that in 1973 he attended about 200 functions and met with around 60 community groups from all quarters of the country. He promoted the arts and urged sensible use of leisure time and avoidance of the stresses of modern life.

During his time at Áras an Uachtaráin, Childers made two overseas trips. The first was to Paris where he led the Irish delegation at the funeral of President Pompidou. The second trip was a four-day state visit to Belgium. He enjoyed an excellent relationship in Brussels with King Baudouin and Queen Fabiola. His visit coincided with Ireland's entry into the EEC.

In his limited leisure time he enjoyed gardening and became especially engaged in the development of a 'swamp garden' in the grounds of Áras an Uachtaráin. Special plants were delivered and despite a full round of Presidential engagements he devoted as much time as he could to the new garden.

*President Childers with his daughter, Nessa (second from right), at a dinner at the Royal College of Psychiatrists in Dublin – this photograph was taken only hours before his sudden death*

On Friday 15 November 1974, the President attended a luncheon given by the French Prime Minister, Jacques Chirac, and a party of 32 officials. He particularly enjoyed the occasion as it afforded him the opportunity to speak French. On the following day he addressed the first annual dinner of the Irish Division of the Royal College of Psychiatrists, which was held only a stone's throw from Leinster House (seat of the Irish Parliament), in the Royal College of Physicians. In his talk he returned, once again, to the theme of the necessity of dealing with the stresses of modern life. On concluding his speech he suddenly collapsed. He was rushed to Dublin's Mater Hospital but it was not possible to revive him and he was pronounced dead just after 1.00 pm on the morning of 17 November 1974.

The news of President Childers's sudden death was greeted with great shock and sadness throughout the nation. The funeral service in St. Patrick's Cathedral was attended by heads of state from many countries. In attendance was the Earl Mountbatten of Burma representing Queen Elizabeth II. Erskine Childers was

*Bust of President Erskine Childers by Séamus Murphy, RHA*

laid to rest in Derralossary near Roundwood in County Wicklow after a State funeral. He had been in office for only 18 months.

*The grave of President Childers at Derralossary, near Roundwood, County Wicklow – his widow, Mrs Rita Childers, who died in 2010, was buried alongside her husband*

# Cearbhall Ó Dálaigh

## Fifth President of Ireland (1974–1976)

### Early Days

Cearbhall Ó Dálaigh was born in Bray, County Wicklow, on 12 February 1911. His paternal grandfather, who hailed from County Cork, had travelled to Britain to improve his lot and joined the British Army in Gravesend. After a posting to India he returned to Ireland and settled down to married life. His son, Richard Daly (Cearbhall's father), was educated at a national school in Dublin. On completion of his schooling, at the age of 13, he went to work for the Dunlop Company. Later, he got a job with a fish and poultry merchant based in the city centre. It was through his work here that he met Agnes Thornton, known as Úna, with whom he fell in love and married. She was a member of Conradh na Gaeilge. She was also a member of an organisation called Inghiní na h-Éireann (Daughters of Ireland) founded by Maud Gonne McBride. The newly married couple set up home in the seaside town of Bray over a shop at number 85 Main Street.

In 1914, when Cearbhall was three years of age, the Ó Dálaigh family moved to Vevey, about a mile outside Bray. They had four children, Cearbhall, Aonghas, Úna and Nuala. In 1915, when he was only four years old, Cearbhall and his brother were sent to the local Loreto Convent. His brother was well behaved but the same could not be said of Cearbhall who caused considerable disruption in class, so much so that he was not allowed back after one particular foray. Later, in 1918, he attended St. Cronan's national school where he settled in well and he remained there until 1920. In that year his father died and the family moved to Dublin. There he went to Synge Street Christian Brothers School and was considered a good pupil if not a genius. He applied himself well and developed an awareness that knowledge held the key to progress in the world. He recalled: 'I had good ... remarkably good teachers ... my greatest distinction at school was as an athlete – I won the All Ireland quarter mile junior championship.'

At the Christian Brothers School his learning of Irish was stimulated and he was encouraged to spend the summer holiday months in Ring College in Waterford learning the language. The college was headed by the famous An Fear Mór (the big man), Seumas O h-Eochadha. The world renowned actor, Cyril Cusack, was also there at that time. At Synge Street, Cearbhall obtained the 'Fáinne' (a silver or gold ring signifying a knowledge of, and willingness to speak, Irish). Here, too, he acquired strong Christian ideals copperfastened by those instilled in him at home. Though he spoke Irish whenever he could, he never put those who were not familiar with the language ill at ease in any way.

Cearbhall Ó Dálaigh entered University College Dublin (UCD) in 1931 and graduated with a BA in Celtic Studies. At this time his professor of Modern Irish was Douglas de h-Íde. Cearbhall took an active part in the Literary and Historical Society, or the 'Yell and Howl' Society as his fellow students named it. As a member of the L&H Society Cearbhall often addressed meetings in Irish. A fellow member, Dick Dunne, described his contributions as follows:

> '... there was a dynamic energy which physically displayed itself in every movement. I don't think I know of anyone who worked so hard; he wrote bilingually scores of articles whilst still engaged in arduous studies in college and in reading for the Bar. As a speaker I would not rate him in the top flight: he was too staccato in his utterance, yet he was effective because his audience felt that he knew what he was talking about.'

In the first issue of the National Student magazine the following 'rann' appeared:

> *Fear Óg darb'ainm O' Dálaigh*
> *Ni Fheictear riamh ach a shalai*
> *Ma tá bean no cailín*
> *Ar bith to be seen*
> *I n-aon cheann ar bith des na hallaí.*

Ó Dálaigh was a regular reader of *The Nation* newspaper and in 1929 started writing for it under the title 'Um Chasig 1916'. He also contributed a series of short stories in Irish. In June of that year he produced an article entitled 'The Clergy and Irish', in which he was critical of the fact that although 'to Maynooth came the talent of Irish speaking villages ... but no lecture halls resounded to its music. There only the flat, much lipped English...' He criticised the Catholic clergy in general for abandoning Irish. He also extended his criticism to Daniel O'Connell whom he quoted as saying: 'I can witness without a sigh the gradual disuse of Irish.'

Ó Dálaigh continued:

> *'The chains of slavery were forged in the smithy of O'Connell's rhetoric and in the quiet churches of the countryside.... The clergy are the lever to move the Nation ... some of the noblest have led the van. Shall the others lag behind? Move the other way? Ireland awaits an answer.'*

Ó Dálaigh expanded his journalistic practice by becoming Irish language editor of the *Irish Press* newspaper for the period 1931 to 1942. His brother, Aonghus, was also a contributor to the same newspaper.

## Romance

Ó Dálaigh was a member of An Cumann Ghaelach. It was through his membership of this organisation that he became friendly with Máirín Nic Dhiarmada, a fellow student at UCD. Máirín's father was a member of Conradh na Gaeilge and later became the organisation's secretary. He had served in India teaching Irishmen in the British Army. He married there and, indeed, Máirín was born there. She was two years old when she was brought to Ireland. After her graduation from UCD she obtained a teaching post in Monaghan and later in Scoil Chaitríona in Eccles Street in Dublin city. In 1931, Máirín was elected *reachtaire* (administrator) of An Cumann Ghaelach. When she met Cearbhall he was 23 years old and she was a few years younger. On 14 June 1934, they were married in Eaglais Mhuire agus Peadair in Rathmines in Dublin. Cearbhall's brother, Aonghus, and Máirín's sister, Maeve, were witnesses. Afterwards they spent some time in the Great Blasket Island in Kerry. At that time there were about 120 inhabitants. They enjoyed getting to know everyone and discovering the delights and beauty of the island. They then travelled through the North's Mourne Mountains and on to Belfast taking in the Antrim Glens and the Giants Causeway. On returning to Dublin they set up home in Grosvenor Road in Rathgar.

## Politics

In 1926, de Valera left Sinn Féin and formed a new party – Fianna Fáil. His followers included Seán Lemass, Sean T. O'Kelly, Frank Aiken, Seán MacEntee, and Jim Ryan. Cearbhall Ó Dálaigh was a great admirer of de Valera, and indeed his father had been friendly with de Valera some years previously. His mother, too, had great respect for de Valera. Cearbhall agreed with de Valera's decision that Fianna Fáil deputies should take their seats in the Irish Parliament by taking the infamous Oath of Allegiance (though at the same time denying its applicability), a decision that was to have a major impact on the politics of the country both immediately and in the longer term.

In 1948, Ó Dálaigh ran for the Dáil under the Fianna Fáil ticket in the Dublin South West constituency, however he lost out to fellow party members Bob Briscoe and Bernard Butler. Fianna Fáil lost the election to a coalition of Fine Gael, Labour, Clann na Poblachta and Clann na Talún. The coalition formed a government under Fine Gael's John A. Costello. In 1951, Ó Dálaigh again put himself forward for election. This time he lost out to Sean MacBride, who was elected on the ninth count under the proportional representation voting system. Ó Dálaigh's final tally was 6,131 votes against 6,288 votes for MacBride.

Prior to this, in 1934, Cearbhall Ó Dálaigh had been called to the Bar. He devilled under Kevin Dixon and later under Colm Condon, both very well known barristers. He was called to the Inner Bar ('took silk') in 1945. A year later, at the age of 35, with a total of 12 years Bar experience behind him, he was appointed Attorney General by then Taoiseach Éamon de Valera. Cearbhall was the youngest appointee to the post in the history of the State. He served in this post for the period 1946–1948.

Ó Dálaigh was destined for loftier office and in 1953 was 'promoted' by de Valera to membership of the Supreme Court. In this capacity he was involved in a number of high profile cases, including a libel case brought by the poet Patrick Kavanagh, and an appeal case in connection with the stamp auctioneer, Paul Singer, of Shanahan's Stamp Auctions Ltd.

In 1961, Ó Dálaigh was made Chief Justice. A hallmark of his period in office was highlighting the importance of the Constitution as regards the protective provisions of citizens' rights. His reputation for intellectual brilliance coupled with his fairness in the administration of the law became widely respected. He promoted the independence of the judiciary combined with a focus on the rights of the individual. On this latter point he discoursed as follows:

*Chief Justice Cearbhall Ó Dálaigh in wig and gown*

'I had from my student days a keenly developed sense of the rights of the individual and the sacredness, perhaps inviolability might be a better term, of the human personality. By this I mean, the freedom of the individual to reject mass opinion: to make an individual choice.'

In his book *Cearbhall Ó Dálaigh*, Risteard O Glaisne quoted professor John M. Kelly as saying:

'... no one understood better the place and function of the courts in a democracy, and on all occasions he was scrupulous and fearless in upholding the liberty and constitutional rights of the ordinary man and woman. It was really during his term as Chief Justice that the Constitution became a living and vibrant thing and those *of us who were fortunate to work with him in the Supreme Court were constantly inspired by his concern to explore fresh ideas and develop new concepts in order to fit the law to the times instead of the times to the law....'*

And again:

*'As a lawyer and a Chief Justice, he was a most outstanding person. He presided over the Court during the very important years in which his spirit was joined by other judges who were of the same cast of mind and had the same intellectual brilliance, but he must get a large part of the credit for the number of important decisions the Court made in the 1960s. Lawyers will remember him for this, and for his extreme courtesy and gentleness as a human being.'*

In the same book, Gerald Hogan, law lecturer in Trinity College Dublin, was quoted as saying:

*'The appointment of Cearbhall Ó Dálaigh as Chief Justice in 1961 heralded the beginning of a new era in Irish jurisprudence. Both he and Justice Brian Walsh were determined to make a fresh start and to release the Irish legal system from the state of almost servile dependency on English judicial developments into which it had lapsed. They recognised that this could be done in a number of ways. First, a more flexible approach might be taken to the question of precedent. Secondly, they encouraged the citation of authorities from other common law countries apart from Britain, such as Australia, New Zealand, and, most notably, the United States. Finally, both judges were alive to the possibilities prescribed by the Constitution. Quite apart from the fact that that document could be invoked to enhance the protection of civil liberties, both Ó Dálaigh and Walsh recognised that if constitutional jurisprudence advanced to a sufficiently developed state it would thereby be possible to effect a complete remoulding of fundamental legal principles and thus establish an entire corpus of law which would have a distinctly native foundation...'*

And again, Hogan says:

> 'There is virtually no body of law which is immune from the growing volume of constitutional case law, and its influence on traditional common law subjects such as tort and evidence has been so great that now- perhaps for the first time ever- one can almost speak of a distinct "Irish law of torts" or "Irish law of evidence".'

Despite his hectic legal schedule, Ó Dálaigh found time to continue his involvement in promotion of the Irish language, Irish music and cultural matters generally. In 1960, he was a founding member and chairman of Cairde na Cruite (the Friends of the Irish Harp). This organisation was formed to restore the Irish harp, the symbol of an ancient culture, to a

*Cearbhall Ó Dálaigh delivering an address to the*
*International Council on Alcoholism*

place of honour and to make more widely known and appreciated all that survived of the heritage of Irish harp music. Ó Dálaigh saw it as acting as a bridge between those people who spoke Irish fluently and those who loved the language but were not as fluent as they would like to be. His wife, Máirín, a Celtic scholar in her own right (her knowledge of old Irish was greatly admired by experts in the field) encouraged him in this direction.

Ó Dálaigh's high profile meant that he was constantly in demand for speechmaking, which was renowned for its delivery, wit and clarity. He was also associated with a large number of charitable organisations, including the Irish National Council on Alcoholism.

## European Court

In 1972, Ó Dálaigh was part of a three-person team that visited Brussels with the aim of seeing how the European Court worked. This was of some importance in the light of Ireland's pending membership of the European Economic Community (EEC), or the Common Market as it was then more usually known.

On 16 August 1972, it was announced in the national Irish press that Cearbhall Ó Dálaigh, Chief Justice and President of the Supreme Court, had been appointed as Ireland's member of the EEC's Court of Justice. Once installed in his new post, Ó Dálaigh impressed his fellow members of the Court. His linguistic skills enabled him to get to grips quickly with the details of the national laws of the member states and their relationship to the laws of the Community. Although it transpired that he would be in his new post for only two years, he made a significant impression on the post and in the production of legal interpretations that, later on, had a key bearing on judgements in European law. He was in Strasbourg on business when he heard of the sad and sudden death of President Childers in Dublin.

## New President

Speculation started in due course as to who might succeed Childers as President of Ireland. Ó Dálaigh's name came to the fore as did those of Dr

Ken Whitaker, a former Secretary of the Department of Finance and later Governor of the Central Bank; Dr Donal Keenan, who was President of the GAA; and Mr Con Cremin, the Irish Ambassador to the United Nations. There was also newspaper speculation that Childers's widow, Rita, might be a non-political agreed candidate. In the end, however, Ó Dálaigh was proposed by Fianna Fáil and this was accepted by Fine Gael and the Labour Party.

*Cearbhall Ó Dálaigh, Prof P.K. Lynch, Éamon de Valera and Patrick J. Hillery*

On Ó Dálaigh's nomination the *Irish Times* had the following to say:

> *'Mr Justice Ó Dálaigh will be a good President.... He is learned and lively.... He knows and is known in the world outside Ireland. Unlike so many eminent jurists his personality has not been dehydrated by his profession and, withal, he is the right age, in his early sixties.... Mr Ó Dálaigh will, of course, move confidently through his ceremonial duties, and will be an accomplished host to the endless queue of visitors to the Park.'*

Rita Childers, however, had some misgivings about the selection process for the Presidency. She said:

> *'I saw how, once again, a woman in Ireland can be regarded as a mere baggage.... Let us all at once put behind us these past wounding ungracious days and give all respect and welcome to Justice Ó Dálaigh and Bean Chéile Ó Dálaigh in their sustenance of the meaning of the Presidency of Ireland. Let us pledge ourselves never again to allow such corrosive, destructive cynicism about 'politics' to contaminate that high office, so that the children and youth on whom our whole future depends may at least have this one above - politics focus to inspire them.'*

Further unpleasantness followed when, in the early part of 1975, Fianna Fáil arranged for a commemorative Mass to be celebrated for the former President Childers. Mrs Childers wrote to Fianna Fáil saying:

> *'The late President would not benefit from the prayers of such a party in its present format.'*

## Inauguration

When Cearbhall Ó Dálaigh was elected President, the Catholic Archbishop of Dublin, Dermot Ryan, invited the heads of the Protestant churches to a meeting to discuss the possibility of holding an ecumenical service to mark the President's inauguration. Dean Tom Salmon of Christ Church Cathedral was nominated by George Simms, Protestant Archbishop of Dublin, to represent him. Ó Dálaigh participated in the meeting and immersed himself fully in the proceedings. Dean Salmon decided on a piece from the Book of Common Prayer for his own contribution which read as follows:

> *'Look, we beseech you, O Lord, upon the people of this land who are called after thy holy Name; and grant that they may ever walk worthy of their Christian profession. Grant unto us all that, laying aside our divisions, we may be united in heart and mind to bear the burdens which are laid upon us. Help us to respond*

*to the call of our country according to our several powers; put far from us selfish indifference to the needs of others; and give us grace to fulfil our daily duties with sober diligence. Keep us from all uncharitableness in word or deed; and enable us by patient continuance in well-doing to glorify thy Name: through Jesus Christ our Lord. Amen.'*

Ó Dálaigh was delighted about this offering and insisted that it be included in the service. Indeed, he proposed to translate it into Irish and say it himself. He was even more chuffed when the Dean gave him his own Irish version of the Book of Common Prayer.

The inauguration took place on 19 December 1974. The following are some excerpts from the new President's speech which was delivered in Irish, French and English:

*'I always like to come prepared for a task. But how do you come prepared for the task of being President of Ireland? How do you follow after such names as de h-Íde, Ó Ceallaigh, de Valera, Childers? In time of difficulty our ancestors would say: 'Níor dhún Dia doras riamh nar oscail Sé ceann eile' (God never closes one door without opening another). I pray God it may be so.'*

*'A lawyer looks at the Constitution (article 12.1) and reads: "There shall be a President of Ireland (Uachtaráin na hÉireann) who shall take precedence over all other persons in the State...." This, I see, is an impossible role. A judge, prima facia, would pronounce the section 'void for impossibility'. But every statute and every Constitution must be read as a whole; and article 5 says "Ireland is a ... democratic State". Here, then, we find the solution of our problem. The President is first, but primus inter pares, first among equals. This makes the office of President of Ireland a possible task, a task that can be grappled with...'*

*'The Press in recent days have repeatedly asked me: "What, Mr President-elect, is your policy going to be as President?" I have invariably answered – and I think, correctly – that Presidents, under the Irish Constitution, don't have policies. But perhaps a*

*President can have a theme. If he can, then I have found an answer for my friends of the Press. The theme of my septennate (más cead san le Dia) will again be that of my early student years, "Community Spirit" – how sorely needed in part of this strife-torn island – with the new European dimension added, and never forgetting our brothers of the Third World.'*

*'We approach the Feast of the Prince of Peace. Can we, could we, may we, find truce in Ireland as we approach the day of Days? And if this be granted, is it too bold to hope thereafter for a temporary extension – to be prolonged indefinitely and to eventuate at last, one day, in a durable, just peace among all who live in our beloved sea-girt land?'*

## Working as President

Throughout his Presidency, Ó Dálaigh was to the forefront in the promotion of, and support for, the Irish language. He encouraged people to use the Irish version of their names and of their businesses. In the state visit to France he surprised members of the Irish press there by addressing them in Irish. Religion was close to his heart too. In 1975, he asked:

*'Is the quality of life in this country favourably or adversely affected by the power of the Catholic Church? My first answer is that all of us are too ready to neglect the beam in our own eye. The quality of life; this is the sum of our individual lives. We know the road that we should travel, but our nature is recalcitrant. And one of the easiest escapes is to criticise one another. Do I know what is the power of the church? It is, I suppose, the voice of churchmen speaking on great public issues, it is, also, perhaps, that in some respects Catholic education has been too protective – that it did not do sufficient to confront the problems and ideologies that modern life presents to young people. If so, parents must also bear a part of this responsibility. Where, regrettably, Christians and others differ in their opinions, there will, in any democracy, be a clash of views; and what are desirable laws, for the common good, can give rise*

*to genuine differences. These are great questions – what rights are personal rights, and to what extent, even in agreed areas, is it wise to insist that the ordinary law should underwrite the moral law?'*

Although primarily engaged in lofty affairs of state, Ó Dálaigh found time to give consideration to more mundane matters like the age old problem of litter on Ireland's streets. He called on Dubliners to form 'five clubs' – groups of five people who would make it their business to tidy up their own local environment. In addition, he proposed early morning collection units to tidy up the previous day's litter, and urged businesses to wash down their store, property frontage and pathway.

## Culture

In cultural matters, too, Ó Dálaigh was, perhaps, before his time in calling for an international charter for artists, saying that the artist had the right to expect a living from society. In 1975, he opened the Cork ROSC exhibition of Irish art, 1900 to 1950. He urged that all Irish artists should decorate Ireland's great public buildings, offices, factories and schools. He said: 'It is acknowledged that modern buildings are incomplete without the work of painters, sculptors and tapestry makers.' He also commented that in modern church buildings there was a marked lack of art. In addressing the Irish Theatre Company, he said:

> *'Theatre is as essential as pure air for a country's cultural health. The Greeks thought of theatre as a purging of the soul. It is this and much else. It is magic, fantasy, vision; the Irish word "Deismireacht" (Refinement) might be the best single word. May the Irish Theatre Company live to speak many words.'*

At a lunch in Áras an Uachtaráin in 1975 to celebrate the 76th birthday of the actor Micheál MacLiammoir, reference was made to tree planting in the grounds of Áras in honour of the work of MacLiammoir and his partner Hilton Edwards. In the book entitled *The Importance of being Micheal*, by Micheal O'hAodha, there is a photograph taken on the occasion in question showing Michael Scott, Hilton Edwards, President

Ó Dálaigh, Micheál MacLiammoir, Siobhán McKenna and Micheál Ó hAodha standing on the proposed site of the tree planting. The positions were marked with small signs as it was not the proper time of year for the planting of ash. However, due to the later resignation of Ó Dálaigh from the Presidency, the trees were not planted until President McAleese came to office.

At the final curtain call of MacLiammoir's one man show, 'The Importance of Being Oscar', Ó Dálaigh, who attended the performance, paid tribute to the actor. The President's genuine interest in the theatre was confirmed by *Irish Independent* journalist Des Rushe when he reported that the President had attended a different theatre almost every night during the 1975 Dublin Theatre Festival and, furthermore, insisted on buying his own tickets. On one occasion the President found the Gate Theatre full on his arrival but he brushed aside embarrassed apologies of the staff that no seat could be found for him. At the Abbey Theatre he attended a performance of Thomas Murphy's controversial play, 'The Sanctuary Lamp', and went on stage afterwards to contribute to a discussion on the play. Rushe went on to say that President Ó Dálaigh filled an office which was above politics and divorced from decision-making and cannot, therefore, do much by way of concrete action.

> *'He has, though, done as much as he can by setting an example of sympathetic involvement. And his dedication has been of benefit to Ireland. Visitors from abroad noted his ubiquitous presence with astonishment and found it incredible that he went everywhere without fuss or guards or armoured cars. It shattered the image of a country allegedly riven by violence.'*

## State Visits

On 13 March 1975, President Ó Dálaigh paid a state visit to France. He was received by President Giscard d'Estaing. Writing in the *Irish Independent*, Michael Denieffe commented favourably on the various ceremonial aspects of the visit, including wreath-laying at the Tomb of the Unknown

Soldier:

> *'Demure, dapper and precise to an inch, President Ó Dálaigh sparked off a glow of sheer atmosphere that moved and warmed the heart of a cold and grey Paris.'*

In October 1975, President O'Dálaigh paid a state visit to Spain. He was met at the airport by King Carlos whom he addressed in Spanish. At the end of his visit, the King also honoured the President by being present at the airport for his departure. The President also visited the European Commission in Luxembourg.

## Herrema Kidnapping

One of the more unusual aspects of Ó Dálaigh's Presidency arose when a Dr Tiede Herrema was kidnapped by terrorist activists. Dr Herrema was a Dutch industrialist working in Ireland. So concerned about the situation was Ó Dálaigh that he drafted a letter to the Taoiseach of the day, Liam Cosgrave, offering himself as a substitute for Dr Herrema 'in the firm knowledge that there can be no government compromise with blackmail. I do not mind dying. My death will vindicate Ireland's honour.' However, in the end, the President decided against sending the letter. On the release of Dr Herrema, there was considerable controversy as to whether or not a compromise had been agreed with the kidnappers. The doctor was, apparently, a personal witness to a document on which a deal

*Portrait of President Ó Dálaigh by Thomas Ryan*

was written regarding the nature of the charges that would be brought against the culprits, Eddie Gallagher and Marion Coyle. In the end, the Government denied that any negotiations had taken place or that any deal had been done.

On the occasion of the conferring of Irish Citizenship as a token of honour on Dr Herrema and his wife on 11 December 1975, the President said:

> 'In Ireland the only token of honour which the State can confer is a grant of citizenship … the power to make the grant, which is vested in the President, has been exercised only once before and never has it been exercised in respect of both husband and wife. In Ireland, the Netherlands and far beyond, the name of "Herrema" is now a household word; it is a synonym for the tenacity, fortitude and comprehension of two very special people.'

## Heinous Crime

On 9 July 1976, Britain's new ambassador to Ireland, Christopher Ewart-Biggs, presented his credentials to President Ó Dálaigh. On the occasion Ewart-Biggs said:

> 'I will do all I can, all the time, to try to ensure that our two countries, whose interests are so closely interwoven, shall always have the comfort of truth and trust together; that we shall know each other's minds as true friends do and that our relationship will be directed to our common future as partners in Europe.'

On 21 July 1976, Ewart-Biggs and an embassy employee, Judith Cooke, were killed by an IRA bomb in Dublin. This shocking act shook the political circles in both Ireland and Britain. President Ó Dálaigh immediately conveyed his sympathy to Queen Elizabeth II: 'I assure Your Majesty of our deep sense of outrage at this heinous crime against both our peoples.' Later he was to attend a service of remembrance in St Patrick's Cathedral in Dublin and undertook one of the Bible readings.

## Crisis

In the wake of the killing of Ewart-Biggs, the Fine Gael-led Government introduced emergency legislation a month later to firm up the fight against terrorists. It brought with it a suggestion that certain constitutional safeguards would be suspended.

The leader of the opposition in the Dáil, Jack Lynch, expressed the view that the current security threat to the country was not so great or serious as to warrant such a suspension. Nevertheless, the Bill was passed in the Dáil by 65 votes to 61. On

*President Cearbhall Ó Dálaigh in pensive mood outside Áras an Uachtaráin*

being passed to the President for signing into law, Ó Dálaigh decided to refer the Bill, after consultation with the Council of State, to the Supreme Court to advise him as to its constitutionality. In a radio interview, the Minister for Justice, Paddy Cooney, said that the urgency of the Bill was being hampered by its referral by the President to the Council of State. The Supreme Court decided that the Bill was not repugnant to the Constitution and the President then signed it into law.

On 18 October, the Minister for Defence, Patrick Donegan, at an inspection of troops in a barracks in Mullingar, said in an RTE interview, departing from his prepared script:

> '... it was amazing when the President sent the Emergency Powers Bill to the Supreme Court. He did not send the powers of the army to the Supreme Court. He did not send the seven years maximum penalty for inciting people to join the IRA to the Supreme Court. In my opinion he is a thundering disgrace. The fact is the army must stand behind the State...'

134

Later, a statement issued through the Government Information Service on behalf of the Minister for Defence stated:

> 'I regret the remarks which arose out of my deep feelings for the security of our citizens. I intend to offer my apologies to the President as soon as possible.'

The editorial of the *Irish Times* of 19 October stated:

> 'The implications of the Donegan affair go very deep. It will be strange indeed if a Taoiseach (Cosgrave) who so rightly condemns subversion allows a Minister – one of the Ministers, too, most closely concerned with the security of the State – to remain in office after offering an outrageous public insult to the President. Apologies are not enough. Until Mr Donegan resigns, the Government's respect for the institutions of the State must be in question. This affair, which carries in it possible seeds of a serious constitutional problem, is the most urgent matter demanding action to restore public confidence.'

After a Ministerial meeting it was decided that Mr Donegan should go the President to tender his apologies.

A Government statement declared that no one would be resigning over the affair. The President refused to see Mr Donegan, who then wrote the following letter of apology to the him:

> 'A Uachtaráin uasail,
>
> I wish to refer to what I said yesterday at Columb Barracks, Mullingar, regarding the reference by you of the Emergency Powers Bill, 1976, to the Supreme Court on the question of constitutionality.
>
> In the statement issued by me last night through the Government Information Service, expressing my regret, I indicated my intention to offer my apologies to you as soon as possible.
>
> Pursuant to that intention, the Secretary of my Department, on my instruction and in my presence, sought from your Secretary this morning an appointment for me with you, so that I could

*offer my apologies to you in person today. As you did not find it possible to accede to my request for an appointment, I hasten to make my apology to you, sincerely and humbly, by this letter.*

*In making my apologies, I would like to refer particularly to what I said regarding the non-reference by you of the Criminal Law Bill 1976, to the Supreme Court. My mention of certain provisions of that Bill was for the purpose of stressing that you did not consider it necessary, after your consultation with the Council of State, to refer that Bill to the Court. I wish to assure you that my references to that Bill were not intended either directly or indirectly or by implication as in any way reflecting on you.*

*Specifically, I wish to tender to you my very deep regret for my use of the words "thundering disgrace" in relation to you.*

*I repeat my expression of sincere and humble apology.'*

*Patrick Donegan.*

The President's reply was as follows:

*'A Aire Uasail,*

*I received your letter of today's date this evening at 4.45.*

*The Constitution vests the supreme command of the Defence Forces in the President, and all commissioned officers, on the Government's nomination, hold their commission from the President.*

*The exercise of the supreme command, the Constitution directs, is to be regulated by law; and the formula of section 17 (1) of the Defence Act, 1954, is as follows:*

*"Under the direction of the President, and subject to the provisions of the Act, the military command of, and all executive and administrative powers in relation to, the Defence Forces, including the power to delegate command and authority, shall be exercisable by the Government and, subject to such excep-*

*tions and limitations as the Government may from time to time determine, through and by the Minister (for Defence)."*

*The President's role in relation to the Defence Forces is therefore honorary in character; nevertheless, a special relation exists between the President and the Minister for Defence. That relationship has been irreparably breached not only by what you said yesterday but also because of the place where, and the persons before whom, you chose to make your outrageous criticism; I adopt this term from today's leading article in the Irish Times.*

*The gravamen of your utterance is "in my opinion he (the President) is a thundering disgrace". These words, I find, and the following sentence: "The fact is, the Army must stand behind the State." Can this be construed by ordinary people otherwise than as an insinuation that the President does not stand behind the State? Have you any conception of your responsibilities as Minister of State and, in particular, as Minister for Defence?*

*In relation to the reference of Bills to the Supreme Court for a decision as to whether they are repugnant to the Constitution, Article 26 of the Constitution expressly authorises the President, after consultation with the Council of State, to exercise this power. The President may refer any Bill, with three specified exceptions. It has never been suggested that the Emergency Powers Bill fell into any of the excepted categories, quite the contrary.*

*If the office of President, as I conceive it to be, is to have any usefulness, a President would be failing in his duty "to maintain the Constitution of Ireland and uphold its laws"if he were not vigilant in his scrutiny of legislative proposals.*

*I cannot accept that what you have had to say about the "non-reference" by me of the Criminal Law Bill was not intended to be a reflection upon my office.*

*Your speech shows no understanding of the difference between the "non-reference" of the Criminal Law Bill and the "reference" of the Emergency Powers Bill. The sections of the Criminal Law Bill which I specifically mentioned in the summons to the Council of State – section 3 and section 15 (6) – are still open to constitutional scrutiny of the Courts in the ordinary way, notwithstanding that the Bill is now law.*

*The serious constitutional questions which arose in respect of the Emergency Powers Bill were whether the mere invocation of the formula specified in article 28 (3) (3) of the Constitution put all matters, including the question of the existence of a national emergency, affecting the vital interests of the State, beyond the scrutiny by the Courts. The Supreme Court has dealt with the matter and other important topics in its judgement.'*

*Cearbhall Ó Dálaigh.*

In the Dáil, Jack Lynch referred to 'the gross insult offered to the President and the grave reflection on his integrity, capacity and constitutional status as Head of the State by the Minister for Defence, Deputy Donegan'.

The Taoiseach, Liam Cosgrave, replied:

*'While I do not accept that the remarks of the Minister for Defence can be given the particular construction contained in the question, I regret that the Minister should have made any remarks which slighted the President. The Minister has offered a full and unreserved apology to the President.'*

*'Does the Taoiseach intend to ask for the resignation of the Minister or alternatively to dismiss him?'*

*'I have nothing to add to the reply.'*

A Dáil motion on confidence in the Minister for Defence was won by a government majority of five votes (63 to 58).

The President's resignation followed immediately. It is clear from the President's remarks and, later, from those of his wife, that it was the Government's successful motion of confidence in the Minister for Defence, and not the behaviour of the Minister himself, that forced his hand in deciding to resign.

## Notice of Resignation

The following News Release was issued from Áras an Uachtaráin:

> 'Today, 22 October 1976 at Áras an Uachtaráin, an tUachtarán Cearbhall Ó Dálaigh executed under his hand and seal his resignation from the office of the President of Ireland with effect from 6.00 pm today. He directed that signed copies of the instrument be forwarded to the members of the Presidential Commission, viz:
>
> The Chief Justice
> Chairman of Dáil Éireann (An Ceann Comhairle)
> Chairman of Seanad Éireann
>
> Upon whom, pursuant to Article 14 (1) of the Constitution, devolve the exercise and performance of the powers and functions of the President.
>
> He directed also that signed copies of the instrument be forwarded to the Taoiseach, the Tánaiste and the Leader of the Opposition.
>
> Having this afternoon fulfilled a function at Glengara Park School, Dun Laoghaire, an t-Uachtarán directly left for his home in Kilquade.'

## Reaction

Paying tribute to Ó Dálaigh, the actress Siobhán McKenna said:

> '... to me this is the worst thing to have happened to Ireland that I can remember. Éamon de Valera lived out his time; Mr Childers was a marvellous President who unfortunately did not live out his time, but I think that Cearbhall Ó Dálaigh had such a tremendous amount before him.... He is a European in the true sense.... He is a real Irishman ... he is a very cultured man, a very simple

*Cearbhall Ó Dálaigh making a phone call on the evening of his resignation as President of Ireland*

man and a very approachable man…. He has a lot of interest in life, I think it is our loss, not his.'

The *Irish Press* stated:

'Under the Constitution there are three pillars of the system by which Ireland is governed – the President, the Judiciary, the Legislature. The President as the guardian of the freedoms contained in the Constitution was in the position that he faced what was tantamount to a repudiation in the exercise of his autonomous functions by the Dáil. Viewed thus one pillar was down and two to go, the legislature and Judiciary. Only the Judiciary and, in particular, the Supreme Court, in the wake of the Dáil vote stood in the path of a dictatorship by a Dáil majority under which all freedoms could be seriously threatened.'

The newspaper went on to say:

'Cearbhall Ó Dálaigh's departure from public life shows that democracy is not as soundly based as people might think. It is not *automatically conferred on States everlastingly and it is not served by attitudes by those of Mr Donegan, nor of his colleagues in the Cabinet....'*

Mrs Rita Childers backed Ó Dálaigh's decision to resign, and said: 'Mr Cosgrave should say "I am sorry. I made a mistake".' She added:

*'... we had a splendid President and I think the whole matter should be solved by the Taoiseach apologising to him and by Mr Donegan resigning.'*

It is clear that two camps emerged from the Donegan affair: those who supported Cosgrave's decision to back his Minister and those against. Public pronouncements from the second camp seemed to be more forthcoming in stating their views. There were many references to Mr Donegan's rashness and stubbornness. It was felt that his attack on the President was an attack on the Constitution itself. There was even a suggestion that had Donegan refused to withdraw his insult to their Supreme Commander he should have been arrested and charged under the Emergency Powers Act with attempting to subvert the loyalty of the Armed Forces. There were others, however, who believed that Ó Dálaigh should not have resigned and that he should instead have merely treated the incident with contempt.

C.S. (Tod) Andrews, in paying tribute to the President, said:

*'Of all the men, Irish or foreign, whom I have encountered Cearbhall Ó Dálaigh was unique. His essential characteristic was that of an Irish patriot. He was a separatist. He believed that as long as the British remained in the six counties, the nation would not burgeon. That did not mean that he was anti British ... but he wanted an Ireland where the native language and literature, music and arts would play a dominant part in the life of the nation. He was more aware than most men of "The Hidden Ireland" of Daniel Corkery. It was an Ireland in which his inner life was led. He had a scholarly knowledge of the Irish language. He spoke it with what some Gaeilgeoirí regarded as an affected accent. But what he was doing was giving every vowel and every consonant its precise value. His Irish would, I imagine, have been spoken*

141

*by educated people if the language had developed uninterrupt-
edly over the centuries. Cearbhall Ó Dálaigh was extremely but
unaffectedly courteous. He had absorbed all the good manners
of the Europeans with whom he associated. He was essentially a
European and wished every Irish person to regard themselves as
Europeans as well as Irish.'*

The editorial of the *Sunday Independent* of 24 November 1976 ran:

*'In sacrificing his own career as President, he made the position
of future Presidents more secure and gave the office a status no
Government will now challenge or insult with impunity. For
this, if nothing else, the Irish people should be grateful that it
had in Cearbhall Ó Dálaigh, the Supreme Court Judge, a liberal interpreter of citizens' rights under the Constitution. In the
public person holding high office, the dignity and demands of
that office often leave little room for visible evidence of private
character. But Cearbhall Ó Dálaigh enjoyed a singular capacity
to integrate the private and public person; to manifest, as judge
and later as President his private virtues of compassion, humil-
ity and tolerance. In doing so, he added greatly to the dignity of
public office and humanising it through such an abundance of
private virtue.'*

In the course of the selection process for the new President there was
some support for Ó Dálaigh to allow his name to go forward once again,
but he never entertained this seriously as it would have put the Presidency
into the political arena which was what he wanted to avoid.

## Retirement

A short time after the President's resignation, the family moved from
County Wicklow to County Kerry. They settled first in Caherciveen in
1977 and later moved to Tathaile near Sneem. Ó Dálaigh and his wife
were apparently very happy in their new abode and they enjoyed and appreciated the welcome they received from the local people.

In July 1977, Ó Dálaigh was invited to visit China. While there, the Senior Vice President of the Central Committee of the Communist Party hosted a banquet held in Ó Dálaigh's honour in the Great Hall in

*Former President Cearbhall Ó Dálaigh with his dogs outside a pharmacy in Sneem, Co Kerry, after his resignation from the Presidency*

Peking. The event received wide television coverage in the country. Indeed, so successful was his visit that he was invited to make a return trip at a later date.

## Death

Cearbhall Ó Dálaigh died on 21 March 1978, less then two years after resigning the Presidency. He was buried in Sneem, County Kerry, after a state funeral.

## Tribute

Below is an excerpt from the remarks by President McAleese at the Annual UCD Law Society Cearbhall Ó Dálaigh Dinner at Dublin Castle on 25 March 2003:

> *'Last Friday along with many others, I attended a particularly beautiful anniversary Mass in his honour and there it was evident that we were not simply commemorating a great jurist, a remarkable intellect, a principled and ill-fated President, but a man of huge faith, love and generosity that his absence still hurts deeply those who were privileged to know him.... History will be kind to Cearbhall the jurist as it should be for he was a champion. His short Presidency is arguably the most critical in terms of the history of the office but this evening, twenty-five years on from the death of the man described by Brendan Kennelly so brilliantly as "Immediate Man", we pay tribute to the man who loved his country, its native tongue and its people, with great passion, who served them all with humility and devotion and whose friendship was so dearly held that his name could still bring tears to the eyes of those who knew and loved him some twenty-five years after his death.'*

Fr. Loman Mac Aogha OFM referred to Cearbhall Ó Dálaigh's love of children, as expressed on Brendan Kennelly's poem about a thirsty child on the long journey from Dublin to Kerry.

Cearbhall Ó Dálaigh

# Immediate Man

*Is it not a heart lifting*
*Sight to see a laughing*
*Prince of a man rising*
*From his seat in a crowded train*
*And go, immediate man,*
*To return with solace for one*
*Who undistressed in a moment,*
*Will never forget him?*
*The fields and the lakes have names, dear,*
*And every rock, mountain and hill,*
*And don't worry if the stations come quickly or slowly,*
*Or there are too many hurrying people.*
*Take your ease and consider them all,*
*Think of the names and know what you feel,*
*He gets off at Killarney, this man of style.*
*Over the years she has mentioned his smile,*
*His greyhound words, his wise eyes,*
*His contemplative hands, impulsive ways,*
*The sense he transmitted that we are witnesses*
*To stations, fields, lakes we should name and praise.*

Brendan Kennelly

# Patrick Hillery

## Sixth President of Ireland (1976–1990)

### Family Background

Patrick John Hillery was born on 2 May 1923 in Spanish Point, Miltown Malbay, in County Clare. The Hillery family was of tenant farmer stock for the best part of the nineteenth century. Patrick's grandfather, Pat Hillery, was put off his land outside Miltown Malbay by the local landlords, the Moroney family. He then settled in the town itself. He supported the Land League, which was formed to support tenant farmers from the excesses of the landlords and to secure, as far as possible, fair rents and security of tenure. He was jailed for a short time because of his involvement in the League. He died in 1899 at the age of 46. His wife, Margaret, was a business woman of some repute. The eldest of their five children was Michael.

He was a bright lad and won a scholarship to the Royal College of Surgeons in Dublin. He qualified as a doctor in 1912 and set up as a general practitioner in Miltown Malbay. In 1919, he married Ellen MacMahon, a local girl whose family were successful business people in the area. Michael and Ellen set up home in nearby Spanish Point. They were both supporters in the fight for Irish independence in 1920. Michael offered his medical skills to the local IRA unit, and Ellen provided nursing to wounded volunteers and arranged shelter for them in her family home in Miltown Malbay. After the War of Independence, and following the split in Sinn Féin over the treaty conditions, Michael Hillery took no further part in politics and devoted himself exclusively to his medical practice. This entailed looking after patients from both sides of the new domestic political divide. He and Ellen had four children, of whom Patrick Hillery was one.

Patrick Hillery's initial education was in the local national school. When he was twelve years old he was sent to Rockwell College in Cashel, County Tipperary. The school was run by the Holy Ghost Order of priests and was his father's alma mater. Patrick was content there and took a special interest in sport, especially hurling, Gaelic football and rugby. His initial enthusiasm for his studies waned somewhat, but he managed to obtain satisfactory results which allowed him to enter University College Dublin (UCD) in 1939 to study medicine. It was discovered, however, that at the age of 16 he was too young to enter certain laboratories, the university rules prescribing that for safety reasons 17 was the minimum appropriate age. He had to return home and wait a further year before commencing his studies. He was very successful in each of his six years of study and even managed to obtain an honours science degree while completing his medical studies. He graduated in 1947 with first class honours. During his time in UCD he took no interest in politics, even though there would have been ample opportunities to have done so.

After graduating from UCD, Patrick Hillery undertook a one year internship in the Mater Hospital in Dublin and then moved to the National Maternity Hospital, also in Dublin. Seeking to widen his experience, he went to Canada in 1948 and took up duty in  the Hotel Dieu (Hospital) in Ontario, followed by a move to the Saskatchewan Hospital. After a year he got word that his father was ill and returned to Ireland. He spent a short time working as a family doctor locally before taking up a post, once again, in Dublin. This time the post was in Peamount Hospital near Newcastle. This enabled him to obtain training in the treatment of tuberculosis, which was by then a widespread scourge throughout the country.

## Early Politics

While Hillery was in Canada, the Fianna Fáil party, founded by Éamon de Valera, lost power and an inter-party government under Taoiseach John A. Costello of Fine Gael took over. However, the Government collapsed in 1951 and another general election was called. Although Patrick, now back in Ireland, had shown no interest in politics, he was nominated to run for Fianna Fáil by local activists in his native County Clare. Reluctantly, he allowed his name to go forward to the Fianna Fáil convention. He never thought he would be selected, especially as his nomination was very much a last minute one and he had not engaged in any canvassing. It came as bit of a shock to him to learn that he had indeed been selected and, furthermore, on the same ticket as de Valera himself.

Hillery's election campaign was a low key affair which was in marked contrast to the more usual loud and barracking style of electioneering. This seemed to strike a chord with the local electorate and, together with the fact that he and his family were so well known in the area, resulted in his beating two seasoned fellow party contenders and taking a second seat for the Fianna Fáil party. The first place went to de Valera who, as expected, topped the poll. Hillery's primary interest still lay very much in his medical practice, and for the next eight years he combined this with his duties as a Dáil backbencher.

In June 1951, de Valera was elected Taoiseach by a very slim majority with the help of five independent TDs. The impact of this on Patrick Hillery personally was that his local constituency work was doubled as he was now expected to undertake de Valera's constituency duties as well.

A general election was called in 1954 and Hillery was re-elected with ease, although at the national level Fianna Fáil lost out overall and Fine Gael's John A. Costello was once more elected Taoiseach of a coalition government. The Dáil was still dominated by the two main sections representing both sides in the Civil War, with bitterness and distrust never far below the surface.

## Romance

In 1955, Patrick married Beatrice (known as Maeve) Finnegan. She was born on 3 September 1924 in Sheffield, England, where her Irish-born parents lived. During her teen years Maeve lived with her grandmother in Galway – Sheffield not being considered a safe place during the Second World War. On completing her secondary education in Galway in 1940, she applied to University College Galway (UCG) for 'pre-med' studies. As with Patrick, she was too young and had to wait a year before she was allowed to enrol. She spent the final three years of her study at the same university as Patrick in Dublin. In fact, they were both in the final year together but did not meet until some years later. On her graduation in 1947, Maeve worked in a number of Dublin hospitals before moving back to Sheffield to take up a post in the Royal Hospital. In 1955, however, she returned once again to Dublin but was unable to secure a permanent post, finding that being a female professional in the male-dominated medical world was a definite disadvantage, notwithstanding her expertise as an anaesthetist. She decided to emigrate to Canada having secured a post in a Montreal hospital. Before doing so, however, she met Patrick Hillery by chance when she was undertaking locum duties in Harcourt Street Children's Hospital in Dublin. He was working there to gain some experience in paediatrics. She abandoned her plan to emigrate and they became engaged shortly after they met. They got married on 27 October 1955.

## More Politics

The Hillerys' first child, John, was born in June 1957 and in October of that same year Hillery's father, who had just retired from his medical practice, died. A further general election was held that year resulting in a win for Fianna Fáil with Hillery returned once again. De Valera tried to convince Hillery that he should accept the position of Parliamentary Secretary (now called 'Junior Minister'), but he declined as he had no ambitions in that regard. His aim remained to dedicate himself to his medical practice as far as his political duties would allow.

In 1959, Fianna Fáil again won a general election. Shortly after that de Valera announced that he intended to resign and become a candidate for the Presidency, in anticipation of the end of President O'Kelly's term of office. De Valera's announcement came as a blow to Hillery in that it now meant that he would have to put aside his intention to return to full- time medical practice as his departure would leave Fianna Fáil without a TD in the area and he could not, it seemed, allow that to happen.

## Promotion

The appointment of Sean Lemass as Taoiseach on 23 June 1959 had a dramatically successful effect on Ireland's economic life. At this time. Hillery was still harbouring thoughts of being able to return to his home town and again take up his medical practice. His elevation to the Ministry of Education put paid to that. He was enticed by the Lemass-style of politics, which he saw both as pragmatic and a move away from the old style of bickering based on old Civil War divisions. The transition to his new responsibilities did not come easily to him, but his determination and skill soon saw him on top of the job. Constant travelling between Miltown Milbay and Dublin now became impractical. The family, therefore, moved to Dublin and bought a house in Shankill.  Despite his hectic schedule, Hillery made a point of devoting special time to his wife and small son.

When Patrick Hillery was made Minister for Education the role was considered a relatively junior one compared to some other ministerial posts.

The majority of primary and secondary schools were under the control of the Catholic Church, with a small proportion controlled by the Protestant churches. The role of the Department was, therefore, largely in the area of private schools and its funding was limited. Hillery quickly became aware of the need to improve education, particularly in the areas of teacher/pupil ratios, teacher training and refurbishment of school buildings. He drew up a plan to try to deal with these issues within the constraints of the Department's limited funding. He also concentrated his endeavours in the area of scholarships, which were under the aegis of local authorities and which he considered inadequately funded. He convinced the Government to pass new legislation to provide significant State funding to the local authorities for scholarships.

The previous de Valera-led government had approved, in principle, the transfer of University College Dublin (UCD) from its city centre site at Earlsfort Terrace to a greenfield site at Belfield, about 2.5 kilometres outside the city centre. Hillery supported this proposal and obtained the necessary Dáil approval to set it in motion. An earlier proposal to amalgamate UCD and Trinity College (TCD) had come to nothing, mainly because the existence of separate universities suited the educational authorities and, significantly, the church authorities. The latter's influence arose because the Catholic Church considered that TCD was a haven of Protestantism and therefore an unsuitable establishment for those of the Catholic faith. The college welcomed students of all faiths or none. This was in contrast to the earlier state of affairs, prior to 1793, when TCD authorities had banned Catholics from entering their university.

A general election was held in 1961 and Hillery polled well enough to bring in a second Fianna Fáil candidate, Seán Ó Ceallaigh, with him. Hillery's second term, from 1961 to 1965, saw him push forward with improvements on the educational front, particularly in proposed radical changes which would form the foundations upon which his initial successor, George Colley, and later Donagh O'Malley, would introduce major impacts in the way schooling was organised throughout the country. This was facilitated in particular by the approval, acquired by Hillery, for Ireland to participate in an OECD national pilot study on the long-term educational needs of Ireland. There was, of course, the risk of adverse reflection on him and on the Department with the inevitable highlighting in the study of shortcomings in the country's educational system. Hillery considered the risk well worthwhile because it would give him the necessary leverage to come forward with proposals for the much needed reforms which he saw as critically necessary for educational improvements in Ireland.

In June 1962, Hillery arranged that the pilot study be undertaken by a national survey team under the auspices of both the OECD and the Department of Education. The study started in October of that year. It was completed just before Hillery's term in Education came to an end, but the substance of the study was already beginning to register in the appropriate ministries in Leinster House. Simultaneously, Hillery pushed ahead with a plan to deal with the need for the provision of second level education in small farm areas, especially those in the west of Ireland. He also made reforms in the area of special education for physically and mentally disadvantaged children. His proposal for the establishment of comprehensive schools received the firm backing of Lemass. This support was very important if he was to have any chance of obtaining the necessary funding. His aim was to promote equality of educational opportunity and to improve standards in the various strands of education. In particular, he wanted to provide educational opportunities for those with a more technical bent and to make the necessary education equal in standard with that of the more traditional academic studies. His proposals received favourable press comments but a negative response from the Catholic Church, which saw the move as an intrusion into what they saw as their preserve – one which, up to then, the State was more than happy to leave in their hands. The Church also feared that non-denominational or co-educational schools would leave a serious gap in the religious education of pupils in those establishments. Hillery used his diplomatic skills to the full in successfully persuading the Catholic Church to accept a pilot scheme, and this paved the way, eventually, for significant progress to be made in this area.

Hillery's overall stamp in education was to lift the Education ministry to a level equal with other senior ministries in the Government. His period of tenure also marked the transfer of responsibilities previously held exclusively by the churches to the Department.

## New Ministry

A general election was held in 1965 with Fianna Fáil again returned to power. This time Lemass appointed Hillery as Minister for Industry and Commerce, a lofty post for him at the young age of 42. This brief was held previously by Lemass himself and was, therefore, an indication of the high level of confidence the Taoiseach had in Hillery.

Hillery's appointment coincided with the possibility of Ireland's entry into the European Economic Community (EEC). This heralded a move away from protectionist economic policies to the more competitive but wider arena of the EEC. This path was marked out in the Government's Second Programme for Economic Expansion, which was published in 1963. The subsequent period was notable for a deterioration in industrial relations which resulted, in 1966, in a wave of strikes. Proposed legislation to enhance industrial relations, drawn up by Hillery with backing from the Taoiseach, was not well received by the trade unions which wanted a continuation of the prevailing system of voluntary wage bargaining. The new proposals in the Industrial Relations (Amendment) Bill envisaged enhanced authority for the Labour Court by giving it power to enforce binding arbitration of disputes to include all industrial workers. The Trade Union Bill foresaw the withdrawal of legal protection from picketing in any unofficial action. The proposals were seen by the unions as too restrictive and an impasse ensued.

## New Responsibilities

In June 1966, Hillery proposed the establishment of a new government department – a Department of Labour. Lemass was sufficiently enthusiastic about the proposal that he appointed Hillery as Minister of the new department in July of that year. Hillery's new position brought him new challenges as well as some inherited ones. These included dealing with the thorny matter of industrial relations, retraining of workers, health and safety matters and manpower policy generally, especially in the light of a hoped for upward surge in economic activity as a result of the introduction of new technologies. In 1967, a major advance was made in the area of protection of workers by the introduction of the Redundancy Payments Act. The purpose of the Act was to provide compensation to those who lost their jobs. In that same year the Industrial Training Authority (AnCO), now restyled FÁS, was introduced to promote training and retraining of workers.

Earlier in 1966, Lemass had disclosed to Hillery that he intended to step down as Taoiseach and to retire from politics. He sounded Hillery out to see if he would be interested in succeeding him as Taoiseach, but Hillery said that he had no ambitions at all in that regard. When, in November 1966, Lemass did announce his intention to retire it brought to the surface certain tensions within the Fianna Fáil party. These were focused on the two main contenders for the post, namely, George Colley and Charles Haughey. In order to avoid any trouble Lemass proposed Jack Lynch to stand for the leadership of the party and, therefore, ultimately, to become Taoiseach. Lynch agreed to go forward and was successful. He was elected Taoiseach on 10 November 1966. Hillery was retained in his post as Minister for Labour by the new Taoiseach.

A disastrous and prolonged Electricity Supply Board (ESB) strike took place in 1968 and Hillery was forced to intervene, an action he had avoided as a matter of principle up to then. Another major strike, this time by maintenance workers, took place the following year. Hillery then came forward with proposed legislation with the aim of stabilising the current voluntary bargaining system in place of mooted radical proposals such as a statutory incomes policy. The new proposals resulted in the appointment of a Rights Commissioners to deal with disputes arising from perceived breaches of workers rights. This allowed pressure to be taken off the Labour Court system which could now concentrate on issues such as pay claims.

Meanwhile, on the family front, when son John was twelve, Patrick and Maeve adopted a baby girl, Vivienne. She was born on 11 April 1969 and the adoption procedures were completed soon after that. The expanded family brought additional responsibilities on Hillery, ones which he wholeheartedly welcomed.

## New Political Duties

A general election in 1969 saw Fianna Fáil re-elected with an overall majority. Hillery was elected too but this time he was second in his Clare constituency to newcomer Sylvester Barrett. Whilst the election was a personal triumph for Taoiseach Jack Lynch, he was nevertheless considered, in some Fianna Fáil quarters, as no more than a caretaker leader. Those of this opinion were, undoubtedly, Government ministers Kevin Boland (Local Government), Neil Blaney (Agriculture) and Charles Haughey (Finance). In July, Lynch reshuffled his Government and Hillery was appointed to the post of External Affairs, later renamed Foreign Affairs.

## Northern Troubles

Hillery's arrival in his new post coincided with an upsurge in violence and instability in the North of Ireland. This resulted from the repression by the Royal Ulster Constabulary (RUC) of civil rights protests by the nationalist minority community. The planned marches by loyalist Apprentice Boys in Derry on 12 August did not bode well for the impending summer marching season by loyalist groups. With this in mind, Hillery travelled to London on 1 August to meet with the British Foreign Secretary, Michael Stewart. Hillery urged that the parade be confined to loyalist areas, but was informed that this was a British matter and none of the Republic of Ireland's business. The parade went ahead on 12 August and the anticipated violence occurred in Derry and Belfast. The RUC and the semi-military B-Special forces attacked nationalist areas leaving a trail of destruction in their wake. Inhabitants were forced to evacuate and it was clear that the situation was out of control. The nationalist minority felt undefended and, therefore, under significant threat. In response, the Irish Government arranged for the Irish army to set up field hospitals along the border to treat the injured. The old Coombe Hospital in Dublin, then vacant, and other public buildings in the city were cleared to provide shelter for evacuees. Taoiseach Jack Lynch made a television address in which he said 'the government could not stand by and see innocent people injured and perhaps worse'. He sought negotiations with the British Government to discuss all aspects of the situation, but the discussions came to nothing. The number of British troops in the North was increased significantly. Initially, they were seen as endeavouring to keep the peace between loyalists and nationalists, or indeed by some as providing protection to the nationalists in particular. It was not long, however, before British troops were seen by nationalists as being exclusively on the side of the loyalists. Their presence became a major bone of contention among the minority population.

## United Nations

Hillery went to the United Nations to raise with the Security Council the possibility of a peacekeeping force being sent to the North of Ireland, and also to have the situation in the North placed on the agenda of the General Assembly of the UN. As regards the former, Hillery knew well that Britain, as a permanent member of the Security Council, would have a veto on his proposals and that they would, of course, exercise it. Ireland had support from the Soviet Union and Pakistan but, critically, the USA said that they would abstain from any such vote. Additionally, intense pressure on other members by Britain ensured that there would be no support coming from any other quarter. Finland came to the rescue by proposing that Ireland be allowed to address the Security Council before the matter of the agenda was adopted. This would enable Hillery to make his points while satisfying British concerns about the topic actually becoming an agenda item. Hillery was well aware, too, that a lost vote would have been immensely damaging to Ireland's case. Further lobbying by Hillery resulted in the Finnish proposal being accepted. In his address Hillery adopted a moderate and unemotional tone. On the one hand, he accepted the practical reality of the fact that part of the North was under British control whilst reiterating Ireland's de jure rights. He stated that reunification was the only lasting solution to the problems but that Ireland was intent on achieving this by purely peaceful means. He drew attention to the fact that the threat to peace came from within Northern Ireland and was caused by the denial of civil rights to the nationalist minority there. The failure of the Stormont authorities to implement meaningful reforms contributed significantly to the problems.

In response, the British ambassador, Lord Caradon, pointed out that the British troops were welcomed by the Catholic minority and were seen as peacekeepers. He contended that the matter was a British domestic one which was being addressed by them. He finished by saying that he would not object if the Council decided to adjourn without voting on the composition of the agenda. This was agreed, to the satisfaction of all concerned. Lynch sent his congratulations to Hillery on his achievements. However, his praise was not universally shared on the domestic front as Government Ministers such as Boland and Blaney seemed to believe that action rather than words was what was required.

Six weeks later Hillery was again back in New York, this time to attend the General Committee of the General Assembly of the UN. For Hillery, the matter of having the North of Ireland placed on the agenda was once again to the fore. The likelihood of obtaining the agreement of the 25 member nations to this was remote in the extreme. In the end, the outcome was that, once again, Ireland would be allowed to address the Assembly but it was also agreed that the topic be deferred to the next meeting. In fact, the matter was not raised again although, in theory, Ireland retained the possibility of raising the topic at a later stage if needs warranted it. Lord Caradon, however, now hinted to Hillery that direct talks between Britain and Ireland were a distinct possibility.

## Social and Democratic Labour Party (SDLP)

In 1970, a new political party on the nationalist side in the North side was born. It was a conglomeration of a broad range of politicians dedicated to a non-violent approach to solving the North's problems. It was convened by John Hume, later a Nobel Peace Prize winner. Its first leader was Gerry Fitt, later Lord Fitt. The arrival of this moderate party on the political scene was welcomed by the Dublin Government.

Under Prime Minister Harold Wilson a number of secret inter-governmental meetings were held, ostensibly on Anglo-Irish Free Trade matters, but also on matters related to the troubles in the North. Meanwhile, Hillery had matters closer to his own back yard on his mind, namely, the ongoing worry about elements in the Government who were pushing a harder line on northern matters. He was concerned that this might have an adverse impact on the Government's moderate approach to the North. Hillery made his views very clear: he was totally opposed in principle to any military intervention by the Irish army. Additionally, he was convinced that there was no way that the army could succeed against the combined might of the RUC, the B-Specials and the British army troops, not to mention the Ulster Volunteer Force (UVF), the counterpart of the IRA. In his book *Patrick Hillery: The Official Biography*, author John Walsh quotes Hillery as follows: 'You could start the war by giving guns to people who recklessly would start without sufficient brains or case for the finish.' He thought, also, that supplying arms to the nationalists would be seen by the Unionists as an act of war and that massive civil disturbance would ensue, not to mention forced intervention by the Irish Government and open conflict with Britain. He did allow, however, that it was necessary to prepare for a possible doomsday scenario and that the Irish army would need to be prepared to withstand any UVF forays over the border into the Republic. The hardliners in the Government considered this a weak response.

## Arms Importation

In early 1970, an attempt was made to import arms through Dublin destined for the newly emerged Provisional IRA. It failed due to the absence of a 'users certificate' which was required by the customs authorities. The importation move was led by a Captain James Kelly, an officer in the Irish Military

Intelligence, together with John Kelly of the Belfast Citizens Defence Committee and Albert Luykx, a Belgian businessman based in Dublin.

A Public Accounts Committee investigation into the use of a relief fund for the victims of distress in Northern Ireland concluded that a major part of the funds had been used to buy arms. Captain Kelly asserted that the importation had been supported at the highest level, and in particular by Jim Gibbons, the Minister for Defence. Gibbons strongly denied this. Hillery was unaware of the importation plan as was Lynch. Lynch was, of course, aware that the Haughey/Boland/Blaney triumvirate was anxious for more extreme action on the North. The Taoiseach raised the attempted importation with Haughey and Blaney but they protested their innocence. At a cabinet meeting on 1 May, the arms importation attempt was referred to by Lynch who reiterated the Governments' policy of attaining unity solely by peaceful means. But he desisted from taking action against any of his Ministers thought to have been involved. Details of the failed attempt to import arms were passed by sources within the Gardaí to Liam Cosgrave, Fine Gael leader of the opposition. On the 5th of May, Cosgrave brought the matter to the attention of Lynch who was now forced to act.

A press announcement on the morning of the 6th May disclosed that Haughey and Blaney had been dismissed from the Government. Kevin Boland, Minister for Local Government, resigned immediately in sympathy with his colleagues. Hillery was, meanwhile, on a mission in London and had to return straight away to give moral support to Lynch. At a cabinet meeting the possibility of seeking a vote of confidence in the Taoiseach was discussed, but they were unsure about the level of support that Lynch could rely on and were concerned about the danger of creating a split in the Government. It was decided, instead, to ask the party to confirm the Taoiseach's right to appoint Ministers. This tactical approach, which was suggested by Hillery, was successful. The nomination of new Ministers to replace the dismissed ones was the subject of a long debate in the Dáil. In it Hillery defended the Taoiseach's actions in the sackings. Nevertheless, a confidence debate on Jack Lynch did take place in a Dáil debate which was held on the 13th and 14th of May 1970. Speaking in support of the

Taoiseach, Hillery said that it was necessary to seek reconciliation among Irish people and that it was not desirable that one tradition in the country should seek to dominate another one. He continued:

> 'We have seen how such an attempt failed in the North. Shall we, for our part here, now attempt to translate that failure to the whole of our country, or shall we take the alternative of trying to understand that the only solution to the Irish question is that which recognises the value of all our Irish traditions? Starting from such recognition we could work to bring them together peacefully.'

Hillery went on to state that supplying arms to the paramilitary forces in the North would undermine Government policy and damage Ireland's reputation internationally. It would also threaten 'the life and peace of all our country'.

Lynch won the vote of confidence by 72 votes to 64. It was notable that the deposed Ministers supported him in the vote.

In a private visit by President de Valera to Hillery's home in Sutton in Dublin to see their new baby daughter, the President told Hillery that the support of Lynch was the right decision and that they should 'stick with it'.

## More Trouble

The arms importation attempt débacle was, however, by no means at an end. On 28 May 1970, Haughey, Blaney, Captain Kelly and Luykx were charged with conspiracy to import arms. All the defendants were ultimately acquitted, and with this verdict on 23 October 1970 came a call from Haughey for Lynch to resign. At this time the Taoiseach and Hillery were attending the annual session of the UN General Assembly in New York. When word of Haughey's statement was disclosed, the Fianna Fáil party machinery moved into action and a huge welcoming party was present at Dublin Airport to greet the Taoiseach on his return from the USA. This served to ensure that Haughey's call for Lynch's resignation was dissipated, at least for the moment. Underlying unrest among the dissidents rumbled on, however, but a dramatic visit by Hillery in July 1970 to the nationalist Falls Road area in Belfast had the effect of upstaging them as regards ownership of nationalist sentiment. This was particularly so because no advance warning of the visit as given by Hillery to either the Unionist authorities or Westminster, to the great annoyance of both.

The Fianna Fáil Árd Feis, held in February 1971, had special emphasis on differences of approach to the Northern situation and on the issue of leadership. On the former it was clear from the outset of the meeting that supporters of Blaney were well organised. Standing orders resulted in rowdy discussion on the amount of time to be allowed to each speaker. The election of officers went the way of the leadership but, when discussion on the Secretary's Report was held, it became clear that successive speakers were supporters of Blaney and when Lynch's supporters took to the podium they were shouted down. There were reported scuffles in the hall and the atmosphere was very heated. Lynch asked Hillery to respond on behalf of the leadership. This request came out of the blue to Hillery, but he readily accepted and decided to speak from the main platform rather than on the podium. Not long into his speech he was interrupted by the appearance of Boland on the podium whose appearance brought loud applause. Despite constant interruptions by Boland's supporters, Hillery continued his speech vigorously. He said:

> *'Our policy is Jack Lynch's policy, de Valera's policy, Sean Lemass's policy and we will continue that policy in spite of any bully boys within or without the organisation. We can have elections, we can have elections for our officers, but we won't frighten Jack Lynch out of here by a few bully boys. We can change our policy, but we will change it there (in the elections) and not over there (pointing to Boland's supporters). And Fianna Fáil will survive as it did before.'*

These words were met by shouts of, 'We want Boland, we want Boland', to which Hillery responded in raised and emotional tones, so different from his usual quiet manner, 'Ye can have Boland but ye can't have Fianna Fáil!'

Hillery's address had a marked impact on the Árd Feis and bolstered support in a major way for Lynch's leadership. It showed a tough side of Hillery and enhanced his reputation in the party generally. Hillery and his colleague Joe Groome were re-elected as Joint Honorary Secretaries of the party, thus ensuring that Boland lost out. George Colley was elected Honorary Treasurer to the exclusion of Blaney. Charles Haughey, later the same day, told Hillery that he had nothing to do with Boland's protests and Hillery accepted this.

Kevin Boland left Fianna Fáil in 1971 and founded a new party, Aontacht Éireann, which survived only a short time. Neil Blaney was expelled from Fianna Fáil in 1972. He retained his seat as an Independent Fianna Fáil member of the Dáil and continued to maintain considerable support in his native Donegal. Charles Haughey fell into line and, at least outwardly, accepted the leadership of Jack Lynch.

The aftermath of the Fianna Fail Árd Feis resulted in a period of stable government and allowed Hillery to continue to promote the party line on Northern policy. In discussions with the British Government, now Conservative, Hillery continued to press for reforms for the minority in the North and for the banning of the provocative Orange Order loyalist parades in so far as they were routed through or near nationalist areas. He warned the Secretary of State, Douglas-Home, that any acceleration of violence would put in danger the survival of the Irish Government and its moderate approach to Northern matters.

The British Government continued to prop up the Stormont regime, fearing that to replace it with direct rule from Westminster would be more harmful. The Northern Prime Minister, James Chichester-Clark, eventually accepted a British Government-proposed reform programme for the North. This included the creation of a new Housing Executive with minority representation. When Chichester-Clark sought additional troops from Westminster, following the killing of three soldiers in May 1971, Prime Minister Heath refused. Chichester-Clark resigned and was replaced by Brian Faulkner. When Faulkner refused a public inquiry into the killing of two people by British troops in Derry, the SDLP withdrew from Stormont resulting in an increase in political tension.

## Internment up North

On 9 August 1971, Lynch was informed by British Prime Minister Heath that the British Government, in compliance with a request from Faulkner, intended to introduce internment without trial that same day. About 400 people, exclusively from the nationalist minority, were arrested, of whom approximately 340 were detained without trial. Many of those had no involvement in political violence. There was an immediate upsurge in violence in protest against internment, and it had the not surprising effect of bolstering membership of, and support for, the IRA. At a meeting between Hillery and Home Secretary Reginald Maudling, the Irish Foreign Minister warned that the policy of internment could lead to war in the whole of Ireland and that the rise in

*Dr Patrick Hillery, Ireland's Minister for External Affairs, being interviewed in London in 1971 after meetings with UK politicians about Northern Ireland*

support for the IRA had been caused by the policy of sustaining Unionist dominance over the nationalist minority. He said that Britain needed to replace force with politics and that that could be achieved only by introducing a system of power-sharing. Maudling was amenable to the power-sharing proposal but only if and when violence ceased. Hillery advised him that this approach was not realistic. No progress was made in the discussions. Thenceforth, the principle of power-sharing became the cornerstone of the Irish Government's approach to solving the North's problems.

On 30 January 1972, a civil rights march in Derry was fired on by British soldiers of the Parachute Regiment and 14 people were killed, all of whom were unarmed. The event was referred to thereafter as 'Bloody Sunday' (which reflected back to an incident in Dublin in November 1920, also called 'Bloody Sunday', when British troops opened fire on a crowd of spectators and players attending a football match in Dublin's Croke Park killing 12 people; this was in revenge for the killing of 14 undercover British intelligence agents by Sinn Féin.) A huge wave of emotion was created by this action throughout the country. Additionally, it swelled the membership of the IRA even further. It also marked a low point in Anglo-Irish relations. The Irish cabinet decided that Hillery should go to the United Nations, USA and Canada with the aim of raising awareness of the problems at an international level. At a press conference held by Hillery at Kennedy Airport in New York, which received widespread media coverage, Hillery urged friendly nations to bring pressure to bear on the British Government to turn back from the disastrous policies it was following in the North of Ireland. In Dublin, a massive protest march to the British Embassy took place, culminating in the burning down of the embassy by a small minority of protesters. At a further press conference, this time in the UN, Hillery pushed for a power-sharing administration and a realisation by Britain that the British army presence in the North had become 'an instrument of coercion' in nationalist eyes. Despite Hillery's best efforts, Britain's insistence that this was a British domestic matter prevailed once again.

Hillery now devoted himself to visiting all the EEC States as part of the run up to Ireland's (and Britain's) membership of the Community. On Northern matters, Hillery adopted a deliberately low key approach and applied gentle persuasion on the member states in the hope that they would lean diplomatically on Britain regarding Irish concerns. In Britain, the negative affects of internment without trial and the disastrous outfall from

Bloody Sunday resulted in Prime Minister Heath advising Brian Faulkner that he intended introducing direct rule of Northern Ireland from Westminster and phasing out internment. Faulkner opposed this move but Heath prorogued Stormont on 30 March 1972 and direct rule was then imposed. William Whitelaw was named as Secretary of State for Northern Ireland. The end of a brief break in the violence was marked by a resumption of the IRA campaign in July. A spate of bombings in Belfast resulted in 11 people being killed with dozens injured. The Loyalist paramilitaries were not slow to respond and the position was once again tense.

## EEC Entry Problems

In the course of Ireland's preparation for accession to the EEC, a proposal from Jean Monnet, a founding father of the Community, that all applications (including Ireland's) be halted until Britain's membership was first in place caused huge worry in Ireland. This would mean disaster from an economic standpoint as Ireland was hugely dependant on trade with the UK. If Monnet's proposal was agreed, Ireland's position outside the seven member states (including Britain) would result in its trade with Britain being blocked by tariff barriers. Hillery commenced an immediate and vigorous diplomatic campaign to counter Monnet's proposal. In particular, he lobbied both Joseph Luns, President of the Council of Ministers, and the German Foreign Minister. He also lobbied the hugely influential Maurice Schumann who was the French Foreign Minister. Hillery was successful and in October 1969 the Commission agreed to the opening of negotiations for membership with all the applicant countries (Ireland, Britain, Denmark and Norway).

The negotiations, led by Hillery for Ireland, began on 30 June 1970. They were long and arduous. Hillery pushed for the retention of export tax relief and won out. He also succeeded in obtaining a slower than originally proposed run down of motor assembly in Ireland, as well as gaining immediate access to European Agriculture Guidance and Guarantee Fund without any phasing-in period. It was also necessary to agree a transitional period to allow industry and agriculture to adapt to EEC membership requirements. This was set at a five-year period. He also received conces-sions in relation to Anglo Irish free trade provisions during the transitional period. He got acceptance of Ireland's needs in relation to support in re-gional development matters. Fisheries policy caused significant difficulties for Ireland. The EEC wanted equal access to members' coastlines for all members. For Ireland and Norway (Norway eventually decided against joining the EEC), this would have been very damaging because both coun-tries were heavily reliant on the fishing industry. In the end, a compromise was reached with Ireland. It meant that Ireland could enforce a six mile limit for ten years and a twelve mile limit for northern and western coasts. Other matters, such as a sugar production quota, took time to negotiate too, but in the end were agreed.

In summary, it was clear that membership would result in significant benefits for Irish agriculture (through the Common Agriculture Policy (CAP)) and, although there would be short-term difficulties for Irish in-dustry, there would be worthwhile long-term benefits for that sector too.

In compliance with the Irish Constitution, it was necessary to hold a referendum to approve, or otherwise, Ireland's membership of the EEC. A comprehensive campaign to obtain a 'yes' vote was launched by the Gov-ernment. Responsibility for this fell largely on the Department of Foreign Affairs. Briefings were held with agricultural and industrial bodies. It was also necessary to inform the general public and, indeed, members of his own party, of the critical aspects of membership. Hillery pointed out that our failure to join would leave us isolated in Western Europe economically as well as politically. The Fianna Fáil party rallied to his call and Fine Gael too adopted a fully positive attitude towards the EEC. Those opposed to joining the EEC included the Labour Party, the trade unions, 'Provisional' Sinn Féin and 'Official' Sinn Féin (later to become Sinn Féin/Workers Party (in 1977) and later still, the Workers Party (1982), then renamed the Democratic Left (1992) and finally to merge with the Labour Party).

The referendum was held on 10 May 1972. The 'yes' vote took 83 per cent of the poll and the turnout was 71 per cent, a record.

## European Commissioner

In January 1973, Ireland's accession to the EEC was completed. Hillery had already been nominated as Ireland's first European Commissioner. He also became one of five Vice Presidents of the new Commission. This heralded the end of Hillery's involvement in Irish politics and he moved to Brussels to take up his desired brief as Commissioner for Social Affairs. His new job was not without its problems. The portfolio was underdeveloped and he found a distinct lack of interest on the part of other national governments for action on social issues. However, in the end he did receive support from West Germany and France for the development of social action programmes over the following three years. Back in Ireland, a general election in February 1973 resulted in a new coalition government of Fine Gael and Labour with Liam Cosgrave as Taoiseach. Hillery's rapport with the new government was good and he enjoyed an especially good relationship with Garret Fitzgerald, the new Minister for Foreign Affairs, and also with Frank Cluskey of the Labour Party in his capacity as Parliamentary Secretary at the Department of Social Affairs.

For Hillery, the principal areas of action in social policy were in the improvement of living and working conditions, training and retraining, including the upgrading of vocational training, promotion of employment, equality of treatment for migrant workers and abolition of discrimination against women in the workplace. Success in these areas necessitated intensive lobbying of member governments by Hillery. He was careful to include briefings of trade unions in these matters too. In October 1973, the Commission approved his social action programme. He then had to secure the acceptance of the Social Affairs Council and this he did, after lengthy discussions, on 12 December 1973. Hillery moved to introduce many of the reforms, but the processes slowed down with the advent of the 1973 oil crisis which resulted in the Commission's programmes generally being delayed.

The Treaty of Rome embodied in its articles the principle of equal pay for men and women. A number of countries, however, had not implemented this, including Ireland and Britain. Consequently, Hillery drew up a draft directive on the topic which was approved by the Council of Ministers in December 1974. In February of the following year it was formally issued and signed by Garret Fitzgerald as President of the Council of Foreign Ministers (Ireland was then, by rotation, holding the Presidency of the EEC). The reaction among Irish employers was negative. They claimed that trying to deal with the economic downturn arising from the oil crisis prevented them from granting equal pay to women. To do so would lead to job losses. The Cosgrave government, therefore, decided to seek derogation from the directive, but Hillery opposed it and was backed by the Commission. Despite pressure from the Irish Government, Hillery held his ground. His strong view was that he was acting as a European representative and not an Irish one, as indeed was called for by the very terms of his job. Although Hillery suggested that Ireland might be able to obtain financial assistance from the EEC's Social and Regional Funds, it cut no ice with the Irish government. The Commission then announced its refusal to allow Ireland to delay in implementing equal pay. This drew heavy criticism from Dublin. Ritchie Ryan, the Irish Minister for Finance, made it clear that Hillery, together with his fellow Commissioners, were to blame. The criticism was not well received in Brussels. The European Commission said that no legal exception could be made in the matter of implementing equal pay. They fully backed Hillery and said that under the terms of his office he could neither seek nor take instructions from any government.

Allied to the matter of equal pay was a draft directive, issued later by Hillery, for the establishment of equal treatment for women in access to employment, vocational training and working conditions. He further proposed the abolition of inequality in the level of social welfare payment as between men and women. There was significant opposition to the draft directive from Britain and West Germany on cost grounds. Hillery was forced to revise the directive and a modified version was passed by the Social Affairs Committee in February 1976. Hillery also made progress in support for the rehabilitation of people with either physical or mental disabilities. This included the provision of sheltered workshops. A lack of funding meant that his success in the matter of combating poverty was limited. The same applied to the area of improved conditions for migrant workers from outside the EEC. Nevertheless, important principles had been established upon which future progress could be made.

## President of Ireland

In October 1976, President Ó Dálaigh resigned from the Presidency in sudden and dramatic circumstances. The Fianna Fáil party approached Hillery and asked him to allow his name to go forward for the presidency. This was not the first time that Hillery had been considered for the post. When President Childers died suddenly in office Hillery was considered as a suitable successor but he declined to show interest. Now, once again, his name came up. On this occasion his term of office at the Commission was almost at an end. In fact, Taoiseach Cosgrave had informed him that he would not be proposed for a second term. Hillery would have preferred a new European role, possibly in the European Parliament, but back in Ireland momentum for him to go forward for the Presidency as an agreed candidate was gathering pace. In the end, he was approached directly by Jack Lynch and he agreed to accept the proposal. It was a somewhat reluctant acceptance, however, but his loyalty to Lynch counted for much in his coming to the decision to accept. Undoubtedly, some in Fianna Fáil were happy to see him 'out of the way' as he had also been considered as a possible successor to Lynch, although he had no ambitions in that direction. At the suggestion of Charles Haughey, an internal contest for the Presidential nomination was held in Fianna Fáil between Hillery and Joseph Brennan, the Deputy Leader of the Party. Hillery won by 55 votes to 15. His candidature for the Presidency was supported by Fine Gael and Labour and, when the deadline for nominations closed on 9 November 1976, he was declared elected.

## Inauguration

Patrick Hillery was inaugurated as President of Ireland on 3 December 1976. His acceptance speech included praise for the former President,

*Taoiseach Jack Lynch (right) presents the Seal of Office to President Patrick Hillery*

Cearbhall Ó Dálaigh. In a later Irish radio interview he said that Ó Dálaigh had been right to resign, that in fact he had no real alternative but to do so. Hillery now saw his own role as the need to bring stability back into the presidency and to re-establish its constitutional independence.

The transition from being at the very heart of European politics to the largely symbolic position of a strictly non-political national role was not easy for the new President. In addition, he had to suffer a lack of enthusiasm on the part of the Government in the matter of dealing with mundane requests such as seeking transport arrangements for his family members and for getting staff to and from Áras an Uachtaráin. His proposals were initially refused but, after he threatened to move out of the Áras, were ultimately acceded to. Funding for the running of the office of President was inadequate, so much so that some office staff salaries had to be paid out of his own personal resources until he managed to have this matter rectified as well. The 'presidential allowance' which was to cover the day to day costs of the household staff and other running costs remained unchanged at a low level.

*President Hillery and Mrs Hillery at entrance of Áras an Uachtaráin*

In 1977, Fianna Fáil won a general election with the largest ever overall majority. The relationship between the new government and the Presidency was now warmer, though it had no impact on the financial status of the Áras. Hillery, however, continued with his busy schedule of public engagements. These included visiting local communities and voluntary organisations all around the country. In his work he avoided courting publicity, believing that a period of quiet stability was what was called for. Later, however, when he began to consider that media coverage was appropriate, he proposed to Taoiseach Haughey that funds be provided to the establishment of a press office. He was refused. Press coverage did arise, however, when the President made overseas visits. His position as a former Commissioner of the EEC and his status as a former Vice President of that institution helped in this regard.

## State Visits

The President's state visits included trips to France, West Germany, Luxembourg, Bahrain, Tanzania, Denmark, Japan as well as a number of visits to the Vatican following the deaths of Pope Paul VI and Pope John Paul I. He also attended the enthronement of Pope John Paul II. A visit to India was the first ever of an Irish head of State to that country. From the Irish public's perspective, the presidential style adopted by Hillery was perceived as being low key. This was due in part to the fact that his role, by definition, was divorced from any political policy and because it was not in his character to court publicity for its own sake.

*Pope John Paul II greeting President Hillery*

## The Pope in Ireland

The first ever visit of a Pope to Ireland brought a significant amount of media coverage. This was the arrival of Pope John Paul II on 29 September 1979. On his first day in Dublin, His Holiness called to Áras an Uachtaráin for an official meeting with the President. The Pope's visit was a huge success and he was greeted with great enthusiasm at each of the venues (Dublin, Drogheda, Galway, Knock and Limerick). His appeal to the IRA 'on bended knees' to cease their violence was an exception as it met with no success. The President and his wife Maeve saw the Pope off at Shannon Airport at the end of his stay.

## Media Rumour

Almost immediately after the visit by the Pope, Hillery found himself having to deal with a media rumour concerning his marriage and alleged illicit relationships, including one which he was supposed to have conducted in the Áras itself. In order to defend his national and international reputation, Hillery felt it necessary to call a press conference to refute the rumours. He did so on 3 October 1979, dismissing any suggestion of marriage problems or of liaisons with any other woman. He stated further that he had no intention of resigning from the Presidency. The rumours were completely untrue and their source could never be verified, although biographer John Walsh said that Hillery had his suspicions as to who was behind the rumours. In any event, his denials at the press conference were accepted both by the general public and the press and the whole matter quickly faded away.

## Ongoing Work

On 5 December 1979, Jack Lynch announced that he was stepping down as Taoiseach. An election for his successor followed with two contestants, George Colley and Charles Haughey. Haughey won by 44 votes to 38 and was duly elected Taoiseach. The President was contacted by a journalist who asked him if he intended to resign to join the new Government. Once again, Hillery found it necessary to issue a statement confirming that he was staying in office. His relationship with the new Government was lukewarm. The President considered that Haughey thought of him as a competitor for popular opinion. This opinion manifested itself in early 1980 when the President received an invitation to attend the inauguration of Dr John Armstrong as the new Church of Ireland Archbishop of Armagh. The Department of the Taoiseach advised Hillery to decline the invitation as the Taoiseach himself planned to attend. Hillery did what he was asked to do.

Later in the same year, the President received an invitation to attend a British Legion Remembrance Day Service in St. Patrick's Cathedral (Protestant) in Dublin. The nature of the service had been altered by Dean Griffin to include all Irish soldiers who had died 'in the cause of justice and peace'. This would now include members of the Irish army who had served on UN peacekeeping missions in addition to the traditional remembrance of soldiers of the British army who had died in the world wars.

*President Hillery addressing a lunch hosted by the German President, Karl Carstens, in Luttrellstown Castle, Co Dublin, 1980*

The President's secretary sought permission to attend from the Taoiseach's office, but was informed that it would be inappropriate for the President to attend a memorial service for the armed forces of another country. The Secretary issued a reply along these lines to the British Legion without, however, first consulting the President. The British Legion and Dean Griffin were dismayed and upset by the reply. The President's reply received wide publicity. Hillery was greatly embarrassed by the wording of the 'no' issued on his behalf. He received no help from the Taoiseach by way of explanation and had to try to make amends by contacting leading members of the Protestant clergy privately to explain his position. Given the activities of the British army at that time in the North and in the border areas it may have been the case that Hillery would, in the end, have decided against attending but, no doubt, he would have couched his reply in more diplomatic tones as befitted his office.

## Fall of Fine Gael Government

The role of the President is, in the normal course of events, divorced from the politics of the day. However, under Article 13.2.2 of the Constitution,

*President Hillery at the Children of the Year Awards*

the President has the right to refuse a dissolution of the Dáil to a Taoiseach who has ceased to command the support of a majority in the Dáil. Such a refusal would have the effect of forcing the requesting Taoiseach to resign and would allow the possibility of the formation of an alternative government from within the existing Dáil, thereby obviating the need for a general election. In John Walsh's previously mentioned book on Hillery, reference is made to an incident in the National Concert Hall in Dublin where Charles Haughey made it his business to approach the President to ask if he was aware that he had the power to, in effect, refuse the holding of an election if it were sought by a Taoiseach. Hillery said that he was so aware. He was aware, too, of the precarious position of the Fine Gael-led Government.

In fact, the Government fell on 27 January 1982 over a proposal to apply Value Added Tax to children's clothes and footwear. Two independent TDs withdrew their support from the Government and, by a margin of one vote, the Government's majority in the Dáil was gone. The Fianna Fáil front bench, at the instigation of Haughey, called for the President not to dissolve the Dáil if requested to do so by the outgoing Taoiseach Garret FitzGerald, and therefore to allow Fianna Fáil to form an alternative Government without having to hold an election. Hillery considered the matter but was not convinced that Haughey would be able to gain the support for the necessary majority – one of the independents had stated previously that he would never support Haughey. Hillery's overriding consideration was to avoid the Presidency being seen as being engaged in any way in day to day politics. In particular, he did not consider discussions with political leaders about the formation of a government as being part of his brief. He decided, therefore, to make himself unavailable for any possible approaches that might entail pressure being put on him to exercise his powers under article 13.2.2. He instructed his Aide de Camp that he was not prepared to speak to anyone except the Taoiseach, Garret Fitzgerald.

It later transpired that on the night of the critical Dáil vote, about eight telephone calls were made to the Áras an Uachtaráin. It was thought that the calls were made by Haughey, Brian Lenihan, Haughey's secretary and others. All requests for discussions were turned down after which Haughey sent a written message in which he advised that he was the leader of the largest party in the Dáil and that he wished to speak to the President on a constitutional matter that was urgent. He further said that he proposed to

*President Hillery and Mrs Hillery visiting Mater Public Hospital, South Brisbane, Australia, in June 1985*

call to the Áras at 22.30 hours to see the President and that he was waiting for an answer from him. None was forthcoming.

Shortly after 10.00 pm on the night of the Dáil vote the Taoiseach arrived at the Áras. The President accepted FitzGerald's request for a dissolution of the Dáil (meaning that a general election would have to be held). It was so held on 18 February 1982 and was won by Fianna Fáil with the support of three Sinn Féin/Workers Party members and independent TD Tony Gregory. This Government did not last long and within eight months Haughey presented himself at the Áras with a request for a dissolution of the Dail. It was, once again, granted by the President. The general election which followed saw Fine Gael under Fitzgerald, together with Labour, once more back in power.

## Second Term for President

In May 1983, Patrick Hillery was 60 years of age. His seven year term of office was due to end in December of that year and he was looking forward to retiring after what was, by any standards, a very full public life. At this time Ireland was in the grip of a severe economic downturn and after three

*President Hillery greeting President Ronald Reagan and Nancy Reagan*

general elections in quick succession none of the main political parties was in the mood for a presidential election. Consequently, the leaders of the three main political parties approached Hillary and asked him to consider a second term in office. He declined as he had his sights firmly fixed on retirement. Persistent and unanimous pressure was put on him. Once again, he put the public interest first and eventually agreed to go forward as an agreed candidate despite his personal preferences to the contrary.

Hillery was re-elected unopposed in November 1983. He was the first President to be returned unopposed for two terms of office. His inauguration took place on 3 December 1983. It was a reasonably low key affair in sympathy of the gloomy economic mood of the country. Prior to his agreeing to go forward for a second term he had received assurances that a significant increase in the presidential allowance would be granted to enable him to deal with the serious underfunding of the running costs of the Presidency. This, however, did not come to pass, although he did receive a reasonable increase in his travel allowance.

Hillery resumed his presidential duties with his customary level of dedication. He promoted community groups, especially those associated with youth and the poorer sections of society and, as before, undertook his duties for the most part out of the glare of publicity, which was mainly due to a lack of funding for a press office.

The President convened the Council of State four times in all and referred the corresponding Bills to the Supreme Court for consideration as to their constitutionality. In two cases the Court directed the Government to redraft the Bills in question.

The Fine Gael government, under Taoiseach Fitzgerald, remained in office until 1987 and during this period FitzGerald briefed the President on a regular basis and enjoyed a good relationship with Hillery. On 10 March 1987, Haughey took office once again and this time the relationship between the Taoiseach and the President was more distant. For example, when Hillery asked for permission to attend the World Cup soccer quarterfinals in Rome between Italy and Ireland he was refused. Haughey, however, did attend.

*President Hillery on board the British training ship 'Lord Nelson', June 1990*

## Personal Tragedy

The Hillery family suffered a personal tragedy in 1987. Their daughter, Vivienne, was diagnosed with non-Hodgkin's lymphoma. The results of the initial treatment were encouraging but in those days the treatment was not as successful as it has since become and their daughter died in March of 1987 at the tender age of 17. It was a devastating blow to the family. Despite Hillery's high public profile, he managed to deal with their traumatic loss privately.

## Continuing Duties

Hillery's State visits in his second term included trips to Australia and New Zealand in 1985, and to China in 1988. He also visited Austria, Italy and the Netherlands. An especially notable trip for him was a visit to the European Commission in 1987. He was happy to be back in familiar ground and was warmly received by Commission President, Jacque Delors. Hillery underlined Ireland's support for the Single European Act (for a single European market) and made the case for an increase in regional and social funding for poorer countries. Hillery received considerable publicity when, in addressing the European Parliament, he was interrupted by the Democratic Unionist Party's Rev. Ian Paisley, a Member of Parliament for Northern Ireland. When Hillery was introduced as President of Ireland, Paisley shouted, 'not of the whole of Ireland', and when Hillery started

*President Hillery greeting visitors at Michael Collins Memorial House,*
*Clonakilty, Co Cork, October 1990 – to the President's right is Peter Sutherland*

speaking Paisley heckled him, but the President of the Parliament, Lord Plumb, called for the ushers to eject Paisley and they quickly did so. Hillery continued with his speech. He registered Ireland's national interests and endorsed Delors's plans to develop greater social and economic development throughout the Community. He also supported the process of integration and the promotion of greater decision making powers at community level. At the conclusion of his speech he received prolonged applause for what was a very well received address.

*Bust of President Patrick Hillery by Marjorie Fitzgibbon, HRHA*

Patrick Hillery's term of office came to an end in December 1990. Perhaps the most significant event of his Presidency was his achievement in re-establishing the independence of the role of the Presidency from the Government of the day. By doing so he reaffirmed the intention of his predecessor in the post, Cearbhall Ó Dálaigh, in this regard.

Patrick Hillery died on 12 April 2008 in St Francis' Hospice in Raheny in Dublin. He was almost 85 years of age. A state funeral followed and he was buried in St Fintan's Cemetery in Sutton, a suburb of Dublin. His remains lie beside his daughter who had died 21 years previously.

Paying tribute to the former President, President Mary McAleese said:

> 'He was involved in every facet of policy-making that paved the way to a new, modern Ireland. Today we detect his foresight and pioneering agenda everywhere ... free educational system, a dynamic, well educated people, a successful economy and a thriving membership of the European Union, one of the single most transformative events for this country.'

State papers released in 2002, under the British Public Record Office's Thirty Year Rule, revealed how Hillery was viewed in Britain. A briefing paper for the Secretary of State for Northern Ireland recorded:

> 'Dr Hillery is regarded as a powerhouse of ideas, one of the few members of Fianna Fáil who has new policies and is eager to implement them.... Dr Hillery has a pleasant manner. He can appear diffident and casual but has an undoubted intellectual capacity and a strong will; since the Government crisis of 1970 he has appeared much more assured ... even brash ... and has handled the Dáil with confidence.'

Minister for Finance and Tánaiste, Brian Cowen (then due to take over as Taoiseach from Bertie Ahern), at his graveside address said of Hillery:

> 'He was a humble man of simple tastes, he has been variously described as honourable, decent, intelligent, courteous, warm and engaging. He was all of those things and more.'

In a letter to the *Irish Times* of 15 April 2008, John Hurley (a former president of the Association of Secondary Teachers of Ireland) said:

> 'And while the public Dr. Paddy will be remembered, one of my abiding memories will be of the day Anthony Daly lifted the McCarthy Cup for us success-starved supporters in 1995. I was fortunate enough to have a seat near the President and I glanced over at Dr. Paddy to see the tears streaming down his face. And that is why his passing is sad, particularly for all us Clare people. He was quintessentially one of our own.'

# Mary Robinson

## Seventh President of Ireland (1990–1997)

### Early Years

Mary Robinson was born on 21 May 1944 in Ballina, County Mayo. Her maiden name was Bourke. The Bourkes (Burkes and de Burgo) were originally of Norman stock. Some of them were of landed gentry. Some were Catholic while others were Protestant. In 1815, John Bourke of Ballycastle, County Mayo, married Elizabeth Paget of the same county, both of landed gentry background. They had four sons, all of whom went into the British Army, two of them rising to the rank of General. One of the sons, William Orme Paget Bourke, a Captain in the 18th Regiment of the Royal Irish Regiment, was Mary Robinson's great-grandfather. In 1856, he married Jane Morrogh, a Catholic from Cork. It was a 'mixed marriage' in which the girls were brought up as Protestants whilst the boys were raised in the Catholic faith. William's son, Henry Charles Bourke (Mary Robinson's grandfather), attended Trinity College Dublin and became a well known solicitor. He set up practice in Mayo. This was in the immediate post-Charles Stewart Parnell period, a politically difficult time as the promised Home Rule had not been delivered to Ireland. Henry was a constitutional nationalist and appeared at courts set up by Sinn Féin prior to independence as an alternative to the official British legal system. He married Eleanor Macaulay and the union produced five sons and two daughters. His second son, Aubrey (de Vere), was Mary Robinson's father. He was educated at a boarding school in England, after which he undertook medical studies in Edinburgh. He qualified as a medical general practitioner and set up his practice in Ballina, County Mayo.

Aubrey married a Donegal woman, Tessa O'Donnell, whom he met while she was working in Temple Street Childrens' Hospital in Dublin. Aubrey had worked in England but returned to take up a post in Dublin's Coombe Lying-In Hospital at the commencement of the Second World War. Tessa was a lively, extroverted person with a great interest in sport. She studied medicine at UCD and, as a qualified doctor, set up practice in Donegal's Arranmore Island before her marriage brought her to Mayo. Aubrey and Tessa had five children, four boys (Oliver, Aubrey, Henry and Adrian) and one daughter, Mary.

Mary was sent to a private school at Ardnaree until the age of ten at which stage she was sent, as a boarder, to Mount Anville, a well known convent school in Dublin run by the Sacred Heart nuns. Her fellow students said that she was an active person and good at games, though not overly fond of what she considered too strict a regime. 'Thoughtful' and 'compassionate' were other descriptions ascribed to the young girl by her school friends. She attained first class academic results, and after her time at Mount Anville she spent a year at a finishing school in Paris. Here she gained a love of the French language and culture. She thoroughly enjoyed Parisian life and found the whole experience stimulating.

After her time in Paris, Mary followed in her grandfather's footsteps by commencing law studies at Trinity College, Dublin. Before this could happen she had to obtain a dispensation from the Catholic Archbishop of Dublin, Archbishop McQuaid, to attend the university. This was because Catholics were banned from attending Trinity College, it being considered by the local hierarchy as an essentially Protestant college and therefore a danger to those of the Catholic faith. This was in contrast to the situation which pertained prior to 1793 when Catholics were banned by the college authorities from attending the university. Having obtained the necessary permission to attend TCD, Mary's parents bought a house in Westland Row in Dublin for Mary and two of her brothers who were also attending Trinity. This was very convenient for them as the house backed on to the grounds of the college. (It was the house in which Oscar Wilde was born in 1854.) Here, Mary and her brothers lived with a nanny who was dispatched from Mayo to look after their domestic needs.

*House in Westland Row, Dublin, which was the birthplace of Oscar Wilde, where Mary Robinson and her brothers resided while students at Trinity College*

Senator David Norris, a fellow student of Mary Robinson's, described Mary as:

*'... stimulating and interesting company but also reserved ... intelligent, attractive woman from a secure social background who was extremely clever and ambitious. This was legitimate for men but not for women who would have been regarded as intellectually aggressive if they behaved in this way. Mary would not defer to men simply because they were men but would pursue an argument right to its conclusion.'*

In 1967, Mary was elected Auditor of the Law Society. Her inaugural address was about contraception, homosexuality and divorce vis- á-vis the law. She questioned the special position of the Catholic Church as contained in the Constitution. While Irish law did not attempt to enforce Catholic morality in relation to adultery, prostitution and drunkenness, 'it did place an embargo on divorce, homosexuality and birth control'. She was of the opinion that the prohibition on divorce should be deleted from the Constitution and that the law relating to it should reflect 'the public opinion of the times'. She said that homosexuality should be legalised if public opinion so wished. She also stated that restrictions on the availability of contraceptives were a legal infringement on the freedom of non-Catholics in the country.

## Harvard Law School

During her time as a student in TCD Mary met and dated Nicholas Robinson. He was one of a family of four boys. His mother died when he was only ten years of age and he attended Mountjoy School as a border. His father was a well known chartered accountant and a member of the Masonic Order. On graduation, Nicholas turned down an opportunity to join a well known Dublin legal firm, Matheson Ormsby and Prentice, and instead went to London to further his real interest which was in producing cartoons. Meanwhile, Mary graduated with first class honours and took up a scholarship to the Harvard Law School in Boston in 1967. At that time the Vietnam War was a controversial issue on campus, as were race issues. Three years previously, President Lyndon Johnson had signed the Civil Rights Act into law, but racial tensions remained and especially so when civil rights leader Martin Luther King was gunned down on 4 April 1968. The atmosphere in Harvard was stimulating for Robinson. In particular, she appreciated the open and questioning attitude of her fellow students. This and the prevailing political situation of the day had a lasting impression on the young graduate from Ireland. Discussions on socialism, equality, civil rights and other social issues were of great interest to Mary. Another event which had a major impact on the students was the assassination of Robert Kennedy just three months into his presidential campaign. Later in that year, Robinson completed her term at Harvard and returned to Ireland.

## Young Lawyer and Senator

Mary spent two years as a junior council on the judiciary's Western Circuit. After the liberalising atmosphere of Harvard, she found her new post a bit staid. Furthermore, she discovered that being young and female was no advantage in the profession. She was pleased, therefore, when in 1969, at the age of 25, she was appointed Reid Professor of Constitutional and Criminal Law at her home university. She was the youngest appointee to the post since its inception in 1888. It was a part-time post and was not well paid. At this same tender age she became a successful candidate for the Seanad. She was, in fact, the first Catholic senator to be returned by TCD.

The operations of the Seanad were a disappointment to Mary as she found them slow moving. Both the timing and frequency of meetings were erratic. Most of its members were elderly and many were loyal political party supporters who had failed to get themselves elected to Dáil Éireann.

In the Seanad debates, Mary pronounced what were considered by many as controversial and radical views, especially for a woman. For example, she advocated the removal of the ban on divorce from the Constitution and a repeal of the ban in the 1935 Criminal Law Amendment Act on birth control by artificial means. She explained to journalist Mary Kenny that she was not promoting divorce, but instead defending the rights of those who considered it right for them. She considered that the law as it stood was being used in the wrong way. She declared:

> *'... if we are a democratic society, then I think that our primary value should be to protect the civil rights and for many people divorce and contraception are part of their civil rights.'*

She was critical of Article 2 of the Irish Constitution which defined the national territory as the whole island of Ireland, its islands and the territorial seas. She was equally critical of Article 3, which proclaimed the right of the Parliament and Government to establish jurisdiction over the whole of the national territory. Her concern was that these claims were objected to by the Unionists in the North.

The Irish Women's Liberation Movement (IWLM) was formed in 1970. Women's liberation groups were active in the USA and around Europe. In that year divorce was recognised in Italy for the first time. In the UK, various Acts of Parliament were passed in relation to women's rights, in particular, in propounding the principle that in marriage assets were deemed to be held jointly by both spouses. In Ireland, the IWLM published a manifesto calling for equal pay, equal education and equality for women before the law. Mary was sympathetic to these principles.

## Marriage

In December 1970, Mary Bourke, then twenty-six years of age, married Nicholas Robinson. He was now a newspaper cartoonist and artist. The ceremony took place in the Catholic Church at Dublin Airport. It was a 'mixed marriage', in that Nicholas Robinson was a Protestant. It was a quiet affair and none of the Bourke family attended. This was thought to be because of some reservation as to Nicholas's ability to provide adequately from a financial point of view, rather than any concern about the fact that he was not a Catholic. In any event, any family concerns about the marriage were put to rest in a short space of time after the wedding.

On 2 October 1972, Mary gave birth to her first child – a baby girl, named Lucy Therese (Tessa). Publicity surrounding this event was deliberately avoided to ensure family privacy, something Mary Robinson ensured throughout her career.

## Continuing Activities

In 1971, a proposed Bill in the Seanad to allow the sale of contraceptives on a restricted basis in the Republic of Ireland became known as the 'Mary Robinson Bill'. It was also supported by senators John Horgan and Trevor West. A special meeting of the Catholic bishops took place in Maynooth in March 1971 which rejected the contention that divorce, contraception and abortion were matters of purely private morality. They further contended that the civil laws of the land should respect the wishes of the people. The Protestant churches, on the other hand, considered that their members had a right to act in accordance with their conscience. This was supported by the Irish Womens' Liberation Movement. The Bill, however, failed to get sufficient support in the Seanad.

On the wider political front, preparations were going ahead for Ireland's membership of the European Economic Community (EEC). Mary Robinson was a member of the Irish Council of the European Movement. Whilst she had some concerns about the possible effects of EEC directives on Irish law, and on what she considered as necessary reforms of the European Parliament, she saw membership as positive as regards bringing north and south closer together, especially in the light of the high level of violence then prevailing north of the border.

Referenda to amend two Articles of the Constitution were held on 7 December 1972. The objective of the first was to lower the minimum voting age from 21 years to 18 years. The second amendment was to remove the recognition of the 'special position' of the Catholic Church and to remove, also, the recognition of the other named mainstream religions. Both amendments were passed. The result of the second one was 84.6 per cent for and 15.4 per cent against. The turnout was 50.7 per cent.

In the Seanad, Robinson forged ahead with her endeavours to secure what she considered to be necessary constitutional reform in the areas of the rights of illegitimate children, marital breakdown, equal pay and other associated issues. Her proposals gained Government support but they were shelved due to the need to deal with an upsurge in violence in the North. This resulted in the urgent need to introduce the Offences Against the State (Amendment) Act to deal more severely with IRA activity. Under the Act, penalties for IRA membership would be applied and membership would be deemed to be a fact on the word of a Garda Superintendent. Bombings in Dublin ensured that it was passed speedily through the Dáil. In the Seanad, however, it was opposed by Mary Robinson on the grounds that it had not been properly debated.

In July, Robinson was called to the Inner Bar of the Middle Temple in London.

In October 1972 it became known that Mary Robinson was again preparing to propose changes to the country's anti-contraception laws. She proposed that contraceptives be made available in relation to family planning through regulations to be drawn up by the Minister for Health. This would see contraceptives being made available only through chemists shops and hospitals or under prescription. The Catholic bishops responded in November by emphasising the moral wrongs of contraception but also said that the law was a matter for the legislature. Mary Robinson then issued a statement saying that she agreed with the bishops as regards the law being a matter for the legislature, but she added that lawmakers had a responsibility to take all relevant factors into account conscientiously for the common good. She added that legislators also had a duty to ensure that the laws of the State would not discriminate against the liberty of the individual to exercise freedom of conscience and to make private moral choices. It was clear, however, that the Catholic Church was opposed to the proposed changes in the law in this area. Robinson's Bill did, however, receive a second reading in the Seanad, but the Fine Gael Government decided to introduce its own legislation instead and the Government Bill was put to the vote in the Dáil on 16 July 1974. To the astonishment of almost everyone in Fine Gael, Taoiseach Liam Cosgrave and six of his colleagues went into the opposition lobby and by doing so effectively defeated his own government's Bill. It is assumed that they opposed the Bill on purely religious grounds.

Robinson, as an independent senator, continued her campaign to push forward as far as she could her proposals on family planning, adoption matters, illegitimate children and associated matters. In a speech to the Irish Association of Civil Liberties in 1974, she said it was an important principle of international law that every State should recognise the right of another State to permit divorce.

When the British Ambassador to Ireland, Christopher Ewart-Biggs, was murdered on 21 July 1976, the Government introduced a Special Criminal Court to deal with the IRA and other subversive groups. They also declared a State of Emergency. This was opposed by Robinson in the Seanad, arguing that the powers under the legislation would be an infringement of individual constitutional rights.

## Labour Party

In July1976, Mary Robinson decided to join the Labour Party and became a Labour Party candidate in the general election of 1977. Another candidate for the same constituency (Rathmines-Dublin) was a 'Left Labour' contender, David Neligan. Robinson endeavoured to convince Neligan that he should drop out of the race in favour of her, but he was not at all happy to do so. Councillor Michael Collins was also considering going forward as a candidate. It was discovered, however, that under the Labour Party rules Mary Robinson was not eligible for consideration as a candidate because she had not been a member of the Labour Party for the necessary minimum period of six months. The Secretary of the Labour Party, Brendan Halligan, found a way around this dilemma by interpreting the rule to mean that the qualifying period of six months meant six lunar months. By this interpretation, and endorsed by the Party's administrative council, Mary Robinson was allowed to seek nomination. Neligan and Collins, however, were also nominated but in the end the administrative council convened an emergency meeting as a result of which Robinson was imposed as the Labour Party candidate.

The general election was won by Fianna Fáil. Mary Robinson failed to get elected by a margin of 406 votes. She was, however, re-elected to the

Seanad, though it appeared that her membership of the Labour Party was not well received by some of her former supporters and she won her seat with a much reduced majority.

Around this time, Robinson became involved in high profile protests against the building of civic offices by Dublin Corporation on Dublin's Wood Quay – a Viking site of considerable archaeological interest, much of which had not yet been explored. In 1979, Robinson was selected as a candidate for the number 9 area of the Corporation and won a seat together with a number of other fellow Wood Quay activists. However, they failed in their efforts to have the site preserved and, much to their disappointment, building on the site was allowed to go ahead. She resigned from the Corporation in January 1983.

## Socialist

Robinson's membership of the Labour Party was based on her interest in socialism. This interest was made clear in the *Trinity News* of November 1977 in which she was quoted as follows:

> *'Socialism is the only possible way in which Ireland can achieve the equality, the social justice and the opportunities for all citizens that are needed.'*

As a lecturer in TCD she joined the Irish Federation of University Teachers and in 1976 she became a member of the Irish Transport and General Workers Union. She got another opportunity to pursue her political interests when a general election was called in 1981. Robinson ran again for office though, on this occasion, in a different constituency, Dublin West. She was once again unsuccessful, polling in ninth place in first preference votes (under Ireland's proportional representation voting system). In the following year she was returned to the Seanad, though once again a new candidate, Shane Ross, won more first preference votes than she did. By this time a second child had been added to the family – son William was born in January 1974 (in May 1981, a third child, Aubrey, was born). In addition to family life, Robinson was engaged in a very busy legal practice as a Senior Council as well as her work as a senator. A further general election in November 1982 saw a Fine Gael/Labour coalition returned to power.

## Law on Abortion

The subject of abortion came to the fore during this period of new government and it was decided to put the matter to a referendum. Proposals to protect the life of the unborn were to be included. In a two and a half hour speech in the Seanad, Robinson argued against the amendment to the Constitution on the grounds that it was contrary to a ruling of the European Union which recognised the right to life of the mother as superior to the right to life of the unborn child. In her arguments she referred to the reservations of the Attorney General on the appropriateness of the wording, the views of the Protestant churches, and the views of the European Commission on Human Rights. The Irish Constitution, by equating both rights (mother and child) to life, would be in breach of the European Convention on Human Rights to which Ireland was a signatory. The Catholic Church issued a statement in August in support of the amendment. It said that it was satisfied that the wording would safeguard the life of both mother and unborn child. The Referendum took place in 1983 and was carried by a majority of 2 to 1. The turnout was 54.6 per cent.

Two years later, a government proposal to abolish illegitimacy was not to Robinson's liking in that she felt that it did not go far enough. For example, it did not give natural fathers automatic rights of guardianship. However, the Government legislation was passed into law in October of 1985.

## Leaving Labour

In 1984, the Fine Gael-led government appointed Attorney General Peter Sutherland to the position of Ireland's EEC Commissioner in Brussels. The junior partner in the Government, the Labour Party, agreed with this posting, but then pressed for the right to nominate the new Attorney General. Taoiseach Garret FitzGerald accepted this. It was widely expected that the post would go to Mary Robinson, but instead it went to John Rogers, a close colleague of Dick Spring, the leader of the Labour Party.

In 1985, the Anglo-Irish Agreement was signed. Under the Agreement the Irish Government was afforded a greater role in determining the future of the six counties of Northern Ireland. Robinson felt that the Agreement would find little or no support amongst the Unionists and, primarily because of this, she decided to resign from the Labour Party which supported the Agreement. She did so in November of that year. Later she was to express her doubts about the Labour Party's commitment to equality and social justice. Her decision to resign was also possibly influenced by her heavy schedule of lecturing, legal practice, family responsibilities and membership of a Parliamentary Committee on European legislation, not to mention her Seanad duties in which she was to remain as an independent senator for a further number of years. On 22 May 1989, however, she informed the electorate through a press release that she would not be contesting her Seanad seat at the next general election. She felt that she needed time to devote to her post as Chairperson of the Legal Affairs Sub-Committee of the Oireachtas Joint Committee on European Community legislation. At this time, too, she was founder and director of the Irish Centre for European Law. In these arenas she foresaw much work, for example, in preparing to meet the challenges and opportunities of the proposed Single European Market.

## Presidency

The second and final term of office of President Hillery was due to finish in December 1990. The Labour Party decided that they would field a candidate. Their leader, Dick Spring, said that, if necessary, he would go forward himself as a candidate. It was, however, to Mary Robinson that the Labour Party turned. She was approached by John Rogers, presumably at the behest of Spring. After much consideration she accepted the nomination. This decision did not go down well with the 'hard' left of the party, who made the point that she was not even a member of the Labour Party anymore. In addition, they had favoured Noel Browne, a controversial former Government Minister, as their preferred choice. From Mary Robinson's viewpoint the idea of being the first woman candidate to run for the Presidency was an exciting prospect. Additionally, if successful, she would have a high profile post from which she could expound upon matters close to her heart. She would not, however, re-join the Labour Party.

A seven month campaign was set in train. The deputy leader of the Labour Party, Ruairi Quinn, was appointed director of the campaign. The party's press officer, Fergus Finlay, was brought on to the campaign committee and was to have a major impact on the style and direction of the campaign. From the very outset Robinson was considered, by political commentators and most people directly involved in politics, as a complete outsider. She had two major disadvantages: firstly, she had failed, not once, but twice to get herself elected as a TD, and secondly, she was a woman. To counteract this she commenced her election campaign significantly earlier than either of her two opponents, the strong favourite, Brian Lenihan of

Fianna Fáil, and Austin Currie of Fine Gael. Her involvement in a number of high profile legal cases during her career, however, was no disadvantage in her campaign. These cases included one in which she challenged the jury system as being discriminatory against women. There was also the Reynolds case in 1973, seeking the right of 18-year-olds to vote, and a case which challenged the way in which married couples were taxed. A further case was that of Josie Airey, the outcome of which was that Ireland was deemed to be in breach of the UN Convention on Human Rights for failing to provide civil legal aid.

## The Campaign

Initially, canvassing votes did not come easily to Robinson as she was, or seemed to be, reserved. However, it did not take her long to feel quite at ease in dealing with voters on a one-to-one basis and on the other aspects of her public relations exercises. Nevertheless, an early poll gave Lenihan a comfortable lead – 24 per cent to 9 per cent, before Currie entered the fray. Currie's background was in northern politics and he was seen as somewhat remote from 'local' politics. The Robinson campaign was extensive and took her through almost every town in the country. The vigour with which she was undertaking her campaign and the intensity of the accompanying public relations was beginning to pay off. She was also learning to engage in subtle 'campaign-speak'. For example, a somewhat

*Mary Robinson and Labour Party supporter Pat Rabbitte*

suspicious Wexford newspaper, the *Enniscorthy Echo*, posed the question to her, 'Would you call yourself a practising Catholic?' Her reply was: 'I have never known what is meant by a practising Catholic but I am not a non-practising Catholic.'

With about a month to go before the election her opponents began to take much more notice of her campaign. Its very intensity could not now be ignored, especially as it was clear that it was bearing fruit. It was not all plain sailing for her. For example, on giving an interview to the rock music magazine *Hot Press* she was asked if she would be willing to preside at the opening of a new stall in a Dublin city centre record store which would, in breach of Irish law, sell condoms. She answered,

> 'Yes.... This is a very young country and I think it would be helpful to have a President who was in touch with what young people are doing.'

She went on to criticise the Catholic Church for what she considered its undue influence and its patriarchal, male-dominated presence. She claimed that the Church had sought to keep down women over the years. She advocated the ordination of women priests and bishops and, indeed, a woman Pope.

> 'It's an awful pity that the Catholic Church hasn't grasped the importance of being on the side of equality and opportunity.'

Though she subsequently claimed to have been misinterpreted as regards her 'Yes' answer (she later claimed that she merely meant that she understood the question), her opponents lost no time in attacking these sentiments. The fact that she was a member of the Trilateral Commission – a think-tank of politicians, businessmen and trade unionists from USA, Europe and Japan – was also attacked as being under the undue influence of the USA. But other events were to put all these matters well and truly in the shade as regards the outcome of the election.

With three weeks to go before election day, the *Irish Times* published a letter in which reference was made to one of a number of articles on the presidential campaign written by a UCD post-graduate student, Jim

Duffy. In one article he referred to alleged attempts by members of the opposition, Fianna Fáil, to persuade President Hillery to refuse a request by the Taoiseach of the fallen Fine Gael/Labour Government to grant dissolution of the Dáil. This would allow Fianna Fáil to form a government without the need to hold a general election. It was held that a number of telephone calls were made to the President's office on the evening of 27 January 1982 in order to influence his decision in favour of Fianna Fáil. It was further said that the present Fianna Fáil candidate for the Presidency, Brian Lenihan, was one of those who made a call. This disclosure had an immediate negative impact on Lenihan's ratings in the polls, and a corresponding positive one for Robinson which had the effect of putting her substantially in the lead.

Lenihan then made a television appearance in which he said that 'on mature recollection' he had not in fact made any calls to President Hillery. Unfortunately for Lenihan, however, a tape recording made by Duffy of an interview he had made with Lenihan disclosed that he had admitted to making such a telephone call. As a result, Fianna Fáil put considerable pressure on Lenihan to resign from the Cabinet. For his part, Lenihan said that he had no recollection of the interview with Duffy. He continued:

> '... or the rubbish spoken by me on the tape. The interview was
> given at a time when my state of health, both physical and, for
> those few short days around the time of the interview, mental, left
> a lot to be desired. What I said on the tape does not accord with
> the facts of what happened on 27 January 1982. I rest my case.'

Haughey, in turn, said that he was under considerable pressure from Desmond O' Malley of the Progressive Democrats, the Government's junior coalition partner, who said that his party could not guarantee support in the Dáil confidence debate unless Lenihan resigned. Lenihan refused to resign, but in the end Taoiseach Haughey sacked him and he was left to run what was left of the campaign on his own. He did made a slight recovery in the polls but it was to no avail. The election result was a clear win for Mary Robinson. When Austin Currie was eliminated his second preference votes went to Mary Robinson in large numbers. The final tally showed 52.8 per cent in favour of Robinson with 47.2 per cent opting for Lenihan. The overall turnout was 64.1 per cent. It was not only the Lenihan incident that swayed votes in favour of Robinson, but the intensity of her seven month long campaign to every corner of the country and the professionalism of her campaign team. She savoured her success and told cheering supporters that she had been voted in by men and women of all parties and of none. She also referred to those who had 'stepped out from the faded days of the civil war and voted for a new Ireland'. She said that above all, she had been supported 'by the women of Ireland , mná na h-Éireann, who, instead of rocking the cradle, rocked the system'.

*President-elect Mary Robinson at breakfast table with husband Nick Robinson.*

## Inauguration

Mary Robinson was inaugurated as President of Ireland on 3 December 1990 at Dublin Castle. The venue is a relatively small one which meant that her personal guest list was modest. Nevertheless, it included visitors from north of the border, representatives of homeless people, and those associated with an interest in women's rights. In her acceptance speech she referred to a fifth province in Ireland which she said she wished to represent:

*President-elect Mary Robinson prior to her inauguration*

'... *not anywhere here or there, north or south, east or west. It is a place within each one of us – that place that is open to the other, that swinging door which allows us to venture out and others to venture in. Ancient legends divide Ireland into four quarters and a "middle", although they differed about the location of this middle or fifth province. While Tara was the political centre of Ireland, tradition has it that this fifth province acted as a second centre, a necessary balance. If I am a symbol of anything, I would like to be a symbol of the reconciling and healing...'*

She went on to make special mention of her wish to reach out to Irish emigrants throughout the continents of North America, Australia and Europe itself. She offered to represent the 70 million people all around the world who claimed Irish descent. She continued:

*'Looking outwards from Ireland, I would like on your behalf to contribute to the international protection and promotion of human rights. One of our greatest natural resources has always been, and still is, our ability to serve as a moral and political conscience*

*in world affairs. We have a long history in providing spiritual, cultural and social assistance to other countries in need – most notably in Latin America, Africa and other Third World countries. And we can continue to promote these values by taking principled and independent stands on issues of international importance. As the elected President of this small democratic country, I assume office at a vital moment in Europe's history. Ideological boundaries that have separated east from west are withering away at an astounding pace. Eastern countries are seeking to participate as full partners in a restructured and economically buoyant Europe. The stage is set for a new common European home, based on respect for human rights, pluralism, tolerance and openness to new ideas. The European Convention on Human Rights – one of the main achievements of the Council of Europe – is asserting itself as the natural Constitution for the new Europe. These developments have created one of the major challenges of the 1990s.'*

She continued:

*'As the elected choice of the people of this part of our island I want to extend the hand of friendship and of love to both communities in the other part. And I want to do this with no strings attached, no hidden agenda. As the person chosen by you to symbolise this Republic and to project our self-image to others, I will seek to encourage mutual understanding and tolerance between all the different communities sharing this island...'*

The new President also referred to the status of women declaring:

*'As a woman, I want women who have felt themselves outside history to be written back into history.'*

Her concluding remarks were:

*'May God direct me so that my presidency is one of justice, peace and love. May I have the fortune to preside over an Ireland at a time of exciting transformation when we enter a new Europe where old wounds can be healed, a time when, in the words of*

*Séamas Heaney, "hope and history rhyme"' May it be a presidency where I the President can sing to you, citizens of Ireland, the joyous refrain of the fourteenth century Irish poet as recalled by W.B. Yeats: "I am of Ireland … come dance with me in Ireland." Go raibh míle maith agaibh go léir.'*

## In Office

Domestic press coverage of the inauguration was extensive and positive. American press welcomed her election and her stand on human rights, in particular, was favourably received. 'Bravo, Mrs Robinson' was the headline of the Moscow newspaper *Pravda*. *The Times* of London said that the President was a politician who was 'serious about understanding unionist fears' in Northern Ireland and who would pursue reconciliation in a practical manner. This, the newspaper considered, was in contrast to Mr Haughey, whom they viewed as 'a veteran exponent of a traditional, nationalist, long on rhetorical appeals to Irish values and short on specific ways to achieve the unification of North and South'. The commentary went on to praise

*President Robinson visiting schoolchildren*

the President's views in favour of contraception and publicly available information on abortion. They also saw her as openly sympathetic to Ulster Unionism. This arose from her declared reservations about the Anglo-Irish Agreement and the Irish Constitutional claim to the North.

It was not long after President Robinson's installation that a certain tension emerged between the Presidency and Taoiseach Charles Haughey. This concerned the President's wish to accept invitations to travel abroad to give lectures or talks. All trips abroad required the prior approval of the Government. In June 1991, the President was refused permission to accept an invitation to deliver the annual BBC 'Dimbleby Lecture'. This was apparently decided on the basis that the content of the lecture had always been political in nature and had previously been given by politicians. The President, however, was under the impression that Haughey wanted to keep a tight grip on her activities.

The President's first official state visit was made in June 1991 to Portugal. She made her first official visit to Northern Ireland in February 1992. Although she had visited there in December 1990 to attend the installation of the new Catholic Archbishop of Armagh, Dr Cathal Daly, this next visit was the first visit of an Irish Head of State north of the border. The Unionist Lord Mayor of Belfast refused to meet her. Refusals also came from councillors of the Democratic Unionist Party and the Ulster Unionist Party. In May 1992, on a visit to Derry, Unionist Councillors once again refused to meet her citing the Republic's Constitutional claim to Northern Ireland.

In September 1991, the President again visited the North. The venue was, once again, Derry and the engagement entailed delivering a keynote speech at an international conference on conflict resolution. The Mayor of the city did not receive the President but instead sent his deputy, Councillor Annie Courtney, to do so. The President's visit was generally well received although she was criticised by relatives of the 14 nationalists killed by the British Army in Derry on 'Bloody Sunday' for refusing to meet them. The reason given by Áras an Uachtaráin was that their campaign was clearly to do with matters of policy. In contrast, the President travelled to England in 1993 to attend a memorial service for the two young boys killed by the IRA in Warrington.

In addition to the President's trip to Warrington, that year brought a heavy schedule of visits abroad for the President. She visited Africa, Australia, New Zealand, Singapore, USA and Spain. One of the major benefits of the visit to the USA was her influencing the Clinton administration to take an active part in the problems in the north of Ireland. Her visit coincided nicely with a visit to the White House of senior Irish politicians who were also there with the same aim of lobbying which, ultimately, was successful.

The thorny question of abortion came to the fore once again in 1992. For many years Irish women had travelled to Britain to have an abortion as the process was illegal in Ireland. A case then arose of a 14-year-old rape victim who had become pregnant as a result of the rape. The family had inquired with the Gárdaí as to whether or not DNA evidence obtained after an abortion would be admissible in court, and was informed that it could not because the procedure by which it would be obtained was illegal. On 17 February 1992, the High Court granted an injunction stopping the girl from leaving the Irish State for a period of nine months. The family appealed the matter to the Supreme Court. On 19 February, in addressing a professional women's group in Waterford, the President said that she shared the sense of frustration and helplessness felt by Irish women and girls that week. She declared:

> *'We are experiencing as a people a very deep crisis in ourselves. I hope we have the courage, which we have not always had, to face up to and look squarely and to say that this is a problem we have got to resolve.'*

Shortly after, on the occasion of her delivering the Allen Lane Foundation lecture, she said there was a need for:

> *'... a comprehensive re-assessment of the place and contribution of a woman in her society. If the imbalances of the past came, as I believe they did, not simply from legislative injustice and economic*

*inequality but from profound resistances and failures of perception, then it follows that to right that balance we must do more than review our legislation and re-state our economic structures. We must also fundamentally re-appraise our view of who and what is valuable in our society. We must look with fresh and unprejudiced eyes at the work of women, the views of women, their way of organising and their interpretation of social priorities. To achieve this, we must, I believe, begin at the beginning and alter our way of thinking....
Once and for all we need to commit ourselves to the concept that women's rights are not factional or sectional privileges, bestowed on the few at the whim of the few. They are human rights.'*

The day after the President made this speech the Supreme Court lifted the injunction against travel and the family travelled immediately to the UK where, it was reported, the girl suffered a natural and spontaneous miscarriage.

On the 5 March 1992, the Supreme Court decided by a majority of four to one that abortion should be permitted in cases where the mother's life was at risk. It held that in the case of the girl who ultimately suffered a miscarriage, her life was at risk in that she suffered suicidal inclinations. Later, a man was convicted of sexual assault and unlawful carnal knowledge. The Government called for a referendum in 1992 which was carried. As a result, the relevant part of the Constitution was amended to read:

*'The State acknowledges the right to life of the unborn and, with due regard to the equal right to life of the mother, guarantees in its laws to respect, and as far as practable, by its laws to defend and vindicate that right.*

*This subsection shall not limit the freedom to travel between the State and another state.*

*This subsection shall not limit freedom to obtain or make available, in the State, subject to such conditions that may be laid down by law, information relating to services lawfully available in another state.'*

## Buckingham Palace

The dawn of a new era in Irish/British relations came into being in May 1993 when the Irish President paid a courtesy call on Queen Elizabeth II at Buckingham Palace. The establishment, in 1921, of an independent Ireland had resulted in the severing of formal links with the British Royal family. Strained relations since then over the problems in the North, and also Ireland's neutrality in World War II, contributed to this situation. In addition, the assassination of Lord Louis Mountbatten by the IRA in Sligo in 1979 resulted in the Irish Government advising against royal visits to Ireland on security grounds. The President's visit was considered a success although an invitation for an official State visit by her to Britain did not materialise.

## Sinn Féin

In June 1993, President Robinson accepted an invitation to visit a variety of community groups in west Belfast. It was clear from the outset that at one of these meetings the attendance would include members of Sinn Féin, including their leader, Gerry Adams. The Belfast Government urged

*Sean Galavan, President Robinson and Ben Culligan at the opening of the National Print Museum in Dublin*

208

the Irish Government to have this meeting stopped. From the Irish Government's viewpoint the prospective meeting with Adams was somewhat of an embarrassment given that, at that time, they themselves were holding Sinn Féin at arm's length, and they also saw that it would be used by the provisional IRA, seen generally as an offshoot of Sinn Féin, for their own propaganda purposes. The task of broaching this subject with the President fell to Dick Spring, Tánaiste and Minister for Foreign Affairs. He met with her and explained the Government's concerns. His understanding was that they would have further talks on the issue when he returned from talks in London at the Anglo-Irish Conference which he had to attend. While in London, however, he heard of a local radio announcement in Belfast confirming that Robinson's visit to Belfast was going ahead. Spring's next meeting with the President was less friendly than the previous one but, in the end, the President declared that she intended to go ahead with the visit.

President Robinson did indeed meet Gerry Adams and the greeting included a handshake, though it took place out of camera shot. The incident was not welcomed in Dublin where it was considered as damaging British/Irish relations and seen as a bonus for the IRA. Opposition members in Dublin were furious and urged the Government to take a firmer hand with the President in these matters. The now infamous handshake was put into perspective, however, when three months later Taoiseach Albert Reynolds shook Adams's hand, as did President Clinton on a later occasion.

Reynolds had taken over from Charles Haughey as Taoiseach in February 1992. His relationship with the President was good. The IRA had called a ceasefire in 1989 but it had lasted only 17 months; nevertheless, relations in the North were now at last improving. The President continued in her quest to underpin this improvement in North/South relations by welcoming residents from the Loyalist Shankill area of Belfast to Áras an Uachtaráin, and she afforded the same welcome to their nationalist counterparts. In the summer of 1995, she received an honorary law degree from Queens University in Belfast. By November of the following year she had made 16 visits to the North. The Unionists were not at all happy about this and the leader of the Ulster Unionist Party, David Trimble, requested that she desist from making these visits which, he claimed, were promoting a republican agenda. The President denied that she was promoting any such agenda but was merely offering the hand of friendship.

As with previous Presidents, the present incumbent had, as part of her duties, to satisfy herself as regards the constitutionality of Bills sent to her by the Government for signing into law. In cases where she had any doubt, and after consulting with her Council of State, she referred Bills to the Supreme Court for its decision. For example, in 1993 she referred the Matrimonial Home Bill. In 1995, she referred a new Abortion Information Bill to the Court which found it in order and the President immediately signed it into law.

## Referendum on Divorce

The coalition government of Fine Gael, Labour and the Democratic Left arranged for a referendum to be held in November 1995 on the introduction of divorce. It had been rejected in an earlier referendum nine years previously. President Robinson commented on a US satellite TV station as follows:

> 'These issues have been discussed in a very open way, to continue to open up as a modern society while retaining Irish qualities. Looking back over the last twenty years I'm much more impressed by the changes in Irish society than identifying certain issues that still need to be addressed ...'

This statement was greatly resented by those in the 'No' campaign as they considered the President's intervention as being outside her Presidential brief. In the end, however, the 'Yes' vote won the day by a slender majority.

## Addressing the Oireachtas

The President decided to exercise her right under article 13.7 of the Constitution, which allows for the President to address both houses of the Oireachtas. The address was given on 8 July 1992. The only previous occasion on which this had been done was in 1959 on the 50th anniversary of the first Dáil by President de Valera. The title of President Robinson's address was 'The Irish Identity in Europe'. She spoke on a broad range of issues, including emigration and unemployment, the changing role of women, and an appeal for understanding to all traditions in the North of Ireland.

## Africa

In 1992, the President made a visit to East Africa. In the course of a press conference in the Kenyan capital, Nairobi, about her trip to Somalia and part of Kenya, she broke down and wept. She had just visited a number of areas devastated by poverty and famine and was horrified by what she saw as a humanitarian disaster. She witnessed the effects of the horrific civil war resulting in the displacement of about one million refugees. Starvation, misery and fear were widespread. She was to say later that she regretted showing such emotion and that her legal training should have enabled her to be more stoical. But her press conference had a powerful impact on those who attended it and those who viewed recordings of it later.

She recorded in her book *A Voice for Somalia*:

*'In the event, because I was hit by a wall of emotion and anger as I tried to convey what I had seen, I thought I had blown the opportunity. That part of me that was a barrister – with the training and discipline of my profession, based on the ability to take a briefing and to advocate a case – knew it was not appropriate to let emotions break through. However, I wasn't just a barrister pleading a case. I was the President of Ireland giving a personal witness and responding to the people of Somalia. Above all, I was a human being devastated by what I had seen.*

*... I saw images on television before I came and found them disturbing ... its much, much more difficult when you come here, because, then its not contained in a little box, you cannot go away for a cup of coffee, you cannot take a telephone call. And to see what we saw for the past three days is unacceptable.... We saw children dying at the very feeding stations that were trying to give them supplementary feeding. We saw mothers whose milk had dried up. We saw them beside children who were covered in*

*sores.... I felt shamed by what I saw, shamed, shamed – on behalf of the European world and the American world and the developed world generally. When we left Nairobi and took the long flight to Paris, I lay back in the plane, closed my eyes and wept quietly for a long time. I felt it was right to weep because I was grieving for the pain of a whole people who had so little quality of life, and for many many children who had such a short life.*

*... by failing to address the starvation and destitution of so many of our fellow human beings we are diminishing the sense of our own humanity.'*

She went to New York and reported directly to the Secretary General of the UN about the plight of the people of Somalia and the need for greater UN efforts in its operations there.

## Oireachtas Again

On 2 February 1995, the President addressed the Oireachtas a second time. On this occasion the theme of her address was 'The Irish Famine'. This was to mark the 150th anniversary of the disaster. On the resultant emigration she said that she recalled her visit of the previous year to the graves of Irish Famine victims (about 15,000 of them) at Grosse Ile in Canada, and the integration of those who survived into French/Canadian culture. On emigration she said that Irishness was not simply territorial but was at its best when reaching out to everyone on the island, and when it could honour those whose sense of identity and cultural values might be more British than Irish.

*'I arrived in heavy rain and as I looked at the mounds which, to-gether with small white crosses, are all that mark the mass graves of the 5,000 or more Irish people who died there, I was struck by the power of commemoration. I was also aware that, even across time and distance, tragedy must be seen as human and not historic and to think of it in national terms alone can obscure that fact.'*

## More Visits

The President made further visits to Africa, making comparisons to the Irish Famine of 1845, and repeated her call for reform of the UN. In 1994, she delivered a speech at Harvard University on the future of the United Nations. She also addressed the UN Commission in New York on the Status of Women. Further trips that year included her attendance at the inauguration of Nelson Mandela as President of South Africa, and visits to Poland, Canada, Zimbabwe, Tanzania, Zambia and Rwanda.

In 1995, the President visited Brazil, Argentina and Chile. Her meeting with the controversial dictator of Chile, General Augusto Pinochet, drew some criticism, as did her failure to visit areas where Irish missionaries were working with the poor. The subject of women's interests were never far from her mind. Also in that same year, she addressed the Council of Europe Conference. Her address included the following comments:

> 'In contrast to many of the formal structures of organised society, which are based on precedent and are hierarchical, women seem to devise instinctively structures which are open, enabling, consultative and flexible. I have observed a similar modus operandi in women's groups and networks in the developing world. Is there not a strong case for thinking that those formal structures and decision- making processes of society – whether political, business, trade union, public service or whatever – could benefit greatly from the style of decision-making and leadership operating in such women's groups? Perhaps they provide the best evidence of the benefits of parity democracy.'

During that same year speculation was abroad about the possibility of Mary Robinson succeeding Boutros Boutros-Ghali, the Secretary General of the UN, who was due to step down in December. In 1996, it became known that Senator Ted Kennedy was in favour of Mary Robinson getting the post and some newspapers in the USA and in Britain also spoke in favour of her. At the International Women's Forum in Boston in October, the US Ambassador to Ireland, Jean Kennedy Smith, spoke about President Robinson as follows:

> *'During her term President Robinson has reshaped the greatest sorrow of Irish history – the Irish Famine – into a catalyst for ensuring that no other people suffer the same anguish. I am among the many who have turned on the evening news to see images of the President walking the alleys of Somalia, Rwanda, or Zaire, comforting near lifeless children, listening to tribal leaders and imploring the nations of the world to stand up to their duty to all humankind…'*

In the end, the post of Secretary General of the UN went to Kofi Annan of Ghana. The post of UN High Commissioner for Human Rights, however, now appeared on the horizon. Her role as President of Ireland was due to finish at the end of 1997. She had the possibility of going forward for the Presidency for a second and final term, and said that she would make her views on this known by the end of March. On 12 March she announced that in fact she would not be running for a second term. She said that her decision had not been an easy one but that future roles for ex-Presidents were limited and the prospect of taking up a UN post would allow her 'to move into another sphere'.

Paying tribute to her Dick Spring said:

> *'She didn't just transform the office she'd won, she transformed Ireland. She transformed our image abroad and she transformed our perception of ourselves. She didn't just make changes or lead the way. She has personified change.'*

Prior to this the President had made a visit to the Vatican and met Pope John Paul II. A State visit to Sweden was also undertaken in April. A general election was held on 6 June 1991, but the Labour Party fared badly and Fianna Fáil and the Progressive Democrats formed a coalition government.

## Final Days as President

On 12 June 1997, the UN Secretary General confirmed that Mary Robinson was nominated for the post of UN High Commissioner for Human Rights. The decision was ratified by the UN General Assembly within the week. Her other routine Presidential business went on. On 1 April she convened the Council of State (for the seventh time during her Presidency) to review the constitutionality of the Employment Equality Bill. It was referred on to the Supreme Court where some elements were deemed to be unconstitutional and needed to be amended. The Equal Status Bill was similarly referred to the Court.

In her final days as President of Ireland she cautioned that racism in the modern Ireland could become a problem unless the Irish people learned to deal with issues associated with immigration and refugees.

President Robinson left office on 12 September 1997, more than two months before her term of office was due to end. She was 53 years of age. Her presidential role was assumed by a Commission comprising the Chairman of each of the Houses of the Oireachtas and the Chief Justice, as provided for in the Constitution,

*Portrait of President Mary Robinson
by Basil Blackshaw*

pending the election of a successor. There was some criticism about her standing down early.

## New Pastures

Mary Robinson was UN Commissioner for Human Rights for the period 1997 to 2002. She brought a sense of urgency to the position. It is probably true to say, too, that she ruffled some feathers along the way. Some of the more traditional bureaucrats were not enamoured by the degree of efficiency with which she worked and which she correspondingly expected from them as well. Her outspokenness was unpopular with some governments. For example, she upset the USA administration by appearing to be, from their perspective, pro-Palestine in the Israeli/Palestine conflict.

Indeed, it was thought by some that it was the view of the USA and Israel on this topic that was responsible for her failing to be nominated for a second term. In the aftermath of the 9/11 atrocity she expressed concern that the US government was using the terrorist attacks to clamp down on

*Mary Robinson receiving 2009 Presidential Medal of Freedom from US President Barack Obama*

human rights and freedom of expression, citing the incarceration of many in Guantanamo Bay without trial or right of redress.

Robinson could claim some success as she felt that in her term of office:

> *'... there is more linkage being made by leaders of developing countries between human rights and economic and social development. They began to realise that if you got human rights right, you accelerated human development and economic development.'*

On leaving her post with the UN, Mary Robinson founded a body called the Ethical Globalization Initiative based in New York. The organisation is supported by a partnership of the Aspen Institute, Columbia University, the State of the World Forum and the Swiss-based International Council on Human Rights Policy. Its goal is to bring the norms and standards of human rights into the globalisation process with an initial focus on Africa. Its mission includes putting human rights at the heart of global governance and policy-making, and to ensure that the needs of the poorest and most vulnerable are addressed on the global stage.

In 2010, Mary Robinson returned to Dublin to establish the Mary Robinson Foundation – Climate Justice. The aim of the foundation is to focus on a human rights-centred approach to climate change.

The final words go to Bishop Desmond Tutu, who said of Mary Robinson: ' She really cares. I love her!'

# Mary McAleese

## Eighth President of Ireland (1997–2011)

### Home Life

Mary McAleese was born Mary Patricia Leneghan, in the Royal Victoria Hospital in Belfast on 27 June 1951. Her father, Paddy Leneghan, hailed from a small farm in County Roscommon but moved to the Ardoyne area of Belfast when he was only fourteen years of age with the aim of enhancing his prospects of finding work. Her mother, Claire (neé McManus), was brought up in Belfast although she spent much of her youth in County Down from whence her parents originally hailed. The McAleese family settled in Skegoniel Avenue, off the Antrim Road. They later moved to Ladbrook Drive, also in the Ardoyne area. Her father worked as a bar manager. Mary was the eldest of nine children. She had three sisters and five brothers. The area in which the family lived was a mixed one of Protestants and Catholics. Later, as the needs of the expanding family dictated, they moved to Mountainview Gardens, originally a predominantly Protestant area of Ardoyne. This area now also contained a largly Catholic enclave. In those days, sectarianism appeared not to be a problem. This was true also of Woodvale Road where they later moved to. As a child, Mary played with her Protestant neighbours just as naturally as

*Mary as a student at Mercy Convent,*
*Crumlin Road, Belfast 1958*

she did with those of her own religious persuasion. She even helped in the Protestant tradition of building bonfires in preparation for the 12th of July celebrations of the victory of the Protestant King William of Orange over the English Catholic King James II at the Battle of the Boyne in 1690. However, she was not allowed to stay to attend the subsequent celebtations, her parents being aware that she might not be welcome.

Mary McAleese's early education was undertaken in the local Convent of Mercy where she successfully passed her '11 Plus' examination. This led in 1962 to a scholarship to St. Dominic's High School on the Falls Road, an early indicator of her academic ability. Here she was made school prefect and leader of the debating team. She was also a founding member in the school of a St Vincent de Paul conference, dedicated to helping the poor of the area. In line with official policy, the school's curriculum on history and geography was largely confined to that of Britain. Ireland did not feature at all. It was left to the family to fill in the gaps in education in these areas.

Although raised a committed Catholic, during her teenage years Mary began to question some aspects of her faith. She became interested in Communism and went as far as obtaining a Communist Party membership application form, but was strongly dissuaded by her mother from joining. While exploring this and other social matters she became acquainted with Fr Justin Coyne by whom she was greatly impressed. Fr Coyne was a priest of the local Holy Cross Monastery. Born in County Meath, he came to Ardoyne in 1961 and was especially popular with young people. He and Mary had many long chats on philosophy, theology and matters of faith generally. His death, five days before her 18th birthday in 1969, was a huge blow to her. She continued to be influenced by his views and teachings even after his death.

Even before the political 'troubles' resurfaced in 1969, Mary would have been acutely aware of the tension between the Nationalist and Unionist communities, not least because it manifested itself, by effective segregation, in determining where one lived. Even within one's own area one was never completely safe.

By 1972, Mary's father was running a pub in the Lower Falls Road. It was bombed in that year killing a twenty-two-year-old mother of three. On another occasion the family was attending Mass only to return home to find their house marked with bullet holes and the windows and doors shattered. In November 1972, the McAleese home was attacked, broken paving stones being hurled at it. The children and their mother barred the doors as best they could. They called the RUC for help only to be told that they would have to wait as the police were busy elsewhere. It later transpired that the attackers dispersed when an armed unit of the IRA made its presence known on the scene. On another occasion the family returned to find that the upstairs windows were smashed and that the bed clothes, walls and ceilings had been riddled with bullet holes. They were now forced to leave the Crumlin Road for good. They moved to Anderstown. This move, however, did not immediatly resolve the public order

221

problems, though they eventually enjoyed relative peace there, probably again due to IRA presence in the area. Later, the family settled in Rostrevor, in County Down, where Paddy Leneghan bought a pub.

Before this, and even while still in her school years, Mary showed an interest in local politics. She saw and understood the practical implications of gerrymandering which ensured, due to the juggling of electoral boundaries, that Unionists almost invariably had a majority on town councils.

## Civil Rights

The Northern Ireland Civil Rights Association was founded in 1967, as was the Derry Housing Action Committee (set up by politician John Hume). The following year the Civil Rights Association took part in a march in support of the Derry Housing Action Committee campaign for a fair deal for nationalists in the allocation of housing. The march was banned by William Craig, Home Affairs Minister in the Northern Ireland Government. Despite this, it went ahead. The participants in the march were attacked by the police. Irish television filmed the resulting violence and it received world wide coverage. A short while after this, a movement called the People's Democracy was founded and Mary McAleese joined it although she was still only a school girl. The People's Democracy was, in fact, a political party. It believed that civil rights could best be achieved by the establishment of an all-Ireland socialist republic. It fielded candidates in the Northern elections up until 1982. Bernadette Devlin was one of its best known leaders. It had a significant impact in the struggle for civil rights for the nationalist minority.

A People's Democracy march which took place on New Year's Day in 1969, from Belfast to Derry, was attacked both by loyalists and off duty members of the 'B-Special' police force (an armed reserve force invariably Protestant and Unionist). August of that year saw widespread terror. Within that period alone 10 people were killed, over 700 were injured, and 1,500 Catholic homes and 300 Protestant homes were burnt down or damaged. The McAleese family decided to leave Ardoyne and they moved to Dublin. In the capital, however, they were disappointed to discover what they considered was a lack of interest in the plight of their fellow country folk north of the border. A month later they decided to move back to Belfast in the hope that things might have calmed down on the political front. They hadn't. Mary's sister, Kate, was attacked by five residents of the nearby Glenbyrn estate. Sixteen-year-old John, who was deaf, and who attended a special education school, was also attacked. Usually he was given a lift home from school by a kindly Protestant Minister but on this particular occasion he travelled by bus. Just before he reached home, and unable to hear three men coming up behind him, he was hit on the head with a bottle, punched and kicked. He survived the attack and was lucky not to be killed. Although John was able to identify at least one of his attackers, the police brought no charges against those who had committed the assault. Notwithstanding this attack and the level of violence around them, Paddy Leneghan made it very clear to his children that he detested violence no matter how strong the provocation and would not tolerate retaliation. At the same time, he also taught his children always to hold steadfastly to their principles.

Matters were, however, to get even worse. On 1 January 1972 – later known as Bloody Sunday – the First Parachute Regiment of the British Army shot and killed 14 unarmed civil rights marchers. The year was to be the worst year of the 'Troubles' with 496 people killed from all shades of the political divide, including British soldiers and members of the RUC.

Prior to this, in August of 1971, the introduction by the British Government of internment without trial was to have a catastrophic affect as the 'innocent' as well as the 'guilty' were incarcerated. It also had the effect of acting as a recruiting flag for the IRA. In 1972, Prime Minister Edward Heath prorogued Stormont. This meant that the Northern Ireland was brought under the direct rule of Westminster and the Northern Government was abolished.

Not only the Leneghan family but Martin McAleese's family, too, was adversely affected by the violent situation in the North. On the day internment was introduced, a gang of loyalists arrived at the McAleese house and gave Martin's family five minutes to leave. Martin's father asked the police for assistance to retrieve some of their belongings, but no help was forth-coming and they had to abandon their house with only two suitcases. They moved to a house in Rathcoole but that had to be abandoned too when Martin's younger brother, Kevin, was attacked and suffered an attempt to have the letters 'UVF' (Ulster Volunteer Force – a Protestant terrorist group) scraped on his arm with a broken bottle. The family then moved to the relative peace of Finaghy, South Belfast.

## University Days

Following the successful sitting of her A-level exams, Mary Leneghan achieved her ambition to attend Queen's University to study law. She commenced in the University's School of Law in 1969 and immersed herself fully in university life. She became president of the College Law Society and, when time allowed, took part in debating. She was also associated with setting up of the first Women's Aid group to be established in Belfast. However, the ongoing level of violence was a constant cause of worry for the young student. Her Christian values held her in good stead during this time. Indeed, it was fortified when, through the Church of Ireland (Protestant) Chaplaincy in the university, she struck up a firm friendship with the Reverend Cecil Kerr. He was renowned for his ecumenical work in the Church. He was also a founder of the Christian Renewal Centre in Rostrevor.

The students of the university – a mix of Catholics and Protestants – blended well together. This was a great relief to Mary and in contrast to what was happening outside the campus walls. Mary worked hard during the four-year period of her study. Her first year results saw her at the top of the list and from this she grew in confidence. During this time she joined the SDLP (but later relinquished her membership when she moved to Dublin). In 1973, Mary graduated with an honours degree in law. The following year she was called to the bar. This was unique in that she was one of a tiny group of women to have received such a call.

## Romance

University life for Mary Leneghan was confined not only to matters of law, for it was here that her relationship with Martin McAleese deepened. She had previously met Martin at an inter-schools debating contest and they had got on well together. Now she took an even greater interest in him and was impressed by his credentials as captain of the GAA Antrim minor football team. Later, however, after her graduation, she struck up a relationship with Rory McShane. He was a founding member of People's Democracy and involved in the civil rights movement. Although they became engaged, the relationship faded when Mary took up the position of Reid Professorship in Trinity College Dublin in 1975 (a post previously held by President Mary Robinson). Literally, the distance between them – he was based in Newry in the North – was not conducive to maintaining a relationship. Martin McAleese, meanwhile, obtained an honours degree in physics but then decided to change his career path to that of accountancy.

For his part, Martin had continued to maintain a serious interest in Mary. Their reunion after her brief relationship with McShane was a great source of satisfaction to him. Mary and Martin were married on 9 March 1976 in the local Catholic Church in Rostrevor. The wedding reception was held in a hotel in Newry – a venue that was frequently the target of loyalists' attacks. During the reception Mary noticed that two of their guests were not present. She was to learn later that they had been killed that same day in a bomb blast in the restaurant they ran. Mary's family kept the news from them and rushed them off on their honeymoon. However, they learned about the fate of their friends from a TV report which they viewed on their stopover in Dublin en route to Kerry. It took considerable convincing by their families to persuade them to continue on with their honeymoon plans but, eventually, they did so. However, their time together was clearly marred by the shocking news.

*Mary (centre) called to the Bar, Belfast 1974*

## Work

The Northern troubles were now in full flight. After the honeymoon Martin
returned to his work in Belfast with the accountancy firm, Stokes Kennedy
Crowley and Company. Meanwhile, Mary, with a year's work as a lawyer

in Belfast behind her, attended her duties at Trinity College in Dublin. Here she gained a reputation as a very competent lecturer and one well adept at keeping order even among the more lively students. Although she was happy to be living in Dublin, which she considered the spiritual home of her nationalist ideals, she missed her family and home life in the North. She continued to be disillusioned by the attitude of those living south of the border who seemed, in many cases, to have insufficient interest in what was happening 'up there'. Nevertheless, she got on with her work.

Her natural independence of mind prompted her to become a founding member of the Campaign for Homosexual Law Reform, together with her fellow Trinity College colleague, David Norris. Other members of the group included Noel Browne (Minister for Health in the period 1948–1951), Dean Victor Griffin and Judge Catherine McGuinness. Later, Mary became a member of the Commission of Inquiry into the Irish Penal System. Here she became a close friend of Séan McBride, a former IRA Chief of Staff and also a former cabinet minister, and winner of both the Lenin and Nobel peace prizes. The report by the Commission was wide ranging and novel but, initially at least, found little favour with the Government of the day. For a short period she was a member of Irish Council for Civil Liberties. She left the Council in 1983 due to a difference of opinion regarding abortion when it backed the 'Pro-Choice' Campaign. Whilst maintaining firm views on the role of women in the Catholic Church, and indeed, on a number of other aspects of her faith, she nevertheless found ultimately that she was content with the Church's basic tenets.

Notwithstanding her very busy schedule, she found time in 1977 to take flying lessons. She received a learner's licence in 1978 and not long afterwards was allowed to fly solo. However, more pressing matters meant that she could not continue with this hobby.

By 1979, Mary was finding her work in Trinity College somewhat staid. She was open, therefore, to exploring other avenues of opportunity. One came when she was offered a position with Radio Telefís Éireann (RTÉ) in March of that year as a presenter/reporter in the Current Affairs Department. Here, too, she soon found a lack of knowledge of Northern mat-

*Mary McAleese on Frontline, RTÉ ,1979*

ters, coupled with an anti-Provisional IRA bias. She was not supportive of violence in any form, but felt that RTÉ should strike a reasonable balance in reporting nationalists' viewpoints. Her criticism applied in particular to the programme 'Today, Tonight' for which she became a reporter. This bias came to the fore in 1981 in the aftermath of the deaths of ten IRA hunger strikers. RTÉ's policy was to play down the topic because they believed that to do otherwise would be seen as giving moral support to the IRA. Mary, however, considered this approach a complete misreading of the feelings on the ground in the North. The foreign media had no such hang-up about affording it due publicity, however, and the hunger strikers quickly attracted world wide interest. RTÉ was forced to undertake rapid catch-up action. Mary was not shy about expressing her views on the situation amongst her work colleagues, but it carried with it the penalty of being labelled a Provisional IRA sympathiser. She greatly resented this. Her views were not helped by revisions to Section 31 of the Broadcasting Authority Act, 1960, which barred interviews by the station with any members of prescribed organisations such as the IRA. The revisions were introduced by the Government Minister responsible for RTÉ, Conor Cruise O'Brien, a man who would later display strong pro-Unionist sympathies, to the extent that he joined the extremist United Kingdom Unionist Party. Nonetheless, Mary did gain a significant amount of experience working on a number of popular current affairs programmes. Ultimately, however, she found that the lack of understanding of the Northern situation by her colleagues, and their lack of any deep interest in it, together with the effective side-lining of Northern matters, were frustrating for her.

In 1981, RTÉ offered Mary a post to work on a programme entitled 'Europa' with co-presenter Conor Brady of the *Irish Times*. Her work entailed travelling to various European cities, usually at weekends. It was a demanding schedule. Additionally, she undertook work in the area of court reporting and her profile was enhanced by her coverage of the Malcolm McArthur murder case. This case was a high profile one by virtue of the fact that McArthur was traced to the residence of the Attorney General, Patrick Connolly, who was then forced to resign his post. The whole matter was of some considerable embarrassment to the Government of the day.

By 1983, Mary felt that many prominent positions in RTÉ were held by members or associates of the Workers Party, a party for which she had scant regard believing that they had definite links with terrorists. The Workers Party had evolved from Sinn Féin/The Workers Party, earlier styled Official Sinn Féin (as distinct from Provisional Sinn Féin).

An altogether new dimension was added to Mary's life in September of 1983 when she gave birth to her first child, baby Emma. She now had to juggle family life with her working life.

In 1984, at the suggestion of John Hume of the SDLP, Taoiseach Garret Fitzgerald set up a body called the New Ireland Forum. This was to provide a focal point and platform for discussions on the problems of the

*Mary McAleese and Conor Brady, presenters of 'Europa' on RTÉ*

North of Ireland. The Catholic bishops invited Mary McAleese to be a member of their delegation and she became their principal spokesperson. In one of her addresses to the Forum, McAleese spoke in favour of the separation of Church and State and of pluralism:

> '*The church does not want a Catholic State for a Catholic people. The Church believes in marriage as a sacrament, as an indissoluble union, as a contract for life. It is entitled to hold that view and to preach that view to its flock. Its sole jurisdiction is in relation to its flock. It does not seek to have any jurisdiction beyond that. It is not entitled to, nor does it seek to tell any government that the Catholic view of marriage should be enshrined in legislation because it is the Catholic view.*'

She also expressed her views on inter-denominational schools as follows:

> '*The notion that consensus comes from contact or even that understanding comes from contact is wrong. It is a dubious and simplistic notion.... I myself lived in an area, which is often described as a flashpoint area, known as Ardoyne. It was a mixed area as I was growing up. I had tremendous contact with*

*Protestant neighbours, played with them. They were in and out of my home but it did not stop one of them from becoming a member of the UDA and now doing a life sentence for killing five Catholics.'*

In relation to Catholic education she said that it:

*'... arises in the context, not of a desire to create a sectarian educational system but out of a genuine desire to extend the home vision, the vision of a Catholic way, the way of life simply to the school....*
*I have very grave doubts from my own direct experience about the ability of the school to break down sectarian prejudice.'*

In 1985, Mary decided to leave RTÉ and concentrate instead on a second term as Reid Professor in Trinity College. She now undertook further studies for a Masters degree, choosing the topic of 'Women in Irish Prisons' for her thesis. She also commenced work on a new book on Irish criminal law.

In 1984, Mary was expelled from the National Union of Journalists. This happened about a month after her appearance at the New Ireland Forum. The grounds given to her were that she was guilty of 'double jobbing', namely, that in addition to her role as a working journalist she was also fulfilling the role of Reid Professor at TCD. There seems to be no written record of this decision, nor was this 'philosophy' applied to others in a similar position.

In the early years of her career Mary had had reservations about various aspects of the Catholic Church, especially, as previously mentioned, regarding its attitude to the role of women in church life. Her views were in the liberal mould. Nevertheless, later she said that the Mass was at the very centre of her faith. She was against the controversial matter of abortion and voted for its banning. She also opposed the proposed introduction of civil divorce. In 1983, she accepted an invitation to join a working group of the Council for Social Welfare, an advisory body to the Catholic Bishops Conference. She worked on a number of policy matters, such as those dealing with the travelling community and the status of children.

## Politics

It was Mary McAleese's work in the New Ireland Forum that brought her to the attention of Fianna Fáil's Charles J. Haughey. He was greatly impressed by both the content of her discourses and the professional way in which she delivered them. She had already been involved with the Fianna Fáil party by virtue of her membership the Women's Committee, which had been formed with the aim of attracting more women into the party. Haughey was attracted to her also because of his own northern roots. Mary joined the Fianna Fáil Peadar Macken/Constance Markievicz Cumann in 1985 and became its secretary. In May of that same year she gave birth to twins, Justin and Saramai. Despite a hectic work and home life, Mary managed to find time to become a founding member of the Irish Commission for Prisoners Overseas. Fellow members on the committee included Bishop Eamonn Casey and Séan McBride. The committee lobbied for justice for the Birmingham Six, the Guilford Four and the Maguire Sisters, all of whom were eventually released when the evidence against them was proved to be false.

Mary McAleese's first foray into formal politics took place in the early part of 1986 when she went forward as a possible Fianna Fáil candidate in the Dublin South-East constituency. However, she failed to get her party's nomination at the selection convention, in fact finishing last of the nominees. She was encouraged by party members to persevere, however, not least because it was now common knowledge that she was a favourite of party leader Haughey.

In demonstration of her determination to continue in party politics, she participated fully in a referendum on the introduction of divorce. The 'Yes' campaign was spearheaded by Taoiseach Garret FitzGerald. Mary was not at all impressed by FitzGerald's contention that the introduction of divorce would be a way of winning over unionist opinion. In her book *Mary McAleese: The Outsider* author Justine McCarthy quoted Mary as follows:

*'The North, it seems, is full of well meaning pluralists on the Unionist's side just waiting for some sign in the heavens that pluralism and democracy are at last on the horizon in the 26 counties and then will be marching over the border in droves.'*

In the event, the referendum, held on 26 June 1986, was defeated by a majority of two-thirds. In November 1995 a second referendum was held on the introduction of divorce and was approved by a small majority, with 50.28 per cent voting 'Yes' and 49.72 per cent voting 'No'.

## Election Time

On the economic front, the country was facing into bad times. The budget deficit had grown to IR£1.4 billion, resulting in necessary cuts in public spending. Coupled with this, unemployment was running at a record high rate. Matters were not helped by the fact that in the North the Troubles were continuing at a worrying level.

On 31 January 1987, President Hillery agreed to dissolve the Dáil at the request of Taoiseach Garret FitzGerald, following the fall of his Government. Just before this, Mary McAleese and Eoin Ryan had been added to the Fianna Fáil ticket in the Dublin South East constituency where the sitting TD was Fianna Fáil's Ger Brady. Their political opponents in the constituency, however, were of a strong calibre. They included outgoing Taoiseach Garret FitzGerald, his Fine Gael running mate Joe Doyle, and Labour's Minister for Labour, Ruairi Quinn. There was concern in the Fianna Fáil ranks that Mary would be seen by the electorate as a 'Catholic Church' candidate and/or a mere 'blow in' from the north. There was some criticism, too, of her campaigning style in that she was perceived as being overly dogmatic in promoting her cause. Whatever the reason, when the General Election was held on 17 February 1987, she lost out narrowly and was eliminated on the eleventh count. The final place went to the Progressive Democrat's Michael McDowell. In the overall count, Fianna Fáil emerged with 81 seats, two short of a majority. Charles J. Haughey was elected Taoiseach but only with the casting vote of the Ceann Comhairle.

## European Matters

The Single European Act was promoted by the European Commission with a view to facilitating cross-community business by removing trade barriers. Although there was some worry in Ireland that the Act could have a negative impact on Ireland's indigenous industries, it was expected to be ratified by the Irish government without any real opposition. However, a small group in Trinity College Dublin came together to oppose it and decided to contest its ratification by taking a case to the courts. The main leaders of this group were lecturers Raymond Crotty and Anthony Coughlan. At the invitation of the latter, Mary McAleese took up the position of co-president of the Constitutional Rights Committee and, through this committee, she too campaigned against the ratification, fearing that its implementation would mean, among other things, that the free movement of services would include a right to abortion.

The Single European Act was due to come into effect on 1 January 1987 but, on Christmas Eve 1986, its opponents won their court case and obtained an injunction against the introduction of the Act. The rest of the European Union membership was to learn that the implementation of the Treaty was being blocked by Ireland. This was an embarrassing position for the Fine Gael Taoiseach, Garret FitzGerald. The Supreme Court ruling was that the government was constitutionally bound to put the Single European Act to a referendum. A subsequent change of government meant that the matter now had to be handled by the new Taoiseach, Charles Haughey. Although when in opposition Haughey had been concerned by the possible adverse impact in Ireland of the Act, he was now a convert to its implementation and told his European partners that he was confident that the matter would be carried in the referendum. He was right. The referendum, held on 24 April 1987, was passed by 70 per cent of the vote. Before this, Mary McAleese continued to oppose the Treaty despite the official policy of her party on the matter. There was little doubt that this was to the displeasure of Haughey.

## The North

The displeasure of Haughey with Mary McAleese continued when she opposed, firstly, the policy of extradition under which those apprehended in the Republic as being suspected of terrorist activities in the North would be handed over to the Northern police authorities, and secondly, the newly proposed Anglo Irish Agreement which was intended to settle political matters north of the border. However, her reservations on the latter waned and she eventually came to accept the Agreement, together with direct rule from Westminster, on the basis that it offered the people in the North some measure of a normal way of life. However, while she did not oppose the proposed granting of self-determination to the people of Northern Ireland, it was in the expectation that, if and when a nationalist majority came to pass in the North, the same principle of self determination would then also apply. On a personal level, however, she and husband Martin remained disillusioned by the general apathy and significant indifference in the Republic to the trials and tribulations of their fellow citizens in the North. They decided, therefore, to break camp and to return to the North. In early August 1987 they bought a house in Rostrevor, County Down.

Mary now faded from active involvement in Fianna Fáil politics. In 1978 Martin had given up his post as financial controller in the Enterprise Travel company in Belfast to study dentistry. Their move to Rostrevor allowed Martin to continue to concentrate on his new profession. Mary, in turn, was able to attend to her TCD duties in Dublin on three days of the week. Around this time Mary was approached by Des Greer, Professor of Law at Queen's University. He told Mary of the creation of a new post, Director of the Institute of Professional Legal Studies. He asked her if she would consider applying for the position. She agreed to do so and after an intensive interview process was offered the post.

In January 1988, Mary commenced work as Director of the Institute of Professional Legal Studies based in Queen's University campus. Her appointment was not well received in Unionist circles. How could someone who was a republican, a prominent Catholic, an opponent of extradition, be selected to such a high profile post? Not only that, but she had beaten applicant David Trimble, her old law lecturer and now a prominent member of the Unionist Party, to the draw. Unionists were loud in their protestations, claiming that she lacked the necessary experience and, furthermore, was from a 'foreign' jurisdiction. Trimble's view was that her selection was a political sop to the Irish Government.

An important element of Mary's work entailed the merging of the educational activities of the two relevant professional bodies in the north – the Law Society and the Bar Council. This warranted delicate and diplomatic negotiations. In this task she achieved a high degree of success. Additionally, the Institute was enjoying an enhanced reputation for its teaching of client counselling, negotiation, mediation and the use of other modern training techniques. Mary's reputation grew and resulted in her receiving a multitude of invitations as a visiting lecturer all around the world. In taking up her post as Director, Mary had had to relinquish her Reid Professorship at TCD. However, she regained the title of 'Professor' in 1993 when Queen's University made her a Professor of Law.

Mary found that the transition from Dublin to Rostrevor was not easy. The area was not immune from the violent activities of the IRA on the one side and the Unionists paramilitaries on the other. Many people had lost their lives in the immediate vicinity. Frequent road checks by armed British soldiers in full battle fatigues were the order of the day. However, they accepted the situation and were prepared for it. Her move back to the North heralded adverse comments in two publications. The *Sunday Independent* contended that she was sympathetic to the Provisional IRA, an allegation that she was worried would put her family in grave danger. In the publication *The Belfast Magazine* it was contended that she had won the post as Director of the Institute of Professional Legal Studies only because of political manoeuvring emanating from the Anglo Irish Agreement. Mary was angry at both publications to the extent that she took legal action against them. In both cases offers of settlement were made to her before the matters came before the court and she accepted them.

## New Academic Heights

In June 1994 McAleese was appointed a Pro-Vice Chancellor of Queens University. She was the first woman and only the second Catholic to be so appointed. With the agreement of the Institute of Professional Legal Studies, her work there had to be confined to mainly policy matters, pending her taking up her new post. One of her early tasks in her new post was to improve the finances of the university. She set about this by approaching some wealthy alumni and applying her considerable persuasive powers. In this she achieved considerable success. She also founded centres of distance learning, the first of which was in Armagh. This made third level education available to many students living outside the Belfast area.

Her duties a Pro-Vice Chancellor included dealing with various external affairs matters which necessitated her travelling to various overseas venues including China, France and the USA. One of her missions abroad took place in October 1995 when she accepted an invitation to a reception at St James's Palace in London to celebrate the 150th anniversary of the founding of Queen's University, an anniversary shared with the other former 'Queen's' universities, namely, University College Cork and University College Galway. President Robinson was also a guest. At the reception McAleese met Queen Elizabeth II who was clearly impressed by the Pro-Vice Chancellor, to the extent that she invited her to small private luncheon in Buckingham Palace the following year. Her working schedule was by now at its busiest. It was added to by her membership of various boards including BBC Northern Ireland (and later, Channel 4 TV), the Electricity Board of Northern Ireland, and the Royal Group of Hospitals Trust.

## Catholicism

On the one hand, Mary McAleese could be considered a 'conservative' Catholic because of her stance opposing such matters as abortion, contraception and divorce. On the other hand, her 'liberal' views are demonistrated by her support for gay rights and of the notion of women priests. In all of this she has maintained a wide circle of priest friends, many of whose views did not always coincide with her own. That she was a keen supporter of ecumenical matters can be evidenced by her attendance, going back to the 1970s, at the Inter Church Conferences in Ballymascanlon, Dundalk. She was also a member of the Bishops' Conference on Social Welfare as well as a contributor to various religious magazines. The hierarchy was not immune from her criticism when she considered it appropriate to voice it. Additionally, in 1994, she joined Brothers and Sisters in Christ (BASIC), an organisation founded for the promotion of women priests. In 1995 they drew up a petition of 20,000 signatures of those in favour of the ordination of women as priests. This was was presented to Cardinal Daly. However, he declined to accept it and McAleese, although a friend of his, was not pleased.

In the early 1990s, Mary wrote to Pope John Paul II regarding a statement issued by him to the effect that those who sought ordination to the priesthood of women were effectively putting themselves out of communion with the Church. She said:

> '*I am grateful that you have spoken on the subject of women priests and that in so doing you have acknowledged the importance of this issue in the modern world. I accept completely the sincerity of the view you have so emphatically expressed but I am nonetheless disappointed … this letter may anger you. I understand that Cardinal Ratzinger has warned that those who do not accept the teaching on women priests are out of communion with the Church. He may be right, but in the deepest recesses of my soul I hear the voice of the Lord whom I love so very much telling me that the disappointment I feel is righteous. It is justified … I remain, until the day I die, convinced beyond the shadow of a doubt that in this regard the Church is wrongheaded and is flying in the face of the will of God.*'

A controversial referendum was held in 1992 dealing with abortion. Specifically, it addressed the availability of abortion in Ireland, the right to travel abroad for abortion, and the dissemination of information on abortion services. Pro-life supporters considered the proposals too liberal whilst the pro-abortion group felt they were too restrictive. Mary McAleese supported the proposals in the referendum but in the end it failed to get the necessary support from the public.

Mary was one of the first journalists to write in Catholic publications about the issue of clerical sexual abuse of children. In 1996 the Catholic hierarchy drafted guidelines on how to deal with child sex abuse. Mary noted that the guidelines did not include mandatory reporting of such offences. She informed a senior bishop that she would campaign against the hierarchy if they did not include it. Her recommendation was acceded to.

In the midst of a heavy workload, Mary managed to find time to maintain her links with the Republic. For example, she acted as advisor to a joint forum on legal training in the Republic. These and other activities ensured that her reputation was growing all the time.

The 1994 IRA ceasefire ended on Friday, 9 February 1996. It was followed immediately by the IRA's bombing of Canary Wharf in London which killed two people and caused huge commercial damage. In the North tensions were rising due to the insistence by Loyalists to have an Orange parade pass through the nationalist Garvaghy Road in Drumcree, County Armagh, against the expressed wishes of the residents. The parade was facilitated by a force of baton drawn RUC.

## Peace Ministry

Mary McAleese was intent on finding a peaceful way through the North's troubles. To this end she accepted an invitation from Fr Alex Reid, a Redemptorist priest, to join him in the Redepmtorist Peace Ministry. Jim Fitzpatrick, the proprietor of *The Irish News* newspaper, was also a member. This three-person group conducted all their talks in secret and was instrumental ultimately in proposing an electoral pact between the SDLP and Sinn Féin in the 1997 general election. Prior to this, Fr Reid had himself been closely involved in starting talks between the Sinn Féin President Gerry Adams and John Hume, the leader of the SDLP.

## New Horizon

In March 1997, the President of Ireland, Mary Robinson, announced her intention not to seek a second term of office when her first period of seven years ended in the autumn. As soon as this came to the notice of Harry Casey, Mary McAleese's former election agent, he asked her to allow her name to go forward as a Fianna Fáil candidate. She was taken aback by this proposal and had major reservations about taking it seriously. A number of matters weighed on her mind, including her earlier election failure. It was with some reluctance that she agreed to give it some further consideration. Foremost on her mind was the possibility that there would be a strong contender for the post in the person of the North's SDLP leader, John Hume. Former Taoiseach Albert Reynolds was also likely to run for the post. Another likely contender was Rosemary Scallon, better known as Dana (the Eurovision Song Contest winner for Ireland). It was also possible that Fine Gael's Mary Banotti and Labour's Michael D. Higgins might also consider entering the race. Other Fianna Fáil contenders were former ministers David Andrews and Michael O'Kennedy (the latter also a former EU Commissioner).

## Candidate

The general consensus in the media was that if John Hume wanted to be President of Ireland he would be unopposed, such was the high regard for him due to his peace making endeavours. Eventually, however, McAleese decided that she would allow her name to go forward pending a decision by Hume. Harry Casey set about canvassing Fianna Fáil supporters and this continued throughout the April–June period of 1997. Strongly involved in supporting Mary was close friend Denis Moloney, a northern solicitor of high repute on both sides of the border. In canvassing support from Fianna Fáil members, the deputy leader of Fianna Fáil, Mary O'Rourke, was at the top of Casey's list. She gave a sympathetic hearing to the idea of Mary McAleese as President. Fianna Fáil TD Mary Hanafin was also contacted but indicated that she might be committed to backing former EU Commissioner Michael O'Kennedy; nevertheless, she agreed to spread McAleese's name to other Fianna Fáil members. Albert Reynolds, meanwhile, had had a number of meetings with the new Fianna Fáil leader, Bertie Ahern, presumably about his interest in running for the Presidency. A new factor emerged, however, which had a mitigating effect on the candidature of Reynolds. In June, Fianna Fáil entered into a coalition government with the Progressive Democrats together with three Independent TDs. It was now very clear that, with the new Government's slim majority, it was critical for Reynolds to hold on to his Longford seat.

Meanwhile, McAleese was concerned that her profile among sitting TDs was still low and would have to be addressed very quickly. The position of John Hume was still anxiously awaited. At the urging of Harry Casey, McAleese wrote to Bertie Ahern setting out her credentials. At a meeting with Ahern in September 1997, he gave no indication as to how he viewed her as a prospective party candidate for the Presidency. He said that the decision was not his to make but that of the Fianna Fáil Parliamentary Party. Also present at that meeting were Chief Whip Seamus Brennan and Martin Mansergh, adviser on Northern matters, both of whom were impressed by McAleese's performance in putting forward her case.

Reynolds, however, now decided to move ahead with his campaign and did so by engaging a public relations firm to handle it. He was not without significant support within his party. Chief amongst them was Charlie McCreevy, the Minister for Finance. However, when Reynolds himself had been Taoiseach he had sacked a number of Ministers who were perceived as being on the other side of a leadership split at that time. Consequently, none of these ex-Ministers, nor their close political colleagues, could be counted on to support him.

After arriving back from France on 8 September 1997, John Hume announced that he would not be a candidate for the Presidency because he felt that he still had work to do in his ambition to bring lasting peace to the North. McAleese now continued her canvassing of Fianna Fáil deputies and senators in Leinster House. She was aware, however, that many deputies felt that they should make the selection from one of their own, namely, from sitting TDs.

The media reported on 14 September that the Labour Party would propose Adi Roche, the well respected founder of the Chernobyl Children's Project, as a candidate. On 16 September, David Andrews announced that he was dropping out of the race.

## Decision Time

On 16 September 1997, the Fianna Fáil parliamentary party met at their headquarters in Mount Street, Dublin, to select their candidate for the Presidency. There were now three Fianna Fáil candidates: Mary McAleese, Albert Reynolds, who was still the firm favourite, and Michael O'Kennedy. The Taoiseach addressed the gathering and advised the members to vote for the best candidate. He was careful not to endorse anyone in particular himself. The usual formalities of proposing and seconding were dispensed with which was fortunate in McAleese's case as this had not been arranged. Each candidate was given three minutes to address the meeting. Mary McAleese was first to speak and addressed the meeting with confidence and clarity. The other two speakers acquitted themselves reasonably well. The first round of voting gave the following result:

| | |
|---|---|
| *Reynolds* | *49* |
| *McAleese* | *42* |
| *O'Kennedy* | *21* |

O'Kennedy was then eliminated and his 'second preference' votes were distributed between Reynolds and McAleese.

One of Reynold's supporters left the meeting for a medical appointment before the second round of voting took place. All the transfers from O'Kennedy went to McAleese. The result of this distribution gave a final result as follows:

| | |
|---|---|
| *McAleese* | *62* |
| *Reynolds* | *48* |

Mary McAleese was now the official Fianna Fáil Presidential candidate.

The result was a clear shock for Reynolds who admitted that he had strongly wanted the chance to run for the Presidency. It would have been the crowning glory to a long and successful political career for him. Nevertheless, he wished Mary McAleese well and said he would support her in her endeavours to get elected. It was subsequently reported that just before he cast his vote, Bertie Ahern showed his ballot paper to Reynolds so that Reynolds could see his own name on it. The interpretation that Reynolds put on that action was that Ahern had guessed that he was going to lose but wanted him to know that he had supported him.

## The Campaign

There were now four candidates in the campaign, all women. They were Mary McAleese, Fine Gael's Mary Banotti, Labour and Democratic Left and Green candidate Adi Roche, and Independent 'Dana' Rosemary Scallon.

The Presidential campaign of Mary McAleese started immediately. It was launched on the day of her selection in Dublin's Shelbourne Hotel in the presence of Taoisech Bertie Ahern and Tánaiste Mary Harney. The Minister for the Environment and Local Government, Noel Dempsey, was appointed campaign manager for the McAleese campaign. He had been a supporter of Albert Reynolds but had been away on Government business when the selection process was held. He cautioned McAleese that she would have to put her trust in his political wisdom and allow him to make decisions with which she might not be fully in agreement. She agreed, somewhat reluctantly. He asked to be fully briefed by her on any aspect that might have a bearing on her campaign. In the course of these discussions McAleese told him about her involvement in secret peace talks on the North. Dempsey considered that this would be a very useful trump card. However, McAleese immediately advised him that he could not use this information under any circumstances as she could not break the confidence of secrecy without having it having a detrimental impact on the peace talks.

It did not take Dempsey long to be convinced that in Mary McAleese he had a winning candidate. He was aware, however, of some areas of concern. For example, McAleese was viewed with reservation by some Catholics who were unhappy with her declared views on the matter of women priests. A further problem was that there was still a degree of apathy within the Fianna Fáil party towards her. After all, so far as rank and file members of the party were concerned, she had up to now been considered an 'outsider'. Dempsey was not slow in concentrating on these important areas. Additionally, Mary McAleese was obviously better known north of the border than in the Republic. Consequently, the campaign concentrated in getting as much radio and television exposure as possible as well as getting appropriate coverage in local and national newspapers in the Republic.

On the public relations front, Dempsey complained to RTÉ that undue exposure had been given to Adi Roche and Mary Banotti. There was a feeling that this stemmed from McAleese's troubled history with RTÉ as an employee, and that she therefore did not have many friends in the decision making echelons of the TV station. In the case of Roche, the McAleese campaign need not have worried unduly because her lack of political experience soon became apparent, to the extent that her initial position at the top of the polls decreased and McAleese's increased.

A new element now arrived on the campaign scene. A retired member of the Gardaí, Derek Nally, entered the campaign. He was a founder member of a group called Victim Support. His public relations director was John Caden, a former producer of the well respected show 'The Gay Byrne Show' on RTÉ radio. In a TV panel discussion programme, Nally, who was taking part with McAleese and others, referred to a newspaper report about a leaked Department of Foreign Affairs document which strongly hinted that McAleese was 'soft' on Sinn Féin. In doing so Nally linked this with the high profile murder of Garda Jerry McCabe by IRA sympathisers the previous year. He challenged McAleese to state where exactly she stood in relation to Sinn Féin. She responded as follows:

> *'I do not believe that one single person should have shed one single drop of blood in this country for the things they have shed them for. I have always been strongly opposed to violence.'*

*The five Presidential candidates (l-r) Mary McAleese, Adi Roche,
Dana Rosemary Scallon, Mary Banotti and Derke Nally with
programme presenters Brian Farrell and Miriam O'Callaghan*

Although this line of attack was maintained by Nally for some time, in
the end it failed to have any lasting impact. Privately, however, McAleese
was furious about it because she was concerned that it could put her family
at risk of physical attack.

Although Nally's campaign began to falter significantly, McAleese had
again to defend herself against the allegation of being 'soft' on Sinn Féin.
The subject arose again when further alleged disclosures in the *Sunday
Business Post* made reference to new details in the leaked Department of
Foreign Affairs document. This created renewed media interest. Dempsey
wanted to counter this by revealing her engagement in the peace discussions but she insisted on holding back on it. However, eventually and
importantly, the superior of Fr Alex Reid issued a statement on behalf of
the peace Ministry:

> *'The Redemptorist Peace Ministry team is non-political, i.e. it
> does not purport to support nor does it in fact support the posi-
> tion of any political party. The benchmark of the Redemptorist
> Peace and Reconciliation team is the call of the Gospel to seek out*

*ways and means of developing and promoting a more peaceful, a more reconciled and a more just society. The Ministry team abhors violence in all its forms. Mr Jim Fitzpatrick and Ms Mary McAleese were invited to join the Peace Ministry precisely because they share these convictions. Their contribution to the Peace Ministry in association with us has been a valuable one. It is deplorable that because of this Ministry they would be in any way slighted.'*

This statement brought immediate relief to the McAleese campaign but more was needed. It came when the SDLP, which up to now had not wished to interfere in 'southern' matters, issued a statement which stated that there was no truth in the allegation that McAleese was a Sinn Féin supporter. The backing of the party's leader, John Hume, carried much weight in the matter. A further boost to her campaign came in the form of an endorsement by the SDLP's Eddie O'Grady. He said:

*'Mary McAlesse can make a real and meaningful contribution to the resolution of conflict in Ireland...'*

He contended that she had a real insight into the Nationalist and Unionist traditions north and south.

Even more significant was the support McAleese received from the leading Unionist politician, John Taylor, when he stated that he had never believed that she was a supporter of Sinn Féin. He also praised her work in the establishment of the new university campus in Armagh.

## The Election

The election for the Presidency of Ireland was held on 30 October 1997. The turnout, at 47 per cent, was the lowest recorded in a Presidential election. In the first round the result was as follows:

| | |
|---|---|
| *Mary McAleese* | *45.2%* |
| *Mary Banotti* | *29.3%* |
| *Rosemary Scallon* | *13.8%* |
| *Adi Roche* | *7.0%* |
| *Derek Nally* | *4.7%* |

The second round count yielded the following final outcome:

*Mary McAleese*     58.67%
*Mary Banotti*      41.33%

In her victory speech in Dublin Castle the President elect declared:

> '*I want us to share as a nation the adventure of this, the most dynamic country in Europe, heading into the next millennium. And I believe this will see the Irish people taking a concrete role as a key player not just on the European stage but globally. It will mark, I believe, the true age of the Irish because I believe we are an unstoppable nation now very definitely in our stride.*'

## The Presidency

Mary McAleese was inaugurated as the eighth President of Ireland on 11 November 1997 in St Patrick's Hall in Dublin Castle. The ceremony started with a prayer service led by the leaders of the five main Christian churches and the Chief Rabbi of Ireland.

In her address the President referred to her delight at what was a special privilege for her in being the first President from Ulster. The general theme of her address was 'Building Bridges'. She said:

> '*These bridges require no engineering skills, but they will demand patience, imagination and courage for Ireland's pace of change is now bewilderingly fast.*'

She continued:

> '*... to speak of reconciliation is to raise a nervous query in the hearts of some north of the border, in the place of my birth. There is no more appropriate place to address that query than here in Dublin Castle, a place where the complex history of the two neighbouring and now very neighbourly islands has seen many chapters written. It is fortuitous, too, that the timing of today's inauguration coincided with the commemoration of those who died so tragically and heroically in two world wars. I think of nationalists and unionists*

247

*President Mary McAleese's Inauguration*

*who fought and died together in these wars, the differences which separated them at home fading into insignificance as the bond of their common humanity forged friendships as intense as love can make them. In Ireland, we know only too well the cruelty and capriciousness of violent conflict. Our own history has been hard on lives young and old. Too hard. Hard on those who died and those left behind with only shattered dreams and poignant memories. We hope and pray, indeed we insist, that we have seen the last of violence. We demand the right to resolve our problems by dialogue and the noble pursuit of consensus ... we need look no further than our own European continent where once bitter enemies now work conscientiously with each other and for each other as friends and partners ... I know the distrusts go deep and the challenge is awesome. Across this island, North, South, East and West there are people of such greatness of heart that I know with their help it can be done. I invite them to work in partnership with me to dedicate ourselves to the task of creating a wonderful millennium gift to the Child of Bethlehem whose 2,000 th birthday we will soon celebrate – the gift of an island where difference is celebrated with joyful curiosity and generous respect ... There will be those who are wary of such invitations, afraid that they are being in-*

*vited to the edge of a precipice. To them I have dedicated a poem*
*written by the English poet, Christopher Logue, himself a veteran*
*of the Second World War.*

*'Come to the edge.*
*We might fall.*
*Come to the edge.*
*It's too high!*
*Come to the edge*
*And they came,*
*And he pushed*
*And they flew.'*

## First Term

The new President started her new role with a full diary of engagements. One of these was her first official visit to Northern Ireland which took place on 5 December 1997. She met members of both sides of the political divide. In Belfast she called on her old school, St. Domnic's. She was also guest of honour at the 20th anniversary of the Institute of Professional Legal Studies of which she had been the Director. In that same month the President, as Supreme Commander of the Defence Forces, visited the Irish troops on United Nation's duty in Lebanon. She paid tribute to the 38 soldiers who died on duty there in the cause of peace. She also praised those who saw service with the UN in conflict areas such as Africa, Asia, the Middle East, Europe and Central America.

Another event, and at the time a more controversial one, occurred in the early part of her Presidency. In attending a Eucharistic service at Dublin's Christ Church Cathedral (Protestant), attended by all the main Christian denominations, she and the members of her family who accompanied her took Communion. The Church of Ireland believed that it was a 'first time' for an Irish President of the Roman Catholic tradition. The *Irish Times* referred to it as breaking new ecumenical ground. However, Fr Denis Faul, a fellow northerner, said that Catholics believed 'the living, risen and glorious Body of Christ was really, truly and substantially present in the Eucharist under the guise of bread and wine, and offered in the sacrifice of the Mass'. He went on to refer to the fact that the Eucharist was central to the unity of the Catholic Church. He said that his view was that the President had breached the Catholic Church's code of canon law in the matter of Eucharistic inter-communion. Such inter-communion was not possible with Protestant Churches. The President's actions were supported, however, by a number of well known 'liberal' Catholic priests such as Fr Austin Flannery, Fr Sean Fagan and Fr Gabriel Daly.

The Irish bishops, after one of their meetings, said that the President's actions had taken everyone by surprise but that they did not wish to censure or embarrass the President but, at the same time, they hoped the issue would not arise again. The controversy continued for a time when an intervention was made on the subject by the Catholic Archbishop of Dublin, Desmond Connell. In referring the to the matter of Catholics taking Communion in Protestant churches he said that 'they have their own Catholic faith and they profess that, and what they are in fact doing in partaking of the Eucharist in a Protestant Church is a sham'. He further said that it was profoundly insulting to the Church of Ireland or to any other Protestant Church to do so. The Archbishop's use of the word 'sham' was not well received by the Protestant churches, although it was later stated that he had not in fact said that the Protestant Eucharist was a sham but rather that Catholic participation in it was a sham. Notwithstanding this, the President received a warm welcome from Archbishop Connell when she attended Mass at St. Andrews church in Dublin's Westland Row marking the commencement of her term of office.

## Peace Park

On 11 November 1998, President McAleese, together with Queen Elizabeth II of Britain and King Albert II of Belgium, opened the Island of Ireland Peace Park at Messines in Belgium. It was created in memory of the 70,000 or so Irishmen from both sides of the border who were killed or wounded or went missing in World War I. In her address President McAleese said:

*'... this was not just another journey down a well-travelled path. For much of the past 80 years, the very idea of such a ceremony would probably have been unthinkable. Those whom we commemorate here were doubly tragic. They fell victim to a war against oppression in Europe. Their memory too fell victim to a war for independence at home in Ireland... I do not think that it is too bold to suggest that this day has been a day of historic significance. The problems we face in building a culture of consensus are difficult but not impossible. We can draw strength from the collegial partnerships built in Europe this past 40 years between once bitter enemies and the enormous goodwill towards Ireland from our friends around the world, not least here in Belgium. None of us has the power to change what is past but we do have the power to use today well to shape a better future. The Peace Park does not invite us to forget the past but to remember it differently. We are asked to look with sorrow and respect on the memory of our countrymen who died with such courage far from the common homeland they loved deeply ... we have built a Peace Park and Round Tower to commemorate the thousands of young men from all parts of Ireland who fought a common enemy, defended democracy and the rights of all nations, whose graves are in shockingly uncountable numbers and those who have no graves, we condemn war and the futility of war.... As Protestants and Catholics we apologise for the terrible deeds to each other and ask forgiveness. From the sacred shrine of remembrance, where soldiers of all nationalities, creeds and political allegiances were united in death, we appeal to all people in Ireland to help build a peaceful and tolerant society.'*

## Good Friday Agreement

On Good Friday, 10 April 1998, a very significant political development took place in the Northern Ireland peace process. It was to become known as the Good Friday Agreement and it chartered a way forward which was satisfactory to most shades of political persuasion in Ireland as a whole. It was signed by the Irish and British Governments and endorsed by all political parties in the North with the exception of the Democratic Unionist Party, although they later gave it backing. Their leader, Rev Ian Paisley, subsequently become First Minister of a new Storement Government. On 23 May 1998, the Agreement was endorsed by voters in Northern Ireland in a referendum. On the same day, voters in the Republic voted in favour of constitutional changes in line with the Agreement, also in a referendum. The 'Yes vote in Northern Ireland was 71 per cent and in the Republic 94 per cent.

In a reaction to the results of the referenda, the President said, on 23 May 1998:

> '*Today is truly a momentous day for Ireland, North and South, we, the people of this island, have said a resounding 'Yes' to the Good Friday Agreement. Ours is the peace. Today is the day we turned our faces firmly towards a new millennium and bequeathed to it the gift of peace. We celebrate and say thank you to those who came out in huge numbers and courageously committed themselves to building a peaceful society where there will be equality and respect between our two rich cultures and traditions … celebrating with us are members of our global Irish family and the many friends of Ireland all over the world. They see a powerful fresh energy at work in this land they love … the Good Friday or Belfast Agreement is the culmination of two years of the most intensive and fraught negotiations . In a wider sense it is the product of over two decades of ever closer partnership between the Irish and British Governments. It had the benefit of powerful insights from past attempts at a settlement. It had the skills and wisdom of our friends abroad, in particular, our American friends whose help has been so invaluable. In the months ahead when the going gets tough, as well it might, when nerves get a little jittery, let us remember and draw renewed strength and generosity from this blessed day, a day when we affirmed, despite our many, many differences, "our indivisibility as Children of God" (John Fitzgerald Kennedy, Dublin, June 1963) – a day when Ireland said "Yes" over two million times to peace through partnership.*'

## Twin Towers

Like many people around the world, the President witnessed on television the planes crashing into the Twin Towers in New York City on 11 September 2001. She was immediately asked by RTÉ to give an interview on the tragedy. With little or no time to prepare a response, and fearful of not saying the right thing in such an emotionally charged atmosphere, she nevertheless agreed. Without notes and with no opportunity for rehearsal she said:

> 'I'm like every other human being with any scrap of decency and any scrap of human compassion. I'm watching the pictures and it's absolutely unbearable. It's just simply unbelievable to be witnessing, actually witnessing, such wanton destruction of human life right in front of our very eyes. It's a crime – it's not just a crime against the American people, it's not just a crime against American civilization. It's a crime against the very foundations of all our humanity and our hearts. Every one of us looking at it and saying, "We know people who could be there, we have friends who could be there". And so it's doing what it's designed to do. It's spreading terror and fear and panic as it was intended to do. To stop us in our tracks and show us just how low, how utterly unbearably, unbelievably low, human beings can sink in their hatred for one another. I think our response to that is and has to be to stand shoulder to shoulder with our American brothers and sisters.'

## Second Term

In September 2004 President McAleese announced her decision to run for a second term of office. She said:

> 'These past seven years have been personally deeply fulfilling and, after consultation with my family I have decided to seek election for a second term. It is my desire and ambition to serve my country and serve it well for a further term as President.'

The Presidential race turned out to be of the 'one horse' kind in that the only potential rival for the post, 'Dana' Rosemary Scallon, failed to get the necessary constitutionally required support of four county councils or the signatures of at least twenty TDs or senators. As a result, and in line with Constitutional procedure, the sitting President was enabled to nominate herself and, consequently, she was returned unopposed.

It was significant that in recognition of the President's work in 'building bridges' she received endorsement from the then Progressive Unionist leader, David Irvine, when he said:

> *'I think given the journey that society in Northern Ireland has been on, she has been a safe pair of hands and I would like to congratulate her on securing a second term. I would not overestimate the contact she has had with a section of loyalism but I think in terms of the outreach work she has done with the unionist community, she has done a good job.'*

On 11 November 2004, Mary McAleese was sworn in for a second term. In her inaugural speech she said:

> *'Cherishing the best of our past we turn to our future not knowing exactly what it holds but with a clear idea of the hard work ahead of us, work for all of us as citizens and not simply for government alone. We are busier than before, harder to please, less heedful of the traditional voices of moral guidance and almost giddy with greater freedom of choice. Our Constitution is an important ethical compass directing us to a practical patriotism, "to promote the common good", to choose responsible citizenship over irresponsible individualism. Our population is growing, new neighbourhoods of strangers are springing up, immigrants bring with them different cultures and embrace the richness of ours, as I have observed in the schools where their children speak to me proudly in Irish. Infrastructure of all sorts is struggling to catch up, including the human infrastructure we offer each other through friendship and community solidarity. The cushion of consumerism is no substitute for the comfort of community. And if our country is to be*

*strong and resilient in the face of its problems and its ambitions in this time of transformation, it needs strong resilient communities ... Community cannot be created by government and it doesn't happen by coincidence. We make it happen ourselves by unselfishly committing our talents, our money and that precious commodity, time, to the service of each other. It will be my mission to nurture and celebrate commitment to community and to responsible citizenship and to encourage self-belief among the most marginalised.*

*Ireland's fortunes are linked to global politics as never before and though we are a small peripheral island we have a fascinating and exceptional engagement with the world that spans every conceivable connection – from centuries old ties of religion and kinship, through championing of the world's poor, to trade in the most sophisticated modern technologies in which we are market lead-*

*President McAleese, Dr Martin McAleese and guests at a Christmas tree-lighting party, December 2004, Áras an Uachtaráin*

255

ers. As President I have a key role in the renewal and development of ties to our global Irish family, Ireland's unpaid ambassadors, who make our name and nature throughout the world ... I will continue to make it my responsibility to assist in the development of our trade in new markets, to get to know new peoples and their cultures and so help to secure both our nation's wellbeing and global solidarity.

... Seven years ago the bridge of peace on this island was a structure in the making. Today more people than ever are committed to its construction and the once massive gulf of mistrust has been reduced to one last step. I use this occasion to ask the hesitant to muster the courage to complete the journey across and let the bright new landscape of hope reveal itself. For my part I pledge to do my best to make us comfortable in each other's company and unafraid of a shared future.'

*President McAleese is presented with copies of 'Columcille the Scribe' and 'New History of Ireland' by members of the RIA, including Seamus Heaney, October 2005*

*President McAleese and Dr Martin McAleese meeting members of Rialto Rainbow*
*Neighbourhood Project at a community reception, Áras an Uachtaráin, April 2005*

## Continuing to Build Bridges

In pursuing the principal theme of her first inaugural speech, that of building bridges in Irish society, the President, through the key activities of
her husband, Martin, arranged a meeting in Áras an Uachtaráin between
Orange Grand Master officials and County Grand Masters in the Republic
together with a variety of Irish Government officials from various Depart-
ments. This was done to support Unionists in the border areas where local
Protestants felt that their needs had been forgotten by their counterparts
in the north and by the Irish Government.

A further example of bridge building was the visit, in September 2005, by the President to the Taughmonagh national school – a 100 per cent loyalist area. The school authorities suggested that they take down the Union Jack flag but the president responded, 'Not at all'. She was very well received by pupils and teachers alike.

As against that the President's actions were not always fully appreciated. Unionist Drew Nelson commented:

> 'She is a complex character. Taking that Communion in Christ Church (Protestant) was a public act of solidarity. Inevitably in the context of the Republic and Northern Ireland, and our own shared and contested history, she has attempted to walk a tightrope in her unusually high number of visits to Northern Ireland. Perhaps President McAleese is trying too hard by being up here far too often. Less is more !'

The President's continuing campaign was aided, in particular, with the help of husband Martin. He was instrumental, in liaison with Unionist Harvey Bicker (later to become a member of Fianna Fáil) and others, in setting up a three-pronged approach to their outreach programme. Firstly, groups of people from Northern Ireland of varying backgrounds with an interest in the sport of golf were received by the President at Áras an Uachtaráin, and then entertained in golf outings to well known golf clubs in the Republic. The second group to be entertained by the President were businessmen and women including farming and fishing representatives. These were brought together in the context of the European Union with visits undertaken to Brussels and seminars arranged in Dublin. Additionally, farming and fishing representatives met with Bord Bia officials in Dublin and with the Republic's Department of Agriculture officials. The third group comprised non-serving military personnel from the north, namely, representatives of the Somme Association, the Irish Regimental Historical Society, Queen's University Officer Training Corps and various regimental associations, who were invited to visit McKee Barracks in Dublin, usually in conjunction with Remembrance Day services in Dublin, with a later visit to Áras an Uachtaráin to meet the President.

In all of these activities the aim of the President was to achieve real peace through outreach culminating in a secular and more united island. Her task was to establish an acceptable co-existence between two diametrically opposed viewpoints, namely, Irish Nationalists (Catholic in the main) and British Unionists (Protestant in the main). In an endeavour to achieve her aims the President made approximately 100 visits to Northern Ireland in the period to mid-2008. One of these visits was in the aftermath of the bombing in Omagh on 15 August 1998 by a breakaway IRA group, in which 28 people were killed. She was shocked by the bombing and distressed, too, by the fact that she knew the town well through the academic outreach programmes which she initiated when she was Pro-Vice Chancellor at Queen's University. In representing the Republic she expressed her revulsion of the barbaric actions and showed her solidarity with the people of the town by her visit.

In her second term of office the President continues to maintain an arduous work schedule. In 2009 alone she attended approximately 130 functions which warranted an accompanying speech or address of some kind. Additional to these was a large number of sporting, social and community func-

*President with children at official opening of City of Dublin YMCA,*
*Aungier Street, Dublin 2, October 2005*

tions at which addresses by her were not needed, but to which importance was lent by her mere presence. Ever supporting her was her husband, Martin. His contribution to the 'bridge building' and peace efforts was recognised early in 2010 when the UDA announced that it had destroyed all its weapons, saying that their endeavours had been made easier in particular by the encouragement of the President's husband and by his work in building up trust between opposing interests in the North.

## Changed Economic Climate

During the course of the President's second term of office the economic situation in Ireland became acutely bad arising from the collapse of the world banking system and an over-reliance on what became an over-heated property boom in Ireland. As the former optimistic mood of the people became significantly dampened, the President remained optimistic that the country was better prepared than previously to cope with the tough impact of the economic downturn.

In her St. Patrick's Day message on 17 March 2009, the President said that some people had been seduced by the 'quick euro' but that it was the others, the vast majority of people, who would get Ireland out of the mess. She said that Ireland had been tested again and again but the last decade's prosperity had given way to the re-appearance of 'ghostly realities' such as lengthening dole queues and emigration. She added:

> *'Now we are sorely tested by the colossal failure of a global and local culture of short term gain and quick profiteering.'*

However, she expressed the view that the vast majority of people in Ireland were sharing what was in their pockets and generously caring for the poor, sick and lonely. She said that most people had not opted for the selfish short-term gain.

> *'These people did not get us into this mess – but they will get us out of it.'*

*President McAleese meets delegates at a Corporate Social*
*Responsibility Conference, Dublin, May 2006*

## Human Rights

Among the very many foreign visits made by the President was one in
June 2009 to the Council of the European Parliamentary Assembly in
Strasbourg. Her address to the Assembly was wide ranging, and part of it
read as follows:

> 'Resort to arms in this day and age is a badge of dreadful human
> failure for we have access to sophisticated and credible dispute-set-
> tling instruments and intermediary bodies. These have been de-
> vised specifically by the international community to help prevent
> the outbreak of conflict and they should be high on the agenda
> where tensions threaten to erupt. The Commissioner for Human
> Rights has been to the fore throughout the member states in at-
> tempting to bring to international attention the tensions and dis-
> trust which regrettably persist between ethnic groups in Europe,
> and directly to try to defuse them. I salute his efforts and construc-

*tive engagements aimed at alleviating these problems and creating space for mutually agreed ways forward. I also salute those in this forum who have consistently practiced restraint and moderation in their public comments on difficult political problems. Your sensitivity has helped cool tempers and to allow more measured, humanly decent options to germinate.'*

## Europe

The nation's voters approved the European Union's Lisbon Treaty in a referendum on 2 October 2009. Two weeks later the President signed the necessary legislation to give effect in Ireland to the implementation of the Treaty. In an earlier referendum on the Treaty, held on 12 June 2008, the majority of voters said 'No'. A poor 'Yes' campaign by the main political parties who were in favour of the Treaty was blamed for the negative outcome. A more vigorous campaign the second time around, together with greater clarification of some issues and some concessions and re-assurances by the EU Commission meant that the 'Yes' vote held sway by a significant majority at the second time of asking. The original 'No' vote had delayed the implementation of the Treaty in the Union and was a cause of much concern in Brussels and in the other member states. The eventual 'Yes' vote allowed a swift ratification process to be completed and facilitated the implementation of the Treaty and its aim of making for a more efficient and stronger European Union.

Speaking in Luxembourg on 15 October 2009 at a gathering comprising the Prime Minister of Luxembourg and distinguished guests, President McAleese said in part of her speech:

*'Just two weeks ago the people of Ireland voted two to one in favour of the Lisbon Treaty having previously rejected it. It was and remains very important to understand that the first "No" vote in 2008, for by no stretch of the imagination, and some people's imaginations were at fever pitch, could it or should it have been interpreted as a vote against the Union. It was, as is now very evident, mostly the expression of concern about certain*

*elements in the Treaty of particular moment or worry to the Irish people. Once those concerns were patiently, forensically analysed and explained by our Government, they were understood and accommodated by our Union partners so that the Irish people were reassured to give the Treaty their wholehearted endorsement. No other European treaty has ever received as many "Yes" votes in Ireland as the Lisbon Treaty did two weeks ago. Those who insisted on seeing the episode as a disaster for Europe were far from correct, for the democratic and consensus-based credentials of the Union and its sensitivity to the customised needs of each of its sovereign members, its assertion of the value of the voices of its citizens, have all proved their worth, their strength, their integrity and ultimately their unity of purpose.'*

## Commission of Investigation

A commission of investigation into clerical child abuse in the Catholic Archdiocese of Dublin in the period January 1975 to April 2004 published its report on 26 November 2009. It was known as the 'Murphy Report'. The Report was critical of the Archdiocese in that, in order to avoid scandal, it covered up sexual abuse of children by a small percentage of priests.

Referring to the Report the President said that she was dismayed at its findings which concluded that:

> *'Clerical child sexual abuse was covered up by the Archdiocese of Dublin and other Church Authorities over much of the period covered by the Commission's remit … the State authorities facilitated the cover up by not fulfilling their responsibilities to ensure that the law was equally applied to all and allowing the Church institutions to be beyond the reach of the normal law enforcement processes.'*

The President commented:

'This failure to prioritise the protection and welfare of children has left a legacy of great hurt for those abused and their families and our first thoughts are with them on this very difficult day. It goes without saying that a key priority now is to ensure that every assistance and support is provided to them. An important public service has been discharged by the Commission and I commend Judge Murphy and her colleagues for their invaluable work. It is reassuring that the Commission is satisfied that the structures and procedures in operation today are effective in terms of the protection and

*President McAleese and child at St Michael's Hospice (House of Peace and Joy) for HIV and AIDS patients, Liberia, December 2004*

safety of young people…. The challenge for everybody involved now must be to ensure that these new agreed structures and procedures continue to function fully, in order to maximize protection of our children. What the Report also reminds us, and what must never be forgotten, is that child abuse is and always has been a criminal offence. The appropriate authorities, therefore, are the Gárda Síochána and the courts, and no one, but no one, is above the law of the land.'

## Christmas Message 2009

In her Christmas message and New Year greetings the President included the following remarks:

'The precious gift of peace once thought to be an impossible dream is quietly growing and changing the face of this island, radiating *a powerful message of possibility to the many parts of the world where conflict wasted lives so needlessly. The prosperity of the Celtic Tiger years has also left its mark, some of it dreadfully chastening but much of it essentially good for it transformed Ireland into a high- achieving, ambitious and confident nation. Now it is our task to consolidate the peace and restore a sustainable, sensible prosperity. That work which is the job of all of us will, in time, bring a welcome flood-tide of good to our people. That is our hope and our prayer for the coming year. May it be for each one of you a year that surprises in ways that lift the heart and the hopes.'*

## Conclusion

President McAleese:

*'There is a slightly rueful Russian saying, that, "These days we live in a country with an unpredictable past". The saying holds equally true in Ireland but not in respect of the subordination of historical fact to power and spin. In Ireland, we say it with opti-mism and excitement, for now we have the confidence that comes from having transcended a cruel history and its lingering long term consequences. We have made friends, good neighbours and partners of what were once seen as old enemies and we are making peace with our past in order to secure the peaceful, prosperous and inclusive future that we deeply desire for all the children of the island of Ireland whatever their faith, perspective or identity.'*

# References

Boylan, Henry. *A Dictionary of Irish Biography*. Gill and Macmillen, Dublin, 1988.

Coffey, Diarmid. *Douglas Hyde – President of Ireland*. The Talbot Press Ltd., Dublin and Cork, 1938.

Coogan, Tim Pat. *De Valera*. Hutchinson, London, 1993.

Collins, Stephen. *The Power Game: Ireland under Fianna Fáil*. O'Brien Press, Dublin, 2001.

Collins, Stephen. *The Cosgrave Legacy*. Blackwater Press, Dublin, 1996.

Daly, Domnic. *The Young Douglas Hyde*. Irish University Press, 1974.

De Valera, Terry. *A Memoir*. Currach Press, Dublin, 2004.

Duffy, Charles Gavan. *The Revival of Irish Literature*. T.F. Unwin, London, 1894.

Dunleavy, Gareth W. *Douglas Hyde*. Bucknell University Press, 1974.

Dunleavy, Janet Egleson and Dunleavy, Garth W. *Douglas Hyde – A Maker of Modern Ireland*. University of California Press, 1991.

Earl of Longford, O'Neill, Thomas P. *Eamon de Valera*. Hutchinson, London, 1970.

Ferriter, Diarmuid. *Judging Dev*. Royal Irish Academy 2007.

Horgan, John. *Mary Robinson – An Independent Voice*. O'Brien Press, Dublin, 1997.

Keating, Tom. *Presidents of Ireland'* Published by Tom Keating, Dublin, 1992.

Kee, Robert. *Ireland. A History*. Weidenfeld and Nicolson, London, 1980.

Lenihan, Brian. *For the Record*. Blackwater Press, Dublin, 1991.

Mackey, Herbert O. *The Life and Times of Roger Casement*. C.J. Fallon, Dublin, 1954.

MacManus, M.J. *Eamon de Valera*. The Talbot Press, Dublin, 1944.

MacMánais, Ray. *The Road from Ardoyne - The Making of a President*. Brandon, Dingle,

2004.

McDunphy, Michael. *The President of Ireland*. Brown and Nolan Ltd. Richview Press, Dublin, 1945.

McAleese, Mary. *Love in Chaos*. The Continuum Publishing Company, New York, 1997.

McCarthy, Justine. *Mary McAleese: The Outsider*. Blackwater Press, Dublin, 1999.

McGarry, Patsy. *First Citizen - Mary McAleese and the Irish Presidency*. O'Brien Press, Dublin, 2008.

Ó h-Aodha, Micheál. *The Importance of Being Micheál*. Brandon, Dingle, 1990.

Ó Ceallaigh, Seán T. *Seán T. Scéal a Bheatha á Insint ag Seán T Ó Ceallaigh*. Foilseacháin Náisiúnta Teoranta, Dublin, 1963.

Ó Glaisne, Risteard. *Cearbhall Ó Dálaigh*. Maigh Nuad, An Sagart, 2001.

O'Connor, John S. *An Ceallach Mar Uachtarán Againn…* Fianna Fáil. Dublin. 1945.

O'Leary Olivia, Burke Helen. *Mary Robinson* Hodder and Straughton. London. 1998.

O'Neill, Tomás and Ó Fiannachta, Pádraigh. *De Valera*. Cló Morainn, Dublin, 1970.

O'Reilly, Emily. *Candidate – Truth Behind the Presidential Campaign*. Attic Press, Dublin, 1991.

Robinson, Mary. *A Voice for Somalia*. O'Brien Press, Dublin, 1992 .

Siggins, Lorna. *The Woman Who Took Power in the Park*. *Mary Robinson*. Mainstream Publishing, Edinburgh and London, 1997.

Walsh, John. *Patrick Hillery – The Official Biography*. New Island, Dublin, 2008.

# Picture Credits

Pages 1, 2, 4, 5, 6, 36 (top), 187, photo by Kevin Kenna

Pages 7, 14, 23, 24, 25, 26, 33, 36 (bottom), 38, 46, 49, 62, 63, 66, 71, 74, 77, 83, 85, 93, 95, 140, 172, 173, 175, 176, 177, 178, 180, 181, 204, 219, National Library of Ireland

Pages 9, 27, courtesy of Deirdre O'Gara

Pages 19, 70, courtesy of the Garda Siochána Museum

Page 28, courtesy of the Douglas Hyde Interpretive Centre

Pages 1, 2, 4, 5, 6, 29, 55, 92, 115, 132, 147, 182, 215, 253, 255, 256, 257, 259, 261, courtesy of Áras an Uachtaráin

Pages 39, 41, 87, 117, 122, 124, 126, 143, reproduced by kind permission of UCD Archives

Pages 57, 164, 185, 201, 202, 216 Getty Images

Page 58 courtesy of New York City Municipal Archives

Page 86 Corbis Images

Pages 102, 103 courtesy of Nessa Childers

Page 106 courtesy of Nessa Childers and *The Irish Times*

Page 107 courtesy of Kevin Batt and the *Irish Independent*

Pages 110, 111, 112 courtesy of Nessa Childers and the *Irish Independent*

Page 114 courtesy of Nessa Childers and the Robby Studio

Pages 171, 230, 245, 248, RTÉ Stills Library

Page 197 courtesy Irish Labour Historical Society

Page 208 courtesy of the National Print Museum

Pages 220, 226, 228 courtesy of President Mary McAleese

*The author and publisher apologise if any permissions were inadvertently omitted and will correct any errors in subsequent editions.*

# Index

# Index